taste of home freezer pleasers COOKBOOK

taste of home BOOKS

REIMAN MEDIA GROUP, INC. • GREENDALE, WISCONSIN

taste of home

Reader's Digest

A TASTE OF HOME/READER'S DIGEST BOOK

© 2010 Reiman Media Group, Inc.
5400 S. 60th St., Greendale WI 53129
All rights reserved.

Taste of Home and Reader's Digest are registered trademarks of The Reader's Digest Association, Inc.

"Timeless Recipes from Trusted Home Cooks" is a registered trademark of Reiman Media Group, Inc.

For other Taste of Home books and products, visit tasteofhome.com.

For more Reader's Digest products and information, visit rd.ca (in Canada)
rd.com (in the United States)

International Standard Book Number (10): 0-89821-814-4
International Standard Book Number (13): 978-0-89821-814-5

Editor in Chief: Catherine Cassidy
Vice President, Executive Editor/Books:
Heidi Reuter Lloyd
Creative Director: Ardyth Cope
U.S. Chief Marketing Officer: Lisa Karpinski
Food Director: Diane Werner RD
Senior Editor/Books: Mark Hagen
Editor: Janet Briggs
Associate Editor: Amy Glander
Art Director: Edwin Robles, Jr.
Content Production Supervisor: Julie Wagner
Design Layout Artists: Emma Acevedo,
Catherine Fletcher, Kathleen Bump
Proofreader: Linne Bruskewitz
Recipe Asset System Manager: Coleen Martin
Premedia Supervisor: Scott Berger
Recipe Testing & Editing: Taste of Home Test Kitchen
Food Photography: Taste of Home Photo Studio
Administrative Assistant: Barb Czysz

The Reader's Digest Associaton
President and Chief Executive Officer: Mary G. Berner
President, U.S. Affinities: Suzanne M. Grimes
SVP, Global Chief Marketing Officer: Amy J. Radin

Cover Photography
Photographer: James Wieland
Food Stylist: Julie Herzfeldt
Set Stylist: Jennifer Bradley Vent

Pictured on the front cover: Potluck Lasagna (p. 83)
Pictured on the back cover (from left to right):
Veggie Calzones (p. 127), Praline-Peach Sundaes (p. 237)
and Taco Corn Bread Squares (p. 235)

Printed in China
1 3 5 7 9 10 8 6 4 2

TABLE OF CONTENTS

The Freezer—A Busy Cook's Friend

It's true! You can enjoy piping hot, homemade suppers even when kitchen time is tight. By stashing delicious, home-cooked meals in the freezer, dinner preparation (and cleanup) is oh-so quick! And with the **343** recipes in **Freezer Pleasers,** finding the perfect dish has never been easier.

With Freezer Pleasers, it's easier than ever to fill your freezer with delicious, home-cooked entrees, snacks, desserts and more. With just a fraction of planning, you'll discover that a freezer full of homemade meals means extra money in your pocket and extra time on your hands!

Take a look inside...you'll discover mouthwatering recipes that include freezing and reheating instructions as well as step-by-step directions and common, everyday ingredients. You'll never waste time hunting for specialty items again! In addition, each dish was tested and approved by the home economists at **Taste of Home**, the world's # 1 cooking magazine, so you know everything is sure to turn out perfect.

With **Freezer Pleasers**, you'll also cut your grocery bill. After all, not only does fixing and freezing meals save time in the long run, but doing so allows you to take advantage of all kinds of supermarket sales. The next time your grocery store discounts ground beef, for instance, whip up Meaty Pasta Casseroles (p. 27) and Peppery Pizza Loaves (p. 91). Then, simply store these all-time family favorites in the freezer for busy nights.

The four sections in **Freezer Pleasers** make it a breeze to fill your freezer with delicious entrees, snacks, desserts and more. That's because each section is arranged to best fit your family's dining style and schedule.

Now and Later recipes yield two or even three meals, but they require you to cook only once. When you want to take advantage of supermarket sales and value packs of meat, stop here and prepare comforting casseroles, soups and other great- tasting foods.

Made for Later features classic make-ahead recipes. These dishes are great for days when you need to serve a hearty main course or special dessert on a particularly busy night. Simply whip up the recipe at your leisure, then freeze it until needed. You'll have peace of mind knowing that there is always something fabulous tucked in the freezer.

Single Servings makes several servings that are frozen individually, so anyone in your family can grab what they need as their schedule allows. For dinner, someone can heat a Freezer Burrito (p. 148) in the microwave; for a quick treat, a Rocky Road Fudge Pop (p. 173) is ready to go.

Creative Leftovers turn tonight's extras into marvelous new dishes tomorrow. You won't hear complaints here about eating the same thing twice. You'll have one wonderful dish to serve the day you cook it and plenty of leftovers to use as starters for other recipes, including main dishes and desserts.

Freezing Basics

Stocking Up

Besides stocking the freezer with the wonderful meals featured in this book, you likely use your freezer to house a variety of uncooked ingredients and foods you use most often, such as ground meat, chicken breast, pork chops and frozen vegetables. These foods help simplify menu planning and dinner preparation on days you cook from scratch. In addition, your freezer may help you take advantage of weekly sales and bulk pricing...a bonus for today's tight grocery budget!

To help you make the most of your freezer, follow the guidelines below on packing foods for the freezer; what foods are suitable for freezing; and best defrosting methods. The **Freezer Storage Chart** on page 8 lists the recommended time foods can be kept in the freezer for optimum quality.

Packaging Choices

The materials used to store food in the freezer protect food from the harsh freezer climate and maintain the food's quality and moisture content. The materials you use should be durable, freezer-safe and moisture- and vapor-proof.

Suitable items for packaging food for freezing are: wide-mouth freezer and/or canning jars, freezer bags, rigid plastic freezer containers, plastic wrap, vacuum-sealed packages, heavy-duty foil and freezer paper. Meat and poultry may be frozen in meat-counter wrapping for short-term freezing, about 1 month.

> Use wide-mouth freezer or canning jars, freezer bags, rigid freezer containers, vacuum-sealed packages, plastic wrap, heavy-duty foil and freezer paper to store food.

Items to avoid when freezing are: glass jars from food products (such as a spaghetti jar or pickle jar), margarine tubs, cottage cheese tubs, milk cartons and food storage bags.

Wrapping It Up

When freezing foods, always start with fresh, high-quality food. Remember that foods past their prime will not improve upon freezing. Any cooked food should be cooled to room temperature before freezing. For convenience, package food in single-meal or single-serving portions.

> For the best quality of frozen foods, start with fresh, high-quality foods. Foods past their prime will not improve upon freezing.

Use freezer jars and rigid containers for soups, stews and other liquid items. Leave some space between the food and lid to allow the food to expand as it freezes. These items can also be stored in freezer bags. Remove as much air as possible before sealing the bags and lay flat when freezing.

Line casserole dishes with heavy-duty foil before placing ingredients in the dish. Once the food is cooked and frozen, use the foil to help remove it from the dish. Wrap securely and freeze.

For added protection, use combination wrapping. For example, wrap first in heavy-duty foil, then in a resealable plastic freezer bag. If you're using a rigid plastic container, first line it with a freezer bag to make it airtight.

Remove as much air as possible when packaging the food. Label and date the packages. Spread out the packages on a flat surface in the freezer (not on a rack) for quicker freezing, and then stack the packages after they are solidly frozen.

Freezer Burn

Freezer burn occurs when food is not wrapped properly and is exposed to the 0° air for an extended time. The food can dry out and/or become icy. Freezer burn is not a food safety issue, but it is a food quality issue. Freezer burn appears as dry, leathery off-colored areas on meat and poultry. The freezer burn areas can be cut off before or after cooking. Discard vegetables and fruits that are icy and/or shriveled.

Avoid Freezing These Items

While just about anything can be frozen, the quality and texture of certain items may be less than desirable after they're defrosted.

Casseroles made with mayonnaise, sour cream, yogurt or cream cheese, as well as gravies and cream-based sauces will separate after thawing. The casserole will have a watery and/or curdled look.

Raw produce with high-water content, such as cabbage, celery, lettuce, other leafy greens, cucumbers, radishes, watermelon, tomatoes and citrus fruits, become limp and waterlogged after thawing.

> **Before freezing, cool food quickly and evenly.**

Cooked potatoes used in dishes like salads, soups or stews become soft, mealy and waterlogged after thawing. Mashed and twice-baked potatoes do freeze well.

Dairy items, such as milk sauces, sour cream and yogurt, mayonnaise, and sauces and gravies thickened with flour and cornstarch will separate during defrosting.

Cooked pasta can be soft and mushy after defrosting. For best results, undercook pasta before cooling and freezing.

Freezer Surprise

Stop your freezer from turning into the lost land of frozen surprises by keeping a list of what's inside. List the item and date it was placed in the freezer. As the item is used, cross it off the list, and add new items to the list when they are placed in the freezer. For convenience hang the list on the freezer.

Freezer Tips

• Use a freezer thermometer to monitor the air temperature. The temperature should be maintained at 0° to preserve food quality.

• Keep the freezer 2/3 full for energy efficiency.

• Leave some space around each package so air can freely circulate.

• Avoid overtaxing the freezer. Whatever is placed in the freezer should be solidly frozen within 24 hours...that means you can add about 2 to 3 pounds per cubic foot. Adding too much food at one time will increase freezing time.

• If you're not sure if something will freeze well, freeze a small amount. After it's thawed and if reheated (if necessary), you can decide if the quality is up to your standards.

• Follow the first in, first out inventory rule. Use the items that have been in the freezer the longest first.

• Many spices change flavor during freezer storage. Add them to the dish when it is being reheated.

• Organize the freezer by food groups so you can easily find what you want.

• Before freezing, cool food quickly and evenly. Transfer warm or hot foods to a shallow pan or divide among several small, shallow containers. Or place the hot pan in the sink on a cooling rack with cool water running underneath it. Help hot liquids like soups and sauces cool more quickly by stirring them frequently.

Defrosting Do's and Don'ts

Do defrost frozen foods in the refrigerator, in cold water or in the microwave. Don't defrost on the kitchen counter, at room temperature, in warm water or outdoors. Baked goods like breads, cakes and cookies are the exception and can be thawed at room temperature. Unwrap them while thawing so they don't get soggy.

> When defrosting in the refrigerator, allow 12 to 24 hours for casseroles, 5 to 7 hours per pound for a beef or pork roast and 24 hours per 4 to 5 pounds for a whole chicken or turkey.

Refrigerator defrosting is safe and fuss-free, but it's the slowest method, so planning ahead is key. Small items like a pound of ground beef can be defrosted overnight. Most items take one or two days. Bulky, large items will take even longer to thaw. Allow 3 to 5 hours per pound for a small beef or pork roast and 5 to 7 hours per pound for a large roast. A whole turkey or large whole chicken will need an entire day for every 4 to 5 pounds. When defrosting in the refrigerator, place the item in a bowl or on a tray to catch any liquid or juices.

Cold water defrosting takes less time than thawing in the refrigerator but requires more attention. To defrost in cold water, place food in a watertight plastic storage bag. (If the bag leaks the food can absorb water, which will affect its texture, and the food may be exposed to bacteria.) Place the bag in cold water. Change the water every 30 minutes until the food is thawed.

Microwave defrosting is suitable for last-minute thawing of small items. To defrost in a microwave oven, unwrap the food and place it on a microwave-safe dish. Follow the manufacturer's directions for recommended times and settings. Microwave defrosting can cause some areas of the food to actually cook, so plan on cooking the food immediately after defrosting.

What to Do When the Freezer Is Not Working

When your freezer stops, look for the reason it is not working. Is the freezer plugged in securely? Did a circuit breaker pop or a fuse blow? Is the outlet working? Is the electrical power out at your house or is it out in the area? Did the freezer have a mechanical failure and needs to be repaired? If the power is out in the house or area, check with the power company as to when the power might be restored. For a mechanical failure, immediately schedule a service call.

If there's a short wait for the power to be restored or a repairman to arrive, the only thing you'll need to do is keep the freezer door shut and the food will be fine. A freezer full of frozen food will keep the food for 2 days, and a freezer that is half full will keep the food for 1 day...as long as the freezer door stays shut. When the freezer is less than half-full, group any meat and poultry away from other foods. This way thawing meats will not drip juices onto other foods. Group remaining items together to help them retain their temperature.

To keep food frozen for longer periods, check with family and neighbors to see if they have some spare freezer space that you can use. Otherwise, you can purchase dry ice to keep the food frozen. Dry ice is very cold and should never be handled without wearing heavy, protective gloves and protective eye gear. Contact with your skin could cause serious problems. Ask that the dry ice be wrapped in newspaper or other protective material before purchasing. Place a layer of cardboard over the food then top with the dry ice. The dry ice will evaporate rather than melt and will not leave puddles of water in the freezer. You may notice a harmless odor, which is given off as the dry ice evaporates.

> If your freezer stops working, check to make sure it is plugged in, the circuit breaker did not pop and the outlet is working. If the freezer still doesn't work after you've exhausted these options, you may need to call for service.

Once the freezer is working again, check the quality of the food. Some foods may be refrozen. You can refreeze meat, poultry, seafood, vegetables and fruits only if the freezer temperature was 40° or lower and the food item is still partially frozen and has ice crystals. Discard any food that has an off odor, off color or shows any signs of spoilage. Also discard softened or melted ice cream and any food that came in contact with meat juices.

Freezer Storage Chart

The times given are for optimum quality at storage at 0°F.

ITEM	MONTHS

BAKED GOODS

Baked breads, rolls, biscuits and unfrosted cakes . . . . .2 to 6

DAIRY

Butter or Margarine . . . . .6 to 9
Cheese (Brie, brick, cheddar, Monterey Jack, mozzarella, Swiss and grated Parmesan or Romano) . .6
Cream (whipping and half-and-half) . . . . .2 to 4
Egg Whites or Yolks, uncooked 12
Milk or Buttermilk 3

MEATS: Beef, Pork, Lamb

Fresh
Chops . . . . .4 to 6
Ground Meat or Stew Meat . . . . .3 to 4
Roasts . . . . .4 to 12
Sausage, fresh . . . . .1 to 2
Steaks . . . . .4 to 12
Cooked Meats/Casseroles . . . . .2 to 3
Process Meats (bacon, ham, hot dogs and luncheon meat) . . . . .1 to 2

POULTRY

Chicken, Turkey, Fresh
Whole 12
Parts 9
Cooked . . . . .1 to 3

FISH & SEAFOOD

Fillets/Steaks
Lean fish (cod, sole, halibut, orange roughy, flounder) 12
Fatty fish (catfish, perch, salmon, whitefish) . . . . .2 to 3
Scallops/Shrimp
Uncooked . . . . .3 to 6
Cooked . . . . .2 to 3

FRUITS

Fresh Berries, Cherries, Peaches and Pears 12
Juice Concentrates, frozen 12

SOUPS & STEWS . . . . .2 to 3

VEGETABLES

Fresh (asparagus, broccoli, carrots, cauliflower and pepper) . . . . .8 to 12

PIES

Fruit, unbaked 8
Fruit, baked . . . . .1 to 2

NOW & LATER

Cook once and eat twice. These time-buster recipes make at least two dishes. Heat one for dinner and pop one in the freezer for a fuss-free meal on a busy night.

Colorful Chicken Casserole, p. 11

Savory

Freezer Berry Jam, p. 65

Sweet

Savory

Colorful Chicken Casserole | *Bernice Morris, Marshfield, Missouri*

Chicken and pasta are combined with a variety of vegetables to make this all-in-one entree. It's a nice change of pace from the usual creamy casseroles.

1	cup chopped celery
1	cup chopped green pepper
3/4	cup chopped onion
2	tablespoons butter
1	cup chicken broth
1	cup frozen corn
1	cup frozen peas
1	teaspoon salt, optional
1/4	teaspoon pepper
3	cups cubed cooked chicken
1	package (7 ounces) ready-cut spaghetti or elbow macaroni, cooked and drained
1	jar (4-1/2 ounces) sliced mushrooms, drained
1	cup (4 ounces) shredded cheddar cheese

1 In a large skillet, saute the celery, green pepper and onion in butter until tender. Add the broth, corn, peas, salt if desired and pepper; heat through. Stir in chicken and spaghetti. Divide between two 2-qt. baking dishes coated with cooking spray. Top with mushrooms and cheese.

2 Cover and freeze one casserole for up to 3 months. Cover and bake the second casserole at 350° for 20 minutes. Uncover; bake 10 minutes longer or until heated through.

3 **To use frozen casserole:** Remove from the freezer 30 minutes before baking. Bake at 350° for 35 minutes. Uncover and bake 15 minutes longer or until heated through. **Yield:** 2 casseroles (4 servings each).

Hamburger Goulash | *Jennifer Willingham, Kansas City, Missouri*

When I was growing up, my birthday meal of choice was always goulash over mashed potatoes. Now I make my mother's tangy recipe for my own family to enjoy.

2-1/2	pounds ground beef
1	medium onion, chopped
2	cups water
3/4	cup ketchup
2	tablespoons Worcestershire sauce
2	teaspoons paprika
1	to 2 teaspoons sugar
1	teaspoon salt
1/2	teaspoon ground mustard
1/4	teaspoon garlic powder
2	tablespoons all-purpose flour
1/4	cup cold water
	Hot cooked noodles or mashed potatoes

1 In a Dutch oven, cook beef and onion over medium heat until meat is no longer pink; drain. Add the water, ketchup, Worcestershire sauce, paprika, sugar, salt, mustard and garlic powder. Bring to a boil. Reduce heat; simmer, uncovered, for 20 minutes.

2 In a small bowl, combine flour and cold water until smooth; stir into the meat mixture. Bring to a boil; cook and stir for 2 minutes or until thickened. Serve half over noodles or potatoes. Cool other half and transfer to a freezer container. May be frozen for up to 3 months.

3 **To use frozen goulash:** Thaw in the refrigerator; place in a small saucepan and heat through. **Yield:** 6 cups.

Hearty Minestrone | *Katie Koziolek, Hartland, Minnesota*

This is my all-time favorite soup. I love to make a large stockpot full of soup and freeze some for later. This hearty dish reminds me of spaghetti and sauce in soup form!

1	pound ground pork
1/2	cup chopped celery
1/2	cup chopped onion
1/2	teaspoon minced garlic
1	can (28 ounces) crushed tomatoes
1	can (16 ounces) kidney beans, rinsed and drained
1	can (15 ounces) garbanzo beans or chickpeas, rinsed and drained
2	cups tomato juice
1	can (15 ounces) tomato sauce
1	can (14-1/2 ounces) beef broth
3	medium carrots, chopped
1	medium zucchini, halved lengthwise and thinly sliced
1	tablespoon Italian seasoning
1	to 1-1/2 teaspoons salt
1/2	teaspoon sugar, optional
1/8	teaspoon pepper

ADDITIONAL INGREDIENTS (for each batch):

1/2	cup water
1	cup uncooked ziti or small tube pasta

1 In a Dutch oven, cook the pork, celery, onion and garlic over medium heat until meat is no longer pink; drain.

2 Stir in the tomatoes, beans, tomato juice, tomato sauce, broth, carrots, zucchini, Italian seasoning, salt, sugar if desired and pepper. Bring to a boil. Reduce heat; cover and simmer for 30-35 minutes or until carrots are tender.

3 Transfer 6 cups of soup to a freezer container; freeze for up to 3 months. Add water and pasta to remaining soup; bring to a boil. Cover and cook until pasta is tender.

4 **To use frozen soup:** Thaw in the refrigerator; transfer to a large saucepan. Stir in water. Bring to a boil; reduce heat. Add pasta; cover and cook until tender. **Yield:** 2 batches (6 servings each).

Hamburger Stroganoff | *Aline Christenot, Chester, Montana*

I've been making this simple yet satisfying meal-for-two for many years. Then I tried freezing the ground beef mixture so I'd have a head start on a future dinner. It works great!

- 1 **pound ground beef**
- 1/4 **cup chopped onion**
- 1 **garlic clove, minced**
- 1 **can (10-1/2 ounces) condensed beef consomme, undiluted**
- 1 **can (4 ounces) mushroom stems and pieces, undrained**
- 3 **tablespoons lemon juice**
- 1/4 **teaspoon pepper**

ADDITIONAL INGREDIENTS (for each dish):
- 2 **cups cooked spiral pasta**
- 1/2 **cup sour cream**
- 2 **tablespoons water**

1 In a large skillet, cook the beef, onion and garlic over medium heat until meat is no longer pink; drain. Stir in the consomme, mushrooms, lemon juice and pepper.

2 Place half of the mixture in a freezer container; cover and freeze for up to 3 months. To the remaining meat mixture, add the pasta, sour cream and water; heat through (do not boil).

3 To use frozen meat mixture: Thaw in the refrigerator. Transfer to a saucepan or skillet and prepare as directed. **Yield:** 2 main dishes (2 servings each).

Sweet Barbecued Pork Chops | *Susan Holderman, Fostoria, Ohio*

I often prepare a double recipe of these tangy chops and freeze half to keep on hand. They're so easy and taste so fresh, family and friends never guess my quick entree was frozen!

- 8 **boneless pork loin chops (3/4 inch thick and 8 ounces each)**
- 2 **tablespoons canola oil**
- 1/2 **cup packed brown sugar**
- 1/2 **cup chopped sweet onion**
- 1/2 **cup each ketchup, barbecue sauce, French salad dressing and honey**

1 In a large skillet, brown pork chops in oil in batches on both sides. Return all to the skillet. Combine the remaining ingredients; pour over chops. Bring to a boil. Reduce heat; cover and simmer for 12-14 minutes or until meat is tender.

2 Serve desired amount. Cool remaining chops; transfer to a freezer container. May be frozen for up to 3 months.

3 To use frozen pork chops: Thaw in the refrigerator overnight. Place in a skillet; bring to a boil. Reduce heat; cover and simmer for 6-8 minutes or until heated through. **Yield:** 8 servings.

Freezer Vegetable Soup | *Elizabeth Moore, Frankfort, Kentucky*

This flavorful soup tastes so fresh you'll never know it's been frozen. You can easily double the recipe when tomatoes are plentiful or toss in extra vegetables from your garden. For heartier fare, beef it up with ground beef, sausage or meatballs.

SOUP BASE:

- 4 cups chopped tomatoes
- 1 cup chopped celery
- 1 cup chopped carrots
- 1 cup chopped onion
- 2 teaspoons sugar
- 1 teaspoon salt, optional
- 1/2 teaspoon pepper
- 1/2 teaspoon dill weed

ADDITIONAL INGREDIENTS (for each batch):

- 2 cups diced potatoes
- 2 cups water

1 Combine soup base ingredients in a Dutch oven; bring to a boil over medium heat. Reduce heat; cover and simmer for 45 minutes. Remove 2 cups of the soup base and cool.

2 Add potatoes and water to Dutch oven. Bring to a boil. Reduce heat; cover and simmer for 20-30 minutes or until potatoes are tender.

3 Transfer cooled soup base to a freezer container. May be frozen for up to 3 months.

4 **To prepare frozen soup base:** Thaw soup base in the refrigerator. Transfer to a Dutch oven. Add potatoes and water; bring to a boil. Reduce heat; simmer, covered, for 30-40 minutes. **Yield:** 2 batches (4 cups each finished soup).

Pearl Onion Mushroom Bake | *Diane Caragio, Livermore, California*

I assemble this saucy side dish days before I need it. Take one out of the freezer in the morning, and it's ready to be baked for dinner. It's great with turkey or ham.

- 24 pearl onions
- 1 cup water
- 3 teaspoons salt
- 3 cups sliced fresh mushrooms
- 10 tablespoons butter, divided
- 2 teaspoons lemon juice
- 1/4 cup all-purpose flour
- 2 cups milk
- 1 cup (4 ounces) shredded cheddar cheese
- 1/2 cup soft bread crumbs

1 In a small saucepan, combine the onions, water and salt. Cover and cook for 20 minutes or until crisp-tender; drain. Transfer to two greased 1-qt. baking pans; set aside.

2 In a skillet, saute mushrooms in 4 tablespoons butter and lemon juice until tender. In a small saucepan, melt 4 tablespoons butter; stir in flour until smooth. Gradually add milk. Bring to a boil; cook and stir for 2 minutes or until thickened. Stir into mushroom mixture.

3 Pour over onions. Melt remaining butter. Add cheese and bread crumbs; toss to coat. Sprinkle over each casserole.

4 Cover and freeze one casserole for up to 3 months. Cover and bake the second casserole at 375° for 15 minutes. Uncover; bake 10 minutes longer or until golden brown.

5 **To use frozen casserole:** Thaw in the refrigerator for 8 hours. Remove from the refrigerator 30 minutes before baking. Bake as directed. **Yield:** 2 casseroles (4 servings each).

Chicken Manicotti | *Jamie Valocchi, Mesa, Arizona*

When a girlfriend came home from the hospital with her newborn, I sent over this freezer casserole. She and her family raved over how good it was. Try substituting olives for mushrooms or using veal instead of chicken.

1 tablespoon garlic powder

1-1/2 pounds boneless skinless chicken breasts

16 uncooked manicotti shells

2 jars (26 ounces each) spaghetti sauce, divided

1 pound bulk Italian sausage, cooked and drained

1/2 pound fresh mushrooms, sliced

4 cups (16 ounces) shredded part-skim mozzarella cheese

2/3 cup water

1 Rub garlic powder over chicken; cut into 1-in. strips. Stuff chicken into manicotti shells. Spread 1 cup spaghetti sauce in each of two greased 13-in. x 9-in. baking dishes.

2 Place eight stuffed manicotti shells in each dish. Sprinkle with sausage and mushrooms. Pour remaining spaghetti sauce over the top. Sprinkle with cheese.

3 Drizzle water around the edge of each dish. Cover and freeze one casserole for up to 1 month. Cover and bake second casserole at 375° for 65-70 minutes or until chicken juices run clear and pasta is tender.

4 **To use frozen casserole:** Thaw in the refrigerator. Remove from the refrigerator 30 minutes before baking. Bake as directed. **Yield:** 2 casseroles (4 servings each).

Three-Cheese Kielbasa Bake | *Kate Beckman, Hemet, California*

This hearty casserole takes advantage of garden-fresh vegetables and handy convenience items. My aunt originally made this for family gatherings. Now I fix it any night of the week.

12 ounces uncooked elbow macaroni
2   pounds kielbasa or Polish sausage, halved lengthwise and sliced
1   tablespoon olive oil
2   medium onions, chopped
2   medium zucchini, quartered and sliced
2   medium carrots, grated
1/2 teaspoon minced garlic
1   jar (26 ounces) spaghetti sauce
1   can (14-1/2 ounces) stewed tomatoes
1   egg, lightly beaten
1   carton (15 ounces) ricotta cheese
2   cups (8 ounces) shredded cheddar cheese
2   cups (8 ounces) part-skim shredded mozzarella cheese
2   green onions, chopped

1 Cook macaroni according to package directions. Meanwhile, in a large skillet, brown sausage in oil over medium heat; drain. Add the onions, zucchini, carrots and garlic; cook and stir for 5-6 minutes or until crisp-tender.

2 Stir in spaghetti sauce and tomatoes. Bring to a boil. Reduce heat; simmer, uncovered, for 15 minutes. Drain macaroni.

3 In each of two greased 13-in. x 9-in. baking dishes, layer a fourth of the macaroni and meat sauce. Combine egg and ricotta cheese; spoon a fourth over sauce. Sprinkle with a fourth of the cheddar and mozzarella. Repeat layers. Top with green onions.

4 Cool one casserole; cover and freeze for up to 2 months. Cover and bake the second casserole at 350° for 15 minutes. Uncover; bake 15 minutes longer or until cheese is melted.

5 **To use frozen casserole:** Thaw in the refrigerator for 24 hours. Remove from the refrigerator 30 minutes before baking. Cover and bake at 350° for 35-40 minutes or until heated through. **Yield:** 2 casseroles (8-10 servings each).

Twice-Baked Ranch Potatoes | *Janice Arnold, Gansevoort, New York*

I make the most of leftover mashed potatoes by creating these creamy stuffed potatoes that freeze well.

    4   large baking potatoes (about 2-1/4 pounds)
    1   package (3 ounces) cream cheese, softened
    2   tablespoons milk
    1   envelope (1 ounce) ranch salad dressing mix
1-1/2   cups mashed potatoes
  1/4   cup shredded cheddar cheese

1 Scrub and pierce potatoes; place on a microwave-safe plate. Microwave, uncovered, on high for 13-15 minutes or until tender, turning several times. Let stand for 10 minutes.

2 In a small bowl, combine cream cheese and milk; beat in salad dressing mix. Add mashed potatoes; mix well. Cut a thin slice from the top of each potato; scoop out pulp, leaving a thin shell. Add pulp to the cream cheese mixture and mash. Spoon into potato shells. Top with cheese.

3 Microwave two potatoes, uncovered, on high for 3-1/2 to 4-1/2 minutes or until heated through. Place remaining potatoes on a baking sheet. Freeze overnight or until thoroughly frozen; transfer to a freezer bag. May be frozen for up to 3 months.

4 **To use frozen potatoes:** Place potatoes on a microwave-safe plate. Microwave, uncovered, at 50% power for 8-9 minutes or until heated through. **Yield:** 4 servings.

Editor's Note: This recipe was tested in a 1,100-watt microwave.

Sweet 'n' Tangy Freezer Pickles | *Jean Vance, Charlotte, North Carolina*

A batch of these crunchy, sweet-sour pickles never last that long at my house!

   10   to 12 medium pickling cucumbers (about 2 pounds), thinly sliced
    3   medium onions, thinly sliced
    1   large green pepper, chopped
    3   tablespoons salt, divided
    2   cups sugar
    1   cup white vinegar
    1   tablespoon celery seed

1 In a large container, combine the cucumbers, onions, green pepper and 2 tablespoons salt. Cover with crushed ice and mix well. Refrigerate for 8 hours. Drain; rinse and drain again.

2 In a large saucepan, combine the sugar, vinegar, celery seed and remaining salt. Bring to a boil; cook and stir for 1 minute.

3 Spoon over cucumber mixture. Pour into jars or freezer containers, leaving 1/2-in. headspace. Cool. Top with lids. Cover and freeze for up to 6 weeks.

4 **To use frozen pickles:** Thaw at room temperature for 4 hours before serving. **Yield:** 4 pints.

Hearty Meat Pie | *Twila Burkholder, Middleburg, Pennsylvania*

A savory mushroom gravy is served alongside this homey meat-and-vegetable pie. I spend a little extra time making two of them, but the reward comes later when I pull the second pie out of the freezer and pop it in the oven. I have a delicious dinner without any fuss.

Pastry for two double-crust pies
- 2 cups grated peeled potatoes
- 1-1/4 cups diced celery
- 1 cup grated carrots
- 1/4 cup chopped onion
- 2 tablespoons Worcestershire sauce
- 1 teaspoon salt
- 1/4 teaspoon pepper
- 3/4 pound lean ground beef

MUSHROOM GRAVY (for each pie):
- 1 can (4 ounces) mushroom stems and pieces
- 2 tablespoons all-purpose flour
- 2 tablespoons canola oil
- 1 teaspoon beef bouillon granules
- 4 drops browning sauce, optional

1 Divide pastry into fourths. On a lightly floured surface, roll out one portion to fit a 9-in. pie plate. In a large bowl, combine the potatoes, celery, carrots, onion, Worcestershire sauce, salt and pepper. Crumble beef over mixture and mix well. Spoon half into crust. Roll out another portion of pastry to fit top of pie; place over filling and seal edges. Cut vents in top pastry. Repeat with remaining pastry and filling.

2 Cover and freeze one pie for up to 3 months. Bake second pie at 375° for 15 minutes. Reduce heat; bake at 350° for 1 hour. Meanwhile, drain mushrooms, reserving liquid. Add water to liquid to measure 1 cup; set aside.

3 In a small saucepan, cook mushrooms and flour in oil until bubbly. Remove from the heat; stir in bouillon and reserved mushroom liquid. Bring to a boil; cook and stir for 1 minute or until thickened. Stir in browning sauce if desired. Serve with pie.

4 **To use frozen pie:** Remove from freezer 30 minutes before baking. Bake at 375° for 70 minutes. Prepare gravy as directed. Serve with pie. **Yield:** 2 pies (6-8 servings each).

Chicken Neapolitan | *Joan Williams, Baltimore, Maryland*

I often prepare a week's worth of recipes on the weekend and freeze them so I can quickly have dinner ready for our hungry teenage boys after one of their many sports activities. Served over noodles, this moist chicken with a flavorful sauce is a favorite.

8 **boneless skinless chicken breast halves (4 ounces each)**
2 **teaspoons salt**
1 **teaspoon pepper**
3 **tablespoons olive oil**
1 **cup chopped onion**
4 **garlic cloves, minced**
1 **pound fresh mushrooms, quartered**
2 **cans (10-3/4 ounces each) condensed tomato bisque soup, undiluted**
3/4 **cup red wine or beef broth**
1 **teaspoon dried basil**
1 **teaspoon dried oregano**
Hot cooked noodles or rice
Sliced ripe olives and minced fresh parsley, optional

1 Sprinkle chicken with salt and pepper. In a large skillet, cook chicken, uncovered, over medium-high heat in oil for 8-9 minutes. Turn chicken; add the onion, garlic and mushrooms. Cook 8 minutes longer or until a meat thermometer reaches 170°.

2 Using a slotted spoon, remove four chicken breast halves and half of the vegetables to a greased 2-1/2-qt. baking dish. Cool.

3 In a large bowl, whisk together the soup, wine, basil and oregano; pour half over chicken in skillet. Cover and simmer for 5-10 minutes or until heated through. Serve over noodles. Garnish with olives and parsley if desired.

4 Pour remaining soup mixture over chicken in baking dish. Cover and freeze for up to 3 months.

5 **To use frozen chicken:** Thaw in the refrigerator overnight. Remove from the refrigerator 30 minutes before baking. Cover and bake at 350° for 35-40 minutes or until heated through. Serve over noodles. Garnish with olives and parsley if desired. **Yield:** 8 servings.

Southern Vegetable Soup | *Christy Hinrichs, Parkville, Missouri*

This chunky, vegetable-filled soup is a surefire way to warm up those cold winter nights.

1/2	**cup chopped onion**
2	**teaspoons minced garlic**
2	**teaspoons olive oil**
2	**cans (14-1/2 ounces each) vegetable broth**
1	**can (28 ounces) crushed tomatoes**
1	**package (16 ounces) frozen mixed vegetables**
1	**cup sliced fresh or frozen okra**
1	**can (4 ounces) chopped green chilies**
2	**teaspoons dried savory**
1	**teaspoon sugar**
1/2	**teaspoon salt**
1/2	**teaspoon dried tarragon**
1/8	**teaspoon white pepper**

1 In a Dutch oven, saute onion and garlic in oil for 3 minutes or until tender. Stir in the remaining ingredients. Bring to a boil. Reduce heat; cover and simmer for 15-20 minutes or until vegetables are crisp-tender.

2 Serve desired amount. Cool remaining soup; transfer to freezer containers. May be frozen for up to 3 months.

3 To use frozen soup: Thaw soup in the refrigerator overnight. Place in a saucepan and heat through. **Yield:** 10 servings (2-1/2 quarts).

Curry-Chutney Cheese Mold | *Carmen Courtney, Ashland, Virginia*

Featuring loads of bacon, green onions and peanuts, this exotic appetizer is a true timesaver due to its make-ahead convenience. I include this spread on my cheese platter when giving a party.

3 packages (8 ounces each) cream cheese, softened
1 cup (8 ounces) sour cream
3/4 cup real bacon bits
1/2 cup finely chopped green onions
2 teaspoons curry powder
1 cup salted peanuts, finely chopped
1 cup raisins, finely chopped
ADDITIONAL INGREDIENTS (for each cheese mold):
1/2 cup chutney
1/2 cup flaked coconut, toasted
Assorted crackers

1 In a large bowl, combine the cream cheese, sour cream, bacon, onions and curry powder. Fold in peanuts and raisins. Lightly press into two 3-cup freezer dishes coated with cooking spray.

2 Cover and freeze one mold for up to 1 month. Cover and freeze the second mold for at least 1 hour; unmold onto a serving plate. Top with chutney and coconut. Serve with crackers.

3 **To use frozen cheese mold:** Unmold onto a serving plate; thaw in the refrigerator. Just before serving, top with chutney and coconut. **Yield:** 2 cheese molds (2-1/2 cups each).

Double Meat Loaf | *Shirley Snyder, Payson, Arizona*

This tender meat loaf with beef and pork is a delicious entree for every day or when company comes to call.

1 egg
1 cup beef broth
1/2 cup quick-cooking oats
1 tablespoon dried minced onion
2 teaspoons dried parsley flakes
1 teaspoon salt
1/2 teaspoon pepper
1-1/2 pounds lean ground beef
1 pound bulk pork sausage
1 can (8 ounces) tomato sauce

1 In a large bowl, combine the egg, broth, oats, onion, parsley, salt and pepper. Crumble beef and sausage over mixture; mix well. Pat into two greased 8-in. x 4-in. loaf pans. Top with tomato sauce.

2 Cover and freeze one meat loaf for up to 3 months. Bake the second loaf, uncovered, at 350° for 55-60 minutes or until a meat thermometer reads 160°.

3 **To use frozen meat loaf:** Thaw in the refrigerator overnight. Remove from the refrigerator 30 minutes before baking. Bake as directed. **Yield:** 2 loaves (4-6 servings each).

Turkey Potpies | *Laurie Jensen, Cadillac, Michigan*

With their golden brown crust and scrumptious filling, these comforting potpies will warm you down to your toes. They bake and cut beautifully.

2	medium potatoes, peeled and cut into 1-inch pieces
3	medium carrots, cut into 1-inch slices
1	medium onion, chopped
1	celery rib, diced
2	tablespoons butter
1	tablespoon olive oil
6	tablespoons all-purpose flour
3	cups chicken broth
4	cups cubed cooked turkey
2/3	cup frozen peas
1/2	cup plus 1 tablespoon heavy whipping cream, divided
1	tablespoon minced fresh parsley
1	teaspoon garlic salt
1/4	teaspoon pepper
1	package (15 ounces) refrigerated pie pastry
1	egg

1 In a Dutch oven, saute the potatoes, carrots, onion and celery in butter and oil until tender. Stir in flour until blended; gradually add broth. Bring to a boil; cook and stir for 2 minutes or until thickened. Stir in the turkey, peas, 1/2 cup cream, parsley, garlic salt and pepper.

2 Spoon into two ungreased 9-in. pie plates. Roll out pastry to fit top of each pie; place over filling. Trim, seal and flute edges. Cut out a decorative center or cut slits in pastry. In a small bowl, whisk egg and remaining cream; brush over dough.

3 Cover and freeze one potpie for up to 3 months. Bake the remaining potpie at 375° for 40-45 minutes or until golden brown. Let stand for 10 minutes before cutting.

4 **To use frozen potpie:** Remove from the freezer 30 minutes before baking (do not thaw). Cover edges of crust loosely with foil; place on a baking sheet. Bake at 425° for 30 minutes. Reduce heat to 350°; remove foil. Bake 55-60 minutes longer or until golden brown. **Yield:** 2 pies (6 servings each).

Flavorful Swedish Meatballs | *Stacy Thomas, Anchorage, Alaska*

Our kids love to roll the ground beef and pork mixture into these moist meatballs. We enjoy them prepared in a creamy gravy. But the frozen meatballs also are great additions to soups and stews, or to stir into spaghetti sauce and serve over pasta.

    2   **eggs, lightly beaten**
  1/4   **cup ketchup**
  3/4   **cup dry bread crumbs**
    2   **tablespoons dried parsley flakes**
    2   **tablespoons Worcestershire sauce**
    1   **teaspoon onion powder**
    1   **teaspoon garlic powder**
    1   **teaspoon pepper**
  1/2   **teaspoon salt**
  1/2   **teaspoon chili powder**
    2   **pounds ground beef**
    1   **pound ground pork**
ADDITIONAL INGREDIENTS (for each batch):
    1   **envelope brown gravy mix**
  1/2   **cup sour cream**
Dash each nutmeg and pepper
Hot cooked noodles

1 In a large bowl, combine the eggs, ketchup, bread crumbs, parsley, Worcestershire sauce and seasonings. Crumble meat over mixture and mix well. Shape into 1-in. balls, about 6 dozen.

2 Place meatballs on greased racks in shallow baking pans. Bake at 400° for 20 minutes or until no longer pink, turning often; drain. Cool. Place about 35 meatballs into a freezer container. May be frozen for up to 3 months.

3 **To prepare Swedish meatballs:** In a large skillet, prepare gravy according to package directions. Add the remaining meatballs; cover and cook for 10 minutes or until heated through. Remove from the heat; stir in the sour cream, nutmeg and pepper. Serve over noodles.

4 **To use frozen meatballs:** Completely thaw in the refrigerator. Prepare as directed. **Yield:** 2 batches (35 meatballs per batch).

South-of-the-Border Quiche | *Paula Marchesi, Lenhartsville, Pennsylvania*

Every holiday we have brunch, and that's when I make a quiche. This is the family's most-requested quiche recipe. When the entire family gets together, I have to make several. There are never any leftovers.

2 **unbaked pastry shells (9 inches)**
2 **teaspoons chili powder**
1 **teaspoon ground cumin**
1-1/2 **cups (6 ounces) shredded cheddar cheese**
1-1/2 **cups (6 ounces) shredded Monterey Jack cheese**
1 **cup (4 ounces) shredded sharp cheddar cheese**
8 **eggs**
2 **cups half-and-half cream**
2 **cans (4 ounces each) chopped green chilies**
2 **cans (2-1/4 ounces each) sliced ripe olives, drained**
1/4 **cup chopped green onions**
2 **tablespoons minced fresh cilantro**
1/2 **teaspoon salt**
1/2 **teaspoon pepper**
Salsa and sour cream, optional

1 Line unpricked pastry shells with a double thickness of heavy-duty foil. Bake at 400° for 5 minutes. Remove foil; bake 5 minutes longer.

2 Sprinkle chili powder and cumin over shells; sprinkle with cheeses. In a large bowl, whisk the eggs, cream, chilies, olives, onions, cilantro, salt and pepper. Pour evenly over cheese.

3 Cover and freeze one quiche for up to 3 months. Cover edges of second quiche loosely with foil; place on a baking sheet. Bake at 400° for 35-40 minutes or until a knife inserted near the center comes out clean. Let stand for 10 minutes before cutting. Serve with salsa and sour cream if desired.

4 To use frozen quiche: Remove from the freezer 30 minutes before baking (do not thaw). Cover edges of crust loosely with foil; place on a baking sheet. Bake at 400° for 55-60 minutes or until a knife inserted near the center comes out clean. Let stand for 10 minutes before cutting. **Yield:** 2 quiches (6 servings each).

Beef Barley Soup | *Lisa Otis, Drain, Oregon*

This satisfying soup is wonderful for a busy day when you want something hot in a hurry. It makes a hearty meal with warm bread and a green salad.

- 2 **pounds ground beef**
- 2 **medium onions, chopped**
- 1/2 **cup chopped celery**
- 3 **cups water**
- 2 **cans (14-1/2 ounces each) beef broth**
- 1 **cup quick-cooking barley**
- 2 **cans (14-1/2 ounces each) diced tomatoes with garlic and onion, undrained**
- 2 **teaspoons Worcestershire sauce**
- 1 **teaspoon salt**
- 1 **teaspoon dried basil**

1 In a Dutch oven, cook the beef, onions and celery over medium heat until meat is no longer pink; drain. Stir in the water and broth; bring to a boil. Reduce heat. Add barley; cover and simmer for 10-20 minutes or until barley is tender.

2 Stir in the remaining ingredients; heat through. Serve one quart immediately. Cool remaining soup. Transfer to two 1-qt. freezer containers; cover and freeze for up to 3 months.

3 To use frozen soup: Thaw in the refrigerator. Place in a saucepan and heat through. **Yield:** 3 batches (3 quarts total).

Mashed Potato Cups | *Jill Hancock, Nashua, New Hampshire*

This recipe makes a tasty side dish that's a nice alternative to the standard potatoes or rice.

- 6 **cups hot mashed potatoes (without added milk and butter)**
- 1/2 **cup milk**
- 1/4 **cup butter**
- 1 **teaspoon salt**
- 1/8 **teaspoon pepper**
- 1-1/3 **cups plus 2 tablespoons shredded Colby-Monterey Jack cheese, divided**
- 2 **tablespoons minced fresh parsley**

1 In a large bowl, beat the mashed potatoes, milk, butter, salt and pepper until smooth. Stir in 1-1/3 cups cheese. Grease two 6-cup muffin pans; divide potato mixture between muffin cups. Sprinkle with remaining cheese; top with parsley.

2 Cover and freeze one pan for up to 3 months. Bake the remaining pan, uncovered, at 350° for 15-20 minutes or until heated through and cheese is melted.

3 To use frozen potato cups: Thaw in the refrigerator. Bake as directed. **Yield:** 2 pans (6 servings each).

Shepherd's Pie | *Paula Zsiray, Logan, Utah*

This classic recipe makes one pie to eat right away and one batch of meat mixture to freeze for another day. Just pull out the frozen beef any time you have some leftover mashed potatoes.

- **2 pounds ground beef**
- **2 cans (12 ounces each) beef gravy**
- **2 cups frozen corn**
- **2 cups frozen peas and carrots**
- **2 teaspoons dried minced onion**

ADDITIONAL INGREDIENTS (for each casserole):
- **2 to 3 cups mashed potatoes**
- **2 tablespoons butter, melted**

Paprika

1 In a Dutch oven, cook beef over medium heat until no longer pink; drain. Add the gravy, vegetables and onion.

2 Spoon half into a greased 2-qt. baking dish or four 2-cup ovenproof dishes. Top with mashed potatoes. Drizzle with butter and sprinkle with paprika. Bake, uncovered, at 350° for 30-35 minutes or until heated through.

3 Cool the remaining beef mixture. Transfer to a freezer container. May be frozen for up to 3 months.

4 To prepare frozen beef mixture: Thaw in the refrigerator; transfer to a greased 2-qt. baking dish. Top with the potatoes, butter and paprika; bake as directed. **Yield:** 2 casseroles (4 servings each).

Meaty Pasta Casseroles | *Debra Butcher, Decatur, Indiana*

I love this recipe because it makes a lot—two hearty casseroles. Every time I fix it, I add something different, such as more garlic, to give it a little extra flavor.

1	**package (16 ounces) penne pasta**
1	**pound ground beef**
1	**pound bulk Italian pork sausage**
1-3/4	**cups sliced fresh mushrooms**
1	**medium onion, chopped**
1	**medium green pepper, chopped**
2	**cans (14-1/2 ounces each) Italian diced tomatoes**
1	**jar (25.6 ounces) Italian sausage and garlic spaghetti sauce**
1	**jar (16 ounces) chunky mild salsa**
1	**package (8 ounces) sliced pepperoni, chopped**
1	**cup (4 ounces) shredded Swiss cheese, divided**
4	**cups (16 ounces) shredded part-skim mozzarella cheese, divided**
1-1/2	**cups shredded Parmesan cheese, divided**
1	**jar (26 ounces) three-cheese spaghetti sauce**

1 Cook pasta according to package directions. Meanwhile, in a Dutch oven, cook the beef, sausage, mushrooms, onion and green pepper over medium heat until meat is no longer pink; drain.

2 Drain pasta; add to the meat mixture. Stir in the tomatoes, sausage and garlic spaghetti sauce, salsa and pepperoni.

3 Divide half of pasta mixture between two greased 13-in. x 9-in. baking dishes. Sprinkle each with 1/4 cup Swiss cheese, 1 cup mozzarella cheese and 1/3 cup Parmesan cheese. Spread 3/4 cup of three-cheese spaghetti sauce over each. Top with remaining pasta mixture and three-cheese spaghetti sauce. Sprinkle with remaining cheeses.

4 Cover and freeze one casserole for up to 3 months. Cover and bake remaining casserole at 350° for 25 minutes. Uncover; bake 10 minutes longer or until cheese is melted.

5 **To use frozen casserole:** Thaw in the refrigerator overnight. Remove from the refrigerator 30 minutes before baking. Cover and bake at 350° for 45 minutes. Uncover; bake 10 minutes longer or until cheese is melted. **Yield:** 2 casseroles (6 servings each).

Jalapeno Chicken Enchiladas | *Kaylin DeVries, Magna, Utah*

These creamy enchiladas are likely to be as popular at your house as they are at mine. I have many requests for this recipe. For weddings, I place the recipe in a nice casserole dish to give as a gift.

2	cans (15 ounces each) tomato sauce, divided
4	cans (10-3/4 ounces each) condensed cream of chicken soup, undiluted
4	cups (32 ounces) sour cream
4	jalapeno peppers, seeded and chopped
1	teaspoon onion salt
1/4	teaspoon pepper
4	cups cubed cooked chicken
3	cups (12 ounces) shredded cheddar cheese, divided
20	flour tortillas (8 inches), warmed

1 In each of two greased 13-in. x 9-in. baking dishes, spread 1/2 cup tomato sauce; set aside. In a large bowl, combine the soup, sour cream, jalapenos, onion salt and pepper. Stir in chicken and 2 cups cheese.

2 Spread about 1/2 cup chicken mixture down the center of each tortilla. Roll up and place seam side down in prepared dishes. Top with remaining tomato sauce; sprinkle with the remaining cheese.

3 Cover and freeze one casserole for up to 1 month. Cover and bake second casserole at 350° for 35-45 minutes or until edges are bubbly.

4 **To use frozen casserole:** Thaw in the refrigerator overnight. Remove from the refrigerator 30 minutes before baking. Bake, covered, at 350° for 40-45 minutes or until edges are bubbly. **Yield:** 2 casseroles (5 servings each).

Editor's Note: When cutting hot peppers, disposable gloves are recommended. Avoid touching your face.

Pizza-Flavored Pasta Sauce | *Angelina Falzarano, Midlothian, Texas*

This chunky, jazzed-up spaghetti sauce with pasta is sure to please hungry kids...and busy moms, too. Served with garlic bread, it really hits the spot when you crave Italian food.

- 1 **pound bulk Italian sausage**
- 1/2 **pound sliced fresh mushrooms**
- 2 **packages (3-1/2 ounces each) sliced pepperoni**
- 3/4 **cup chopped green pepper**
- 1/2 **cup chopped onion**
- 2 **jars (28 ounces each) meatless spaghetti sauce**
- 1 **can (3.8 ounces) sliced ripe olives, drained, divided**
- 2 **tablespoons Italian seasoning**

Hot cooked pasta

1 In a large skillet, cook the sausage, mushrooms, pepperoni, green pepper and onion over medium heat until sausage is no longer pink; drain. Stir in the spaghetti sauce, olives and Italian seasoning.

2 Bring to a boil. Reduce heat; simmer, uncovered, for 10-12 minutes or until heated through. Serve desired amount over pasta. Cool remaining sauce and transfer to freezer containers. May be frozen for up to 3 months.

3 To use frozen sauce: Thaw in the refrigerator overnight. Place in a saucepan and heat through. **Yield:** 9 servings (about 2 quarts).

Sausage Rice Casserole | *Jennifer Trost, West Linn, Oregon*

I fiddled around with this dish, trying to adjust it to my family's tastes. When my pickiest child cleaned her plate, I knew I'd found the right flavor combination.

- 2 **packages (7.2 ounces each) rice pilaf**
- 2 **pounds bulk pork sausage**
- 6 **celery ribs, chopped**
- 4 **medium carrots, sliced**
- 1 **can (10-3/4 ounces) condensed cream of chicken soup, undiluted**
- 1 **can (10-3/4 ounces) condensed cream of mushroom soup, undiluted**
- 2 **teaspoons onion powder**
- 1/2 **teaspoon garlic powder**
- 1/4 **teaspoon pepper**

1 Prepare rice mixes according to the package directions. Meanwhile, in a large skillet, cook the sausage, celery and carrots over medium heat until meat is no longer pink; drain.

2 In a large bowl, combine the sausage mixture, rice, soups, onion powder, garlic powder and pepper. Transfer to two greased 11-in. x 7-in. baking dishes.

3 Cover and freeze one casserole for up to 3 months. Cover and bake the second casserole at 350° for 40-45 minutes or until vegetables are tender.

4 To use frozen casserole: Thaw in the refrigerator overnight. Remove from the refrigerator 30 minutes before baking. Bake as directed. **Yield:** 2 casseroles (6-8 servings each).

Cheesy Vegetable Soup | *Sandra Goetzinger-Andrews, Hiawatha, Iowa*

My sister, Cari, brought this soup to a New Year's Eve family get-together. I was hesitant to try it, but one taste and I was hooked. It makes a large batch, so I freeze leftovers in single-serving containers to take to work for lunch.

6   cups water
1   package (30 ounces) frozen shredded hash brown potatoes
1   package (16 ounces) frozen California-blend vegetables
4   teaspoons chicken bouillon granules
1   pound process cheese (Velveeta), cubed
2   cans (10-3/4 ounces each) condensed cream of mushroom soup, undiluted
1   cup milk

1 In a Dutch oven, bring water to a boil. Add the hash browns, vegetables and bouillon. Reduce heat; cover and simmer for 10 minutes or until vegetables are tender. Stir in the cheese, soup and milk; cook and stir until cheese is melted.

2 Serve desired amount of soup. Cool remaining soup; transfer to freezer containers. May be frozen for up to 3 months.

3 To use frozen soup: Thaw in the refrigerator. Heat in a saucepan, adding additional milk if desired to achieve desired thickness. **Yield:** 14 servings (2-1/2 quarts).

Creamy Chicken 'n' Mushrooms | *Donna Brockett, Kingfisher, Oklahoma*

The convenience of canned soup makes this main dish a quick-and-easy option for the holiday season or any time of year.

8   boneless skinless chicken breast halves (6 ounces each)
4   tablespoons butter, divided
3   cups sliced fresh mushrooms
1/2 cup chopped onion
1/2 teaspoon garlic powder
2   cans (10-3/4 ounces each) condensed cream of mushroom soup, undiluted
1   cup milk
1/2 teaspoon pepper
Hot cooked rice or noodles

1 In a large skillet, brown chicken in batches in 2 tablespoons butter. Transfer to two ungreased 8-in. square baking dishes. Cover and bake at 350° for 20-25 minutes or until a meat thermometer reaches 170°.

2 Meanwhile, in the same skillet, saute the mushrooms, onion and garlic powder in remaining butter until tender. Add the soup, milk and pepper. Bring to a boil. Reduce heat; simmer, uncovered, for 5-6 minutes or until heated through.

3 Drain chicken; top with soup mixture. Cover and freeze one casserole for up to 3 months. Serve the second casserole with rice or noodles.

4 To use frozen casserole: Thaw in the refrigerator overnight. Cover and microwave on high for 8-10 minutes or until heated through, stirring once. Serve with rice or noodles. **Yield:** 2 casseroles (4 servings each).

Supper Suggestions

It's easy to round out this meal and add a little color to the menu. Simply toss a salad of mixed greens with tomato wedges, shredded carrot and sliced red onion. Or for a warm option, microwave a package of frozen green peas, green beans or broccoli spears.

Cheddar Turkey Bake | *Carol Dilcher, Emmaus, Pennsylvania*

This recipe makes two creamy casseroles, so you can serve one for dinner and freeze the second for a night when you're racing the clock.

2 **cups chicken broth**

2 **cups water**

4 **teaspoons dried minced onion**

2 **cups uncooked long grain rice**

2 **cups frozen peas, thawed**

4 **cups cubed cooked turkey**

2 **cans (10-3/4 ounces each) condensed cheddar cheese soup, undiluted**

2 **cups milk**

1 **teaspoon salt, optional**

2 **cups finely crushed butter-flavored crackers (about 60 crackers)**

6 **tablespoons butter, melted**

1 In a large saucepan, bring the broth, water and onion to a boil. Reduce heat. Add rice; cover and simmer for 15 minutes. Remove from the heat; fluff with a fork.

2 Divide rice between two greased 9-in. square baking pans. Sprinkle each with peas and turkey. In a bowl, combine the soup, milk and salt if desired until smooth; pour over turkey. Toss the cracker crumbs and butter; sprinkle over the top.

3 Cover and freeze one casserole for up to 3 months. Bake the second casserole, uncovered, at 350° for 35 minutes or until golden brown.

4 **To use frozen casserole:** Thaw in the refrigerator for 24 hours. Remove from the refrigerator 30 minutes before baking. Bake, uncovered, at 350° for 45-50 minutes or until heated through. **Yield:** 2 casseroles (4-6 servings each).

Three-Meat Spaghetti Sauce | *Ellen Stringer, Bourbonnais, Illinois*

I simmer this hearty sauce in large batches, freeze it and use it for spaghetti, lasagna, mostaccioli and pizza. I adapted the original recipe until I came up with the perfect sauce. I've received many compliments from friends and family. I simmer it in a large electric roaster instead of on the stovetop.

1 pound ground beef
1 pound bulk Italian sausage
1 cup chopped onion
1 can (28 ounces) crushed tomatoes
3 cups water
2 cans (6 ounces each) tomato paste
2 jars (4-1/2 ounces each) sliced
  mushrooms, drained
1 cup chopped pepperoni
2 tablespoons grated Parmesan cheese
2 tablespoons Italian seasoning
1 tablespoon sugar
2 teaspoons garlic salt
1 teaspoon pepper
1 teaspoon dried parsley flakes
Hot cooked spaghetti

1 In a Dutch oven, cook beef, sausage and onion over medium heat until meat is no longer pink; drain. Stir in the tomatoes, water, tomato paste, mushrooms, pepperoni, Parmesan cheese and seasonings. Bring to a boil. Reduce heat; cover and simmer for 30 minutes.

2 Serve desired amount over spaghetti. Cool remaining sauce; transfer in serving-size portions to freezer containers. Sauce may be frozen for up to 3 months.

3 To use frozen sauce: Thaw in the refrigerator overnight. Place in a saucepan and heat through. **Yield:** 11-1/2 cups.

tasteofhome.com

Sloppy Joes | *Sandra Castillo, Janesville, Wisconsin*

I simmer up a big batch of this delicious sandwich filling, then freeze the extras. Just thaw and reheat it for a quick dinner. It's also good for larger gatherings.

2 **pounds ground beef**
2 **medium onions, chopped**
2 **to 3 garlic cloves, minced**
2 **cups ketchup**
1 **cup barbecue sauce**
1/4 **cup packed brown sugar**
1/4 **cup cider vinegar**
2 **tablespoons prepared mustard**
1 **teaspoon Italian seasoning**
1 **teaspoon onion powder**
1/2 **teaspoon pepper**
Hamburger buns, split

1 In a large skillet, cook beef, onions and garlic over medium heat until the meat is no longer pink; drain. Stir in the ketchup, barbecue sauce, brown sugar, vinegar, mustard, Italian seasoning, onion powder and pepper. Bring to a boil. Reduce heat; simmer, uncovered, for 20 minutes.

2 Serve about 1/2 cup meat mixture on each bun. Cool remaining meat mixture. Transfer cooled mixture to freezer containers. May be frozen for up to 3 months.

3 To use frozen sloppy joes: Thaw in the refrigerator; place in a saucepan and heat though. Serve on buns. **Yield:** 12 servings (about 6 cups).

Turkey Meatball Soup | *Taste of Home Test Kitchen*

Ready-made turkey meatballs are combined with fresh and frozen vegetables to come up with this nicely seasoned soup. Small families can enjoy half now and freeze the rest for later. But bigger families may want to double the recipe, so there's plenty leftover for a second meal. Sprinkle bowls with Parmesan cheese just before serving.

3 **cups cut fresh green beans**
2 **cups fresh baby carrots**
2 **cups chicken broth**
1 **teaspoon dried oregano**
1 **teaspoon dried basil**
1 **teaspoon minced garlic**
2 **cans (14-1/2 ounces each) Italian stewed tomatoes**
1 **package (12 ounces) refrigerated fully cooked Italian turkey meatballs**
2 **cups frozen corn**

1 In a large saucepan or Dutch oven, combine the beans, carrots, broth and seasonings. Bring to a boil. Reduce heat; cover and simmer for 10 minutes.

2 Add the tomatoes, meatballs and corn. Cover and cook over medium-low heat for 10 minutes or until meatballs are heated through. Serve desired amount. Cool remaining soup; transfer to freezer containers. May be frozen for up to 3 months.

3 To use frozen soup: Thaw in the refrigerator overnight. Place in a saucepan and heat through. **Yield:** 6 servings.

Chicken Taco Quiche | *Tamie Bradford, Grand Forks Air Force Base, North Dakota*

I wanted to make a quiche but didn't want the usual flavors, so I used ingredients I had in my pantry and refrigerator to come up with this recipe. I was surprised at the great taste and how well the flavors came together. My neighbor asked for the recipe and had the same success!

2 **unbaked pastry shells (9 inches)**
2 **cups cubed cooked chicken**
2 **envelopes taco seasoning, divided**
2/3 **cup salsa**
2 **cups (8 ounces) shredded cheddar cheese**
8 **eggs**
2 **cups half-and-half cream**
2 **tablespoons butter, melted**
1 **can (4 ounces) chopped green chilies**
1/2 **cup sliced ripe olives**

1 Line unpricked pastry shells with a double thickness of heavy-duty foil. Bake at 400° for 4 minutes. Remove foil; bake 4 minutes longer.

2 In a small bowl, combine chicken and one envelope taco seasoning; spoon into pastry shells. Top with salsa and cheese. In a large bowl, whisk the eggs, cream, butter and remaining taco seasoning. Stir in chilies and olives. Pour over cheese.

3 Cover and freeze one quiche for up to 3 months. Cover edges of the second quiche loosely with foil; place on a baking sheet. Bake at 400° for 33-35 minutes or until a knife inserted near the center comes out clean. Let stand for 10 minutes before cutting.

4 To use frozen quiche: Remove from the freezer 30 minutes before baking (do not thaw). Cover edges of crust loosely with foil; place on a baking sheet. Bake at 400° for 70-75 minutes or until a knife inserted near the center comes out clean. Let stand for 10 minutes before cutting. **Yield:** 2 quiches (6 servings each).

Cheddar Beef Enchiladas | *Stacy Cizek, Conrad, Iowa*

I created these enchiladas to satisfy several picky eaters in our house. They were an instant hit and are now requested at least once a week. I especially like that we can enjoy this meal twice by freezing half for a later and busier day.

1 **pound ground beef**
1 **envelope taco seasoning**
1 **cup water**
2 **cups cooked rice**
1 **can (16 ounces) refried beans**
2 **cups (8 ounces) shredded cheddar cheese, divided**
10 **to 12 flour tortillas (8 inches), warmed**
1 **jar (16 ounces) salsa**
1 **can (10-3/4 ounces) condensed cream of chicken soup, undiluted**

1 In a large skillet, cook beef over medium heat until no longer pink; drain. Stir in taco seasoning and water. Bring to a boil. Reduce heat; simmer, uncovered, for 5 minutes. Stir in rice. Cook and stir until liquid is evaporated.

2 Spread about 2 tablespoons of refried beans, 1/4 cup beef mixture and 1 tablespoon cheese down the center of each tortilla; roll up. Place seam side down in two greased 13-in. x 9-in. baking dishes.

3 Combine salsa and soup; pour down the center of enchiladas. Sprinkle with remaining cheese. Bake one casserole, uncovered, at 350° for 20-25 minutes or until heated through and cheese is melted. Cover and freeze remaining casserole for up to 3 months.

4 To use frozen casserole: Thaw in the refrigerator overnight. Remove from the refrigerator 30 minutes before baking. Cover and bake at 350° for 30 minutes. Uncover; bake 5-10 minutes longer or until heated through and cheese is melted. **Yield:** 2 casseroles (5-6 enchiladas each).

Green Bean Chicken Casserole | *DeLissa Mingee, Warr Acres, Oklahoma*

My husband, who claims to be strictly a meat-and-potatoes man, asked for seconds the first time I threw together this comforting all-in-one meal. My daughter and several guests raved about it, too.

1   package (6 ounces) long grain and wild
     rice mix
4   cups cubed cooked chicken
1-3/4 cups frozen French-style green beans
1   can (10-3/4 ounces) condensed cream
     of mushroom soup, undiluted
1   can (10-3/4 ounces) condensed cream
     of chicken and broccoli soup, undiluted
1   can (4 ounces) mushroom stems and
     pieces, drained
2/3 cup chopped onion
2/3 cup chopped green pepper
1   envelope onion soup mix
3/4 cup shredded Colby cheese
ADDITIONAL INGREDIENT (for each casserole):
2/3 cup french-fried onions

1 Prepare wild rice according to package directions. Stir in the chicken, beans, soups, mushrooms, onion, green pepper and soup mix. Spoon into two greased 1-1/2-qt. baking dishes. Sprinkle with the cheese.

2 Cover and freeze one casserole for up to 3 months. Cover and bake the second casserole at 350° for 25-30 minutes or until heated through. Uncover; sprinkle with french-fried onions and bake 5 minutes longer or until onions are golden.

3 To use frozen casserole: Completely thaw in the refrigerator. Remove from the refrigerator 30 minutes before baking. Cover and bake at 350° for 60-65 minutes or until heated through. Uncover; sprinkle with french-fried onions and bake 5 minutes longer. **Yield:** 2 casseroles (4-6 servings each).

Meatball Soup | *Sue Miller, Walworth, Wisconsin*

It's just like a meal in a bowl...or for heartier appetites, serve it with a sandwich. It's great for chilly days.

1 egg, lightly beaten
1/4 cup dry bread crumbs
1/4 cup minced fresh parsley
2 tablespoons grated Parmesan cheese
1/4 teaspoon garlic salt, optional
1/8 teaspoon pepper
1/2 pound lean ground beef
4 cups reduced-sodium beef broth
1 can (16 ounces) kidney beans, rinsed and drained
1 can (14-1/2 ounces) stewed tomatoes
1 medium carrot, thinly sliced
1 teaspoon Italian seasoning
1/4 cup uncooked tiny shell pasta

1 In a small bowl, combine the egg, bread crumbs, parsley, Parmesan cheese, garlic salt if desired and pepper. Crumble beef over mixture; mix well. Shape into 1-in. balls. Brown meatballs in a large saucepan; drain. Add broth, beans, tomatoes, carrot and Italian seasoning. Bring to a boil. Reduce heat; cover and simmer for 10 minutes.

2 Add pasta; simmer 10 minutes longer or until meat is no longer pink and pasta is tender.

3 Serve the desired amount. Cool the remaining soup; transfer in 1-1/2-cup portions to freezer containers. May be frozen for up to 3 months.

4 To use the frozen soup: Thaw the soup in the refrigerator. Place soup in a saucepan and heat through. **Yield:** 5 servings.

Honey-Dijon Chicken | *Barbara Leventhal, Hauppauge, New York*

These moist, tender chicken breasts are nicely browned, then covered in a flavorful sauce that gets its sweetness from honey and pineapple juice. It's delicious served over egg noodles. Even kids are sure to like it.

12	boneless skinless chicken breast halves (4 ounces each)
4	garlic cloves, minced
2	teaspoons dried thyme

Salt and pepper to taste

1	tablespoon canola oil
2	tablespoons cornstarch
1-1/2	cups pineapple juice
1/2	cup water
1/2	cup Dijon mustard
1/3	cup honey

Hot cooked rice or noodles

1 Rub chicken with garlic and thyme. Sprinkle with salt and pepper. In a large skillet, cook chicken in oil or until a meat thermometer reads 170°. In a small bowl, combine the cornstarch, pineapple juice and water until smooth. Stir in mustard and honey. Add to the skillet. Bring to a boil; cook and stir for 2 minutes or until thickened.

2 Spoon half of the chicken and sauce into a greased 11-in. x 7-in. baking dish; cool. Cover and freeze for up to 3 months. Serve remaining chicken and sauce with rice or noodles.

3 To use frozen chicken: Completely thaw in the refrigerator. Remove from the refrigerator 30 minutes before baking. Cover and bake at 350° for 35 minutes or until heated through. **Yield:** 2 casseroles (6 servings each).

Flavorful Southwestern Chili | *Jenny Greear, Huntington, West Virginia*

This satisfying recipe comes from my grandmother. It tastes wonderful, freezes beautifully and makes a complete, last-minute meal. I top bowls with grated cheddar cheese and chopped black olives and serve tortilla chips on the side.

2	pounds ground beef
1-1/2	cups chopped onions
2	cans (14-1/2 ounces each) diced tomatoes, undrained
1	can (15 ounces) pinto beans, rinsed and drained
1	can (15 ounces) tomato sauce
1	package (10 ounces) frozen corn, thawed
1	cup salsa
3/4	cup water
1	can (4 ounces) chopped green chilies
1	teaspoon ground cumin
1/2	teaspoon garlic powder

1 In a Dutch oven, cook beef and onions over medium heat until meat is no longer pink; drain. Stir in the remaining ingredients. Bring to a boil. Reduce heat; simmer, uncovered, for 15 minutes.

2 Serve desired amount. Cool the remaining chili; transfer to freezer containers. May be frozen for up to 3 months.

3 To use frozen chili: Thaw in the refrigerator. Place in a saucepan; heat through. **Yield:** 10 servings (2-1/2 quarts).

Breakfast Bake | *Kim Weaver, Olathe, Kansas*

This light, fluffy egg casserole, sprinkled with smoky bacon, retains its fresh flavor after freezing. While it's ideal for breakfast, it's an easy-to-reheat meal for lunch or dinner, too.

4-1/2 **cups seasoned croutons**

2 **cups (8 ounces) shredded cheddar cheese**

1 **medium onion, chopped**

1/4 **cup chopped sweet red pepper**

1/4 **cup chopped green pepper**

1 **jar (4-1/2 ounces) sliced mushrooms, drained**

8 **eggs**

4 **cups milk**

1 **teaspoon salt**

1 **teaspoon ground mustard**

1/8 **teaspoon pepper**

8 **bacon strips, cooked and crumbled**

1 Sprinkle croutons, cheese, onion, peppers and mushrooms into two greased 8-in. square baking dishes. In a bowl, combine the eggs, milk, salt, mustard and pepper. Slowly pour over vegetables. Sprinkle with bacon.

2 Cover and freeze one casserole for up to 3 months. Bake the second casserole, uncovered, at 350° for 45-50 minutes or until a knife inserted near the center comes out clean.

3 To use frozen casserole: Completely thaw in the refrigerator for 24-36 hours. Remove from the refrigerator 30 minutes before baking. Bake, uncovered, at 350° for 50-60 minutes or until a knife inserted near the center comes out clean. **Yield:** 2 casseroles (6-8 servings each).

Chicken and Bows | *Danette Forbes, Overland Park, Kansas*

I first made this recipe when I was a professional nanny. It comes together quickly at dinnertime when the kids are hungry. Freezing half the mixture means another supper is ready whenever you need it.

1	package (16 ounces) bow tie pasta
2	pounds boneless skinless chicken breasts, cut into strips
1	cup chopped sweet red pepper
1/4	cup butter, cubed
2	cans (10-3/4 ounces each) condensed cream of chicken soup, undiluted
2	cups frozen peas
1-1/2	cups milk
1	teaspoon garlic powder
1/4	to 1/2 teaspoon salt
1/4	teaspoon pepper
2/3	cup grated Parmesan cheese

1 Cook pasta according to package directions. Meanwhile, in a Dutch oven, cook chicken and red pepper in butter over medium heat for 5-6 minutes or until chicken juices run clear.

2 Stir in the soup, peas, milk, garlic powder, salt and pepper. Bring to a boil. Reduce heat; simmer, uncovered, for 1-2 minutes or until heated through. Stir in Parmesan cheese. Drain pasta; add to chicken mixture and toss to coat.

3 Serve half of the mixture immediately. Cool remaining mixture; transfer to a freezer container. Cover and freeze for up to 3 months.

4 **To use frozen chicken mixture:** Thaw in the refrigerator overnight. Transfer to an ungreased shallow 3-qt. microwave-safe dish. Cover and microwave on high for 8-10 minutes or until heated through, stirring once. **Yield:** 2 casseroles (6 servings each).

Editor's Note: This recipe was tested in a 1,100-watt microwave.

Beef Taco Lasagna | *Stacey Compton, Toledo, Ohio*

This recipe makes two big pans, so you have a no-fuss second meal on hand. This appealing lasagna is also great for large get-togethers.

- 24 lasagna noodles
- 2 pounds lean ground beef
- 2 envelopes taco seasoning
- 4 egg whites
- 2 cartons (15 ounces each) ricotta cheese
- 8 cups (2 pounds) shredded cheddar cheese
- 2 jars (24 ounces each) chunky salsa

1 Cook noodles according to package directions. Meanwhile, in a large skillet, cook beef over medium heat until no longer pink; drain. Stir in taco seasoning. In a small bowl, combine egg whites and ricotta cheese. Drain noodles.

2 In each of two 13-in. x 9-in. baking dishes, layer four noodles, 3/4 cup ricotta mixture, half of the beef mixture and 1-1/3 cups cheddar cheese. Top each with four noodles, 3/4 cup ricotta mixture, 1-1/2 cups salsa and 1-1/3 cups cheese. Repeat.

3 Cover and freeze one casserole for up to 3 months. Bake the second casserole, uncovered, at 350° for 35-40 minutes or until heated through. Let stand for 10 minutes before cutting.

4 **To use frozen casserole:** Thaw in the refrigerator for 8 hours. Remove from the refrigerator 30 minutes before baking. Bake as directed. **Yield:** 2 casseroles (8 servings each).

Hearty Ham Loaves | *Audrey Thibodeau, Gilbert, Arizona*

This simple-to-prepare recipe yields two ham loaves. They're so nicely flavored with a variety of seasonings that everyone raves about them.

1 cup crushed butter-flavored crackers (about 25)
2/3 cup finely chopped onion
1/2 cup finely chopped green pepper
2 eggs, lightly beaten
2 tablespoons lemon juice
1 teaspoon ground mustard
1 teaspoon ground ginger
1 teaspoon Worcestershire sauce
1/4 teaspoon pepper
Dash ground nutmeg
Dash paprika
1-1/3 pounds finely ground fully cooked ham
1 pound bulk pork sausage

GLAZE:
1/2 cup packed brown sugar
1/4 cup cider vinegar
1/4 cup water
1 teaspoon ground mustard

1 In a large bowl, combine the crackers, onion, green pepper, eggs, lemon juice and seasonings. Sprinkle ham and sausage over the cracker mixture and mix well. Shape into two loaves. Place in ungreased 9-in. x 5-in. loaf pans. Cover and freeze one ham loaf for up to 2 months. Bake the remaining loaf, uncovered, at 350° for 1 hour.

2 Meanwhile, in a small saucepan, combine glaze ingredients. Bring to a boil; boil for 2 minutes. Remove loaf from the oven; drain. Baste with half of the glaze. Cool remaining glaze and set aside. Bake ham loaf 30-40 minutes longer or until a meat thermometer reads 160°, basting ham loaf occasionally. Cover and freeze reserved glaze for up to 2 months.

3 **To prepare frozen ham loaf with the frozen glaze:** Thaw both in the refrigerator overnight and bake as directed. **Yield:** 2 loaves (6-8 servings each).

Southwestern Casserole | *Joan Hallford, North Richland Hills, Texas*

I've been making this family-pleasing dish for years. It tastes wonderful, and fits nicely into our budget.

1	package (7 ounces) elbow macaroni
2	pounds ground beef
1	large onion, chopped
2	garlic cloves, minced
2	cans (14-1/2 ounces each) diced tomatoes, undrained
1	can (16 ounces) kidney beans, rinsed and drained
1	can (6 ounces) tomato paste
1	can (4 ounces) chopped green chilies, drained
1-1/2	teaspoons salt
1	teaspoon chili powder
1/2	teaspoon ground cumin
1/2	teaspoon pepper
2	cups (8 ounces) shredded Monterey Jack cheese
2	jalapeno peppers, seeded and chopped

1 Cook macaroni according to package directions. Meanwhile, in large saucepan or Dutch oven, cook the beef, onion and garlic over medium heat until meat is no longer pink; drain. Stir in the tomatoes, beans, tomato paste, chilies and seasonings. Bring to a boil. Reduce heat; simmer, uncovered, for 10 minutes. Drain macaroni; stir into beef mixture.

2 Transfer to two greased 2-qt. baking dishes. Top with cheese and jalapenos. Cover and bake at 375° for 30 minutes. Uncover; bake 10 minutes longer or until bubbly and heated through. Serve one casserole. Cool the second casserole; cover and freeze for up to 3 months.

3 To use frozen casserole: Thaw in the refrigerator for 8 hours. Remove from the refrigerator 30 minutes before baking. Cover and bake at 375° for 20-25 minutes or until heated through. **Yield:** 2 casseroles (6 servings each).

Editor's Note: When cutting hot peppers, disposable gloves are recommended. Avoid touching your face.

Sausage Cheese Olive Loaves | *Shana Bailey, Tulia, Texas*

A friend once treated us to one of these attractive rings, and it was so good I asked for the recipe. This hearty bread is perfect for any occasion.

3 loaves (1 pound each) frozen bread dough

1 pound bulk hot pork sausage

1 pound bulk mild pork sausage

1 pound bulk sage pork sausage

1 pound smoked kielbasa or Polish sausage, cut into 1/2-inch pieces

2 cups (8 ounces) shredded cheddar cheese

2 cups (8 ounces) shredded part-skim mozzarella cheese

1 cup grated Parmesan cheese

1 can (6 ounces) ripe olives, drained and sliced

1 jar (5-3/4 ounces) pimiento-stuffed olives, drained and sliced

3 tablespoons butter, melted

1 Thaw bread dough on a greased baking sheet according to package directions; let rise until nearly doubled.

2 Meanwhile, in a large skillet, cook pork sausages over medium heat until no longer pink; drain. Place in a large bowl. Add the kielbasa, cheeses and olives; set aside.

3 Roll each loaf into a 17-in. x 9-in. rectangle. Spread a third of the sausage mixture on each rectangle to within 1 in. of edges. Roll up jelly-roll style, starting with a long side. Pinch seams; place seam side down on greased baking sheets. Form each into a circle; pinch ends together to seal.

4 Bake at 375° for 25-30 minutes or until golden brown. Brush with butter while warm. Serve one loaf warm; refrigerate leftovers for up to 5 days. Cool remaining loaves. Wrap and freeze for up to 3 months.

5 **To use frozen loaves:** Thaw at room temperature for up to 2 hours. Unwrap and place on a baking sheet. Bake at 350° for 30-40 minutes or until heated through. **Yield:** 3 loaves.

Slow-Cooked Chunky Chili | *Margie Shaw, Greenbrier, Arkansas*

Pork sausage, ground beef and plenty of beans make this chili a satisfying meal-starter. I keep the versatile mixture in serving-size containers in my freezer at all times. I can quickly warm up bowls of it on cold days—or use it to fix chili dogs, chili tacos and more.

1 **pound ground beef**
1 **pound bulk pork sausage**
4 **cans (16 ounces each) kidney beans, rinsed and drained**
2 **cans (14-1/2 ounces each) diced tomatoes, undrained**
2 **cans (10 ounces each) diced tomatoes and green chilies, undrained**
1 **large onion, chopped**
1 **medium green pepper, chopped**
1 **envelope taco seasoning**
1/2 **teaspoon salt**
1/4 **teaspoon pepper**

1 In a skillet, cook beef and sausage over medium heat until meat is no longer pink; drain. Transfer to a 5-qt. slow cooker. Stir in remaining ingredients. Cover and cook on high for 4-5 hours or until the vegetables are tender.

2 Serve desired amount. Cool the remaining chili; transfer to freezer bags or containers. May be frozen for up to 3 months.

3 To use frozen chili: Thaw in the refrigerator; place in a saucepan and heat through. Add water if desired. **Yield:** 3 quarts.

Chicken Potpies | *Taste of Home Test Kitchen*

The golden crust and creamy sauce make this veggie-packed pie a sure hit. This mild and comforting family-favorite is in the freezer whenever we need it.

4   cups cubed cooked chicken

4   cups frozen Southern-style hash brown potatoes, thawed

1   package (16 ounces) frozen mixed vegetables, thawed and drained

1   can (10-3/4 ounces) condensed cream of chicken soup, undiluted

1   can (10-3/4 ounces) condensed cream of onion soup, undiluted

1   cup milk

1   cup (8 ounces) sour cream

2   tablespoons all-purpose flour

1/2 teaspoon salt

1/2 teaspoon pepper

1/4 teaspoon garlic powder

1   package (15 ounces) refrigerated pie pastry

1 In a large bowl, combine the chicken, potatoes, vegetables, soups, milk, sour cream, flour and seasonings. Divide between two 9-in. deep-dish pie plates. Roll out pastry to fit the top of each pie. Cut slits in pastry. Place over filling; trim, seal and flute edges.

2 Cover and freeze one potpie for up to 3 months. Bake the second potpie at 400° for 35-40 minutes or until golden brown.

3 To use frozen potpie: Remove from the freezer 30 minutes before baking. Cover edges loosely with foil; place on a baking sheet. Bake at 425° for 30 minutes. Reduce heat to 350°; remove foil and bake 50-55 minutes longer or until golden brown. **Yield:** 2 potpies (6 servings each).

Hamburger Stew | *Marcia Clay, Truman, Minnesota*

A lady from my church gave me this recipe as a way to use my bounty of home-canned tomatoes. My husband loves it, and I like that it's easy to warm up for a carefree dinner in the winter months.

2 **pounds ground beef**

2 **medium onions, chopped**

4 **cans (14-1/2 ounces each) stewed tomatoes**

8 **medium carrots, thinly sliced**

4 **celery ribs, thinly sliced**

2 **medium potatoes, peeled and cubed**

2 **cups water**

1/2 **cup uncooked long grain rice**

1 **to 2 tablespoons salt**

1 **to 2 teaspoons pepper**

ADDITIONAL INGREDIENT (for each batch of stew):

1 **cup water**

1 In a Dutch oven, cook beef and onions over medium heat until meat is no longer pink; drain. Add the tomatoes, carrots, celery, potatoes, water, rice, salt and pepper; bring to a boil. Reduce heat; cover and simmer for 30 minutes or until vegetables and rice are tender.

2 Uncover; simmer 20-30 minutes longer or until thickened. Transfer 3 cups to a saucepan and add water; heat through. Cool remaining stew. Transfer in 3-cup portions to freezer containers. May be frozen for up to 3 months.

3 To use frozen stew: Thaw in the refrigerator for 24 hours. Transfer to a saucepan; add water. Cook until hot and bubbly. **Yield:** about 5 batches (15 cups total).

Chicken Stuffing Casserole | *Cathy Smith, Wyoming, Michigan*

These tasty chicken casseroles are easy to assemble using handy pantry items. They're a great way to use up leftover cooked chicken.

2 packages (6 ounces each) chicken stuffing mix
2 cans (10-3/4 ounces each) condensed cream of mushroom soup, undiluted
1 cup milk
4 cups cubed cooked chicken
2 cups frozen corn
2 cans (8 ounces each) mushroom stems and pieces, drained
4 cups (16 ounces) shredded cheddar cheese

1 Prepare stuffing mixes according to package directions. Meanwhile, in a large bowl, combine soup and milk; set aside. Spread the stuffing into two greased 8-in. square baking dishes. Layer with the chicken, corn, mushrooms, soup mixture and cheese.

2 Cover and freeze one casserole for up to 3 months. Cover and bake the second casserole at 350° for 30-35 minutes or until cheese is melted.

3 **To use frozen casserole:** Remove from the freezer 30 minutes before baking (do not thaw). Bake at 350° for 1-1/2 hours. Uncover; bake 10-15 minutes longer or until heated through. **Yield:** 2 casseroles (6 servings each).

Veggie Lasagna | *Alyce Wyman, Pembina, North Dakota*

This is my daughter-in-law's recipe. It's a tasty and a little different from usual lasagna recipes. You won't even miss the meat!

18   uncooked lasagna noodles
2   eggs
2   egg whites
2   cartons (15 ounces each) reduced-fat ricotta cheese
4   teaspoons dried parsley flakes
2   teaspoons dried basil
2   teaspoons dried oregano
1   teaspoon pepper
8   cups garden-style spaghetti sauce
4   cups (16 ounces) shredded part-skim mozzarella cheese
2   packages (16 ounces each) frozen cut green beans or 8 cups cut fresh green beans
2/3   cup grated Parmesan cheese

1 Cook noodles according to package directions. Meanwhile, in a small bowl, whisk the eggs, egg whites, ricotta cheese, parsley, basil, oregano and pepper; set aside.

2 In each of two 13-in. x 9-in. baking dishes coated with cooking spray, spread 1 cup spaghetti sauce. Drain noodles; place three noodles over spaghetti sauce in each dish.

3 Layer each with a quarter of the ricotta mixture, 1 cup spaghetti sauce, 1 cup mozzarella cheese, three lasagna noodles and half of green beans. Top each with the remaining ricotta mixture, 1 cup spaghetti sauce, remaining lasagna noodles, spaghetti sauce and mozzarella cheese. Sprinkle Parmesan cheese over each.

4 Cover and freeze one lasagna for up to 3 months. Bake second lasagna, uncovered, at 375° for 40-45 minutes or until bubbly and edges are lightly browned. Let stand for 10 minutes before serving.

5 **To use frozen lasagna:** Thaw in the refrigerator overnight. Remove from the refrigerator 30 minutes before baking. Cover and bake at 375° for 1-1/4 to 1-1/2 hours or until bubbly. Let stand for 10 minutes before serving. **Yield:** 2 casseroles (9 servings each).

Ham 'n' Cheese Crepes | *Marion Lowery, Medford, Oregon*

These thin pancakes are easy to freeze and thaw, so you cook up a batch, prepare just enough for two people and save the rest for another time.

- 1/3 **cup cold water**
- 1/3 **cup plus 2 to 3 tablespoons 2% milk, divided**
- 1/2 **cup all-purpose flour**
- 1 **egg**
- 2 **tablespoons butter, melted**
- 1/8 **teaspoon salt**

ADDITIONAL INGREDIENTS (for 4 crepes):

- 1 **tablespoon Dijon mustard**
- 4 **thin slices deli ham**
- 1/2 **cup shredded cheddar cheese**

1 In a blender, combine the water, 1/3 cup milk, flour, egg, butter and salt; cover and process until smooth. Refrigerate for at least 30 minutes; stir. Add remaining milk if batter is too thick.

2 Heat a lightly greased 8-in. skillet; add about 3 tablespoons batter. Lift and tilt pan to evenly coat bottom. Cook until top appears dry; turn and cook 15-20 seconds longer. Repeat with remaining batter, greasing skillet as needed. Stack four crepes with waxed paper in between; cover and freeze for up to 3 months.

3 Spread mustard over remaining crepes; top each with ham and cheese. Roll up tightly. Place in an 8-in. square baking dish coated with cooking spray. Bake, uncovered, at 375° for 10-14 minutes or until heated through.

4 **To use frozen crepes:** Thaw in the refrigerator for about 2 hours. Fill and bake as directed. **Yield:** 4 servings (8 crepes).

Chicken Potato Casserole | *Kersten Campbell, Pullman, Washington*

This savory, satisfying casserole is real comfort food that freezes so well. Thaw it in the fridge overnight, then pop it into the oven the next day for a super-easy supper.

6	large baking potatoes, peeled and cubed
1-1/2	cups water
2	pounds boneless skinless chicken breasts, cut into 1-inch cubes
2	cups (16 ounces) sour cream
3/4	cup shredded cheddar cheese
1/2	cup butter, softened
1/4	cup shredded Parmesan cheese
1	envelope onion soup mix
1/4	cup finely chopped fresh spinach
1/4	cup shredded carrot
1/4	teaspoon salt
1/4	teaspoon garlic powder
1/4	teaspoon pepper
1/4	cup dry bread crumbs

1 Place potatoes and water in a 3-qt. microwave-safe dish. Cover and microwave on high for 12-15 minutes or until tender. Meanwhile, divide chicken between two greased 8-in. square baking dishes.

2 Drain potatoes and place in a large bowl. Add the sour cream, cheddar cheese, butter, Parmesan cheese, soup mix, spinach, carrot, salt, garlic powder and pepper; mash until smooth. Spoon over chicken; sprinkle with bread crumbs.

3 Cover and freeze one casserole for up to 3 months. Bake second casserole, uncovered, at 350° for 45-50 minutes or until chicken juices run clear.

4 **To use frozen casserole:** Thaw in the refrigerator overnight. Remove from the refrigerator 30 minutes before baking. Bake as directed. **Yield:** 2 casseroles (6 servings each).

Editor's Note: This recipe was tested in a 1,100-watt microwave.

Freezer Mashed Potatoes | *Jessie Fortune, Pocahontas, Arkansas*

If you've ever reheated leftover mashed potatoes and been disappointed with the results, you'll welcome this recipe. There's just my husband, Joel, and me, so I like to make these potatoes ahead and use as I need them...without the dirty pans and all the fuss of mashing them. The oven-baked mashed potatoes keep their flavor and creamy texture even after reheating, so you won't feel like you're serving leftovers. Although the recipe calls for reheating in the oven, you can also use your microwave. Simply cook 2-3 minutes on high, stirring twice.

5   **pounds potatoes (about 9 large), peeled and cut into chunks**
2   **tablespoons butter, softened**
1   **cup (8 ounces) sour cream**
2   **packages (3 ounces each) cream cheese, cubed**
1/2   **teaspoon onion powder**
1/2   **teaspoon salt**
1/4   **teaspoon pepper**

1 Place the potatoes in a large saucepan and cover with water. Bring to a boil. Reduce heat; cover and cook for 15-20 minutes or until tender. Drain.

2 In a large bowl, mash potatoes with butter. Beat in the sour cream, cream cheese, onion powder, salt and pepper. Transfer 1-1/2 cups to a 2-cup baking dish coated with cooking spray. Bake, uncovered, at 350° for 30-35 minutes or until heated through.

3 Cool remaining mashed potatoes. Freeze in 1-1/2-cup portions for up to 6 months.

4 To use frozen potatoes: Thaw in the refrigerator. Transfer to a 2-cup baking dish. Bake as directed. **Yield:** 14 servings.

Three-Cheese Lasagna | *Del Mason, Martensville, Saskatchewan*

With all the flavors of lasagna and none of the layering, this recipe is as easy as it is delicious.

2 **pounds ground beef**

1/2 **cup chopped onion**

1 **package (6.4 ounces) lasagna dinner mix**

2-1/4 **cups hot water**

2 **cans (14-1/2 ounces each) diced tomatoes, undrained**

1 **package (10 ounces) frozen chopped spinach, thawed and squeezed dry**

1 **cup sliced fresh mushrooms**

1/2 **cup chopped green onions**

1 **cup (8 ounces) 4% cottage cheese**

1/4 **cup grated Parmesan cheese**

1-1/2 **cups (6 ounces) shredded part-skim mozzarella cheese**

1 In a large skillet, cook beef and onion over medium heat for 10-12 minutes or until meat is no longer pink; drain.

2 Stir in the pasta from the dinner mix, contents of the seasoning mix, water, tomatoes, spinach, mushrooms and onions. Bring to a boil. Reduce heat; cover and simmer for 10-13 minutes or until pasta is tender. Stir in the cottage cheese and Parmesan. Transfer to two greased 8-in. square baking dishes. Sprinkle with mozzarella cheese.

3 Cover and freeze one casserole for up to 3 months. Cover and bake the second casserole at 350° for 15-20 minutes or until bubbly and cheese is melted.

4 To use frozen casserole: Remove from the freezer 30 minutes before baking (do not thaw). Cover and bake at 350° for 1 hour. Uncover; bake 15-20 minutes longer or until heated through. **Yield:** 2 casseroles (4 servings each).

Editor's Note: This recipe was tested with Hamburger Helper Lasagna Dinner Mix.

Pasta Crab Casserole | *Georgia Mountain, Tampa, Florida*

This is an easy dish to freeze ahead for company. A yummy combination of spiral pasta, crab and sauteed veggies is coated with a buttery sauce, then covered with cheddar cheese. All that's needed to complete the meal is warm garlic bread and a tossed green salad.

8	ounces uncooked spiral pasta
2	large onions, chopped
1/2	pound fresh mushrooms, sliced
1/2	cup chopped green pepper
2	garlic cloves, minced
1/2	cup butter
2	packages (8 ounces each) imitation crabmeat, chopped
1/2	cup sour cream
2	teaspoons salt
1-1/2	teaspoons dried basil
1-1/2	cups (6 ounces) shredded cheddar cheese

1 Cook pasta according to package directions. Meanwhile, in a skillet, saute onions, mushrooms, green pepper and garlic in butter until crisp-tender. Remove from the heat. Drain pasta; add to vegetable mixture. Stir in the crab, sour cream, salt and basil.

2 Transfer mixture to two greased 8-in. square baking dishes. Sprinkle with cheese. Cover and freeze one casserole for up to 1 month. Cover and bake the second casserole at 350° for 20 minutes. Uncover; bake 5 minutes longer or until heated through.

3 **To use frozen casserole:** Thaw in the refrigerator for 24 hours. Remove from the refrigerator 30 minutes before baking. Cover and bake at 350° for 55-60 minutes or until heated through. **Yield:** 2 casseroles (4-6 servings each).

Simple Substitutions

If you're a shrimp lover, you can replace the imitation crabmeat in this recipe with a pound of chopped cooked shrimp. And if you'd like, try a different pasta shape in place of the spiral pasta, such as small shells, mini penne or even macaroni.

Homemade Pizza Sauce | *Cheryl Kravik, Spanaway, Washington*

For years, I had trouble finding a pizza my family likes. So I started making my own. The evening I served it to company and they asked for my recipe, I thought, "I finally got it right!" When I prepare my sauce, I usually fix enough for three to four pizzas and freeze it. Feel free to spice up my sauce to suit your family's taste.

2 cans (15 ounces each) tomato sauce
1 can (12 ounces) tomato paste
1 tablespoon Italian seasoning
1 tablespoon dried oregano
1 to 2 teaspoons fennel seed, crushed
1 teaspoon onion powder
1 teaspoon garlic powder
1/2 teaspoon salt

1 In a large saucepan, combine tomato sauce and paste. Add the remaining ingredients; mix well. Bring to a boil over medium heat, stirring constantly. Reduce heat; cover and simmer for 1 hour, stirring occasionally.

2 Use desired amount to make your favorite homemade pizza. Cool the remaining sauce; transfer into freezer containers, leaving 1/2-in. headspace. May be frozen for up to 12 months. **Yield:** about 4 cups.

Editor's Note: Use the sauce with crust and toppings of your choice to make a pizza; 1-1/3 cups of sauce will cover a crust in a 15-in. x 10-in. x 1-in. pan.

Chicken Tetrazzini | *Helen McPhee, Savoy, Illinois*

This is my adaptation of a recipe a friend shared with me more than 35 years ago. It's a nice dish to give to friends who are under the weather.

1	package (12 ounces) spaghetti
1/3	cup butter, cubed
1/3	cup all-purpose flour
3/4	teaspoon salt
1/4	teaspoon white pepper
1	can (14-1/2 ounces) chicken broth
1-1/2	cups half-and-half cream
1	cup heavy whipping cream
4	cups cubed cooked chicken
3	cans (4 ounces each) mushroom stems and pieces, drained
1	jar (4 ounces) sliced pimientos, drained
1/2	cup grated Parmesan cheese

1 Cook spaghetti according to package directions. Meanwhile, in a Dutch oven, melt butter. Stir in the flour, salt and pepper until smooth. Gradually add the broth, half-and-half and whipping cream. Bring to a boil; cook and stir for 2 minutes or until thickened.

2 Remove from the heat. Stir in the chicken, mushrooms and pimientos. Drain spaghetti; add to the chicken mixture and toss to coat.

3 Transfer mixture to two greased 11-in. x 7-in. baking dishes. Sprinkle with Parmesan cheese. Cover and freeze one casserole for up to 2 months. Bake the second casserole, uncovered, at 350° for 20-25 minutes or until heated through.

4 **To use frozen casserole:** Thaw in the refrigerator overnight. Remove from the refrigerator 30 minutes before baking. Cover and bake at 350° for 30 minutes. Uncover; bake 15-20 minutes longer or until heated through. Stir before serving. **Yield:** 2 casseroles (3-4 servings each).

Cheesy Rigatoni Bake | *Nancy Urbine, Lancaster, Ohio*

This is a family favorite. One of our four children always asks for it as a birthday dinner.

- 1 package (16 ounces) rigatoni or large tube pasta
- 2 tablespoons butter
- 1/4 cup all-purpose flour
- 1/2 teaspoon salt
- 2 cups milk
- 1/4 cup water
- 4 eggs, lightly beaten
- 2 cans (8 ounces each) tomato sauce
- 2 cups (8 ounces) shredded part-skim mozzarella cheese, divided
- 1/4 cup grated Parmesan cheese, divided

1 Cook pasta according to package directions. Meanwhile, in a small saucepan, melt butter. Stir in flour and salt until smooth; gradually add milk and water. Bring to a boil; cook and stir for 2 minutes or until thickened.

2 Drain the pasta; place in a large bowl. Add eggs. Spoon into two greased 8-in. square baking dishes. Layer each with one can of tomato sauce, half of the mozzarella cheese and half of the white sauce. Sprinkle each casserole with half the Parmesan cheese.

3 Cover and freeze one casserole for up to 3 months. Bake second casserole, uncovered, at 375° for 30-35 minutes or until a meat thermometer reads 160°.

4 **To use frozen casserole:** Thaw in the refrigerator overnight. Remove from the refrigerator 30 minutes before baking. Cover and bake at 375° for 40 minutes. Uncover; bake 7-10 minutes longer or until a meat thermometer reads 160°. **Yield:** 2 casseroles (6-8 servings each).

Mushroom Pasta Sauce | *Louise Graybiel, Toronto, Ontario*

When I am out of spaghetti sauce and don't have time to make it from scratch, I rely on this easy recipe that makes the most of canned items. It has a sweet taste that kids enjoy.

- 2 cans (14-1/2 ounces each) diced tomatoes, undrained
- 2 cans (10-3/4 ounces each) condensed tomato soup, undiluted
- 2 cans (7 ounces each) pizza sauce
- 1 can (8 ounces) mushroom stems and pieces, drained
- 1 teaspoon dried oregano
- 1 teaspoon dried basil
- 1 garlic clove, minced

1 In a large saucepan, combine all the ingredients. Bring to a boil, stirring frequently. Reduce heat; simmer, uncovered, for 15 minutes.

2 Serve desired amount. Cool remaining sauce; transfer to freezer bags or containers. May be frozen for up to 3 months.

3 **To use frozen sauce:** Thaw in the refrigerator overnight. Place in a saucepan and heat through. **Yield:** about 7 cups.

Turkey Noodle Casserole | *Georgia Hennings, Scottsbluff, Nebraska*

Celery, water chestnuts and mushrooms add texture and crunch to this hearty ground turkey casserole.

2 pounds ground turkey

2 cups chopped celery

1/4 cup chopped green pepper

1/4 cup chopped onion

1 can (10-3/4 ounces) condensed cream of mushroom soup, undiluted

1 can (8 ounces) sliced water chestnuts, drained

1 jar (4-1/2 ounces) sliced mushrooms, drained

1 jar (4 ounces) diced pimientos, drained

1/4 cup soy sauce

1/2 teaspoon salt

1/2 teaspoon lemon-pepper seasoning

1 cup (8 ounces) sour cream

8 ounces cooked wide egg noodles

1 In a large skillet, cook turkey over medium heat until no longer pink. Add the celery, green pepper and onion; cook until tender. Stir in the soup, water chestnuts, mushrooms, pimientos, soy sauce, salt and lemon-pepper. Reduce the heat; simmer for 20 minutes.

2 Remove from the heat; add sour cream and noodles. Spoon half the turkey mixture into a freezer container; cover and freeze for up to 3 months. Place remaining mixture in a greased 2-qt. baking dish. Cover and bake at 350° for 30-35 minutes or until heated through.

3 **To use frozen turkey mixture:** Thaw in the refrigerator. Transfer to a greased 2-qt. baking dish and bake as directed. **Yield:** 2 casseroles (6 serving each).

Spaghetti Ham Bake | *Mary Killion, Hermiston, Oregon*

My sister passed along the recipe for this convenient dish. I appreciate being able to freeze one pan for a hectic day. The generous portions are bound to feed a hungry family.

2 packages (7 ounces each) thin spaghetti, broken into 2-inch pieces
4 cups cubed fully cooked ham
2 cans (10-3/4 ounces each) condensed cream of chicken soup, undiluted
2 cups (16 ounces) sour cream
1/2 pound sliced fresh mushrooms
1/2 cup chopped onion
1/2 cup sliced ripe olives, optional
1-1/2 teaspoons ground mustard
1 teaspoon seasoned salt
2 teaspoons Worcestershire sauce

TOPPING:
2 cups soft bread crumbs
1/4 cup butter, melted
2 cups (8 ounces) shredded cheddar cheese

1 Cook spaghetti according to package directions; drain and place in a large bowl. Stir in ham, soup, sour cream, mushrooms, onion, olives if desired, mustard, seasoned salt and Worcestershire sauce.

2 Transfer to two greased 11-in. x 7-in. baking dishes. In a small bowl, toss bread crumbs and butter; add cheese. Sprinkle over casseroles.

3 Cover and freeze one casserole for up to 2 months. Bake the second casserole, uncovered, at 325° for 30 minutes or until heated through.

4 **To use frozen casserole:** Thaw in the refrigerator overnight. Bake, uncovered, at 325° for 50-55 minutes or until heated through. **Yield:** 2 casseroles (6 servings each).

Wild Rice Chicken Dinner | *Lorraine Hanson, Independence, Iowa*

With chicken, green beans and the nice crunch of water chestnuts and almonds, this casserole has everything you need. Using ready-to-serve wild rice makes putting it together a breeze.

- 2 packages (8.8 ounces each) ready-to-serve long grain and wild rice
- 2 packages (16 ounces each) frozen French-style green beans, thawed
- 2 cans (10-3/4 ounces each) condensed cream of celery soup, undiluted
- 2 cans (8 ounces each) sliced water chestnuts, drained
- 2/3 cup chopped onion
- 2 jars (4 ounces each) sliced pimientos, drained
- 1 cup mayonnaise
- 1/2 cup milk
- 1 teaspoon pepper
- 6 cups cubed cooked chicken
- 1 cup slivered almonds, divided

1 Heat the rice according to package directions. Meanwhile, in a Dutch oven, combine the green beans, soup, water chestnuts, onion, pimientos, mayonnaise, milk and pepper. Bring to a boil. Reduce heat; cover and simmer for 5 minutes. Stir in chicken and rice; cook 3-4 minutes longer or until chicken is heated through.

2 Transfer half of the mixture to a serving dish; sprinkle with 1/2 cup almonds. Serve immediately. Pour the remaining mixture into a greased 13-in. x 9-in. baking dish; cool. Sprinkle with remaining almonds. Cover and freeze for up to 3 months.

3 To use frozen casserole: Thaw in the refrigerator overnight. Remove from the refrigerator 30 minutes before baking. Cover and bake at 350° for 40-45 minutes or until heated through. **Yield:** 2 casseroles (6-8 servings each).

Editor's Note: Reduced-fat or fat-free mayonnaise is not recommended for this recipe.

Rice Mix Equivalents

TIP

Can't find the packages of ready-to-serve long grain and wild rice mix in your grocery store? Instead, you can use 4 cups of cooked, seasoned long grain and wild rice mix, either prepared on the stovetop from boxed mixes or from your favorite recipe.

Sausage Spaghetti Pie | *Linda Remillard, Bonaire, Georgia*

I have made freezer meals for years now, and this is by far my most requested. In fact, I like to make several of these Italian pies at one time so we can have one every week for more than a month! With its lasagna-like flavor, this dish is so tasty when it's hot from the oven.

1 package (1 pound) spaghetti
4 eggs, lightly beaten
2/3 cup grated Parmesan cheese
1 cup chopped onion
1/4 cup butter, cubed
2 cups (16 ounces) sour cream
2 teaspoons Italian seasoning
2 pounds bulk pork sausage
2 cups water
1 can (12 ounces) tomato paste
1 cup (4 ounces) shredded part-skim mozzarella cheese
1/2 cup shredded cheddar cheese

1 Cook spaghetti according to package directions; drain and place in a large bowl. Add eggs and Parmesan cheese. Transfer to three greased 9-in. pie plates; press mixture onto the bottom and up the sides to form a crust. Set aside.

2 In a large saucepan, saute onion in butter until tender. Remove from the heat; stir in sour cream and Italian seasoning. Spoon into the crusts.

3 In a large skillet, cook sausage over medium heat until no longer pink; drain. Stir in water and tomato paste. Bring to a boil. Reduce heat; simmer, uncovered, for 5-10 minutes or until thickened. Spoon over sour cream mixture. Sprinkle with mozzarella and cheddar cheese.

4 Cover and freeze two pies for up to 1 month. Cover and bake third pie at 350° for 35-40 minutes or until heated through.

5 **To use frozen pies:** Completely thaw in the refrigerator. Remove from the refrigerator 30 minutes before baking. Bake as directed. **Yield:** 3 pies (6 servings each).

Hamburger Noodle Bake | *Patricia Teller, Lewiston, Idaho*

This is an old family favorite I made when my boys were growing up. There were never any leftovers.

5	cups uncooked egg noodles
2	pounds ground beef
1	cup chopped onion
1/2	cup chopped green pepper
2	cans (10-3/4 ounces each) condensed tomato soup, undiluted
2	cups (8 ounces) shredded cheddar cheese
1-1/2	cups water
1/2	cup chili sauce
1-1/2	cups soft bread crumbs
3	tablespoons butter, melted

1 Cook noodles according to package directions until almost tender; drain. In a large skillet, cook the beef, onion and green pepper over medium-high heat for 10-12 minutes or until meat is no longer pink; drain. Stir in the noodles, soup, cheese, water and chili sauce. Transfer to two greased 8-in. square baking dishes.

2 Toss the bread crumbs and butter; sprinkle over casseroles. Cover and freeze one casserole for up to 3 months. Bake the second casserole, uncovered, at 350° for 35-40 minutes or until bubbly and golden brown.

3 To use frozen casserole: Remove from the freezer 30 minutes before baking (do not thaw). Cover and bake at 350° for 60 minutes. Uncover; bake 10-15 minutes longer or until heated through. **Yield:** 2 casseroles (4 servings each).

Ham 'n' Cheese Quiche | *Christena Palmer, Green River, Wyoming*

When I was expecting our daughter, I made and froze these cheesy quiches as well as several other dishes. After her birth, it was nice to have dinner in the freezer when my husband and I were too tired to cook.

2 pastry shells (9 inches)
2 cups diced fully cooked ham
2 cups (8 ounces) shredded sharp cheddar cheese
2 teaspoons dried minced onion
4 eggs
2 cups half-and-half cream
1/2 teaspoon salt
1/4 teaspoon pepper

1 Line unpricked pastry shells with a double thickness of heavy-duty foil. Bake at 400° for 5 minutes. Remove foil; bake 5 minutes longer.

2 Divide the ham, cheese and onion between the shells. In a bowl, whisk eggs, cream, salt and pepper. Pour into shells. Cover and freeze one quiche for up to 3 months. Cover edges of the second quiche with foil and bake at 400° for 35-40 minutes or until a knife inserted near the center comes out clean. Let stand for 5-10 minutes before cutting.

3 **To use frozen quiche:** Completely thaw in the refrigerator. Remove from the refrigerator 30 minutes before baking as directed. **Yield:** 2 quiches (6 servings each).

sweet

Freezer Berry Jam

Freezer Berry Jam | *Rita Pischke, Whitemouth, Manitoba*

We live on the farm where my husband was raised. Whenever we find wild blueberries nearby, I make this gorgeous ruby-red jam. It's wonderful as a breakfast sauce over toast or biscuits.

4 **cups blueberries**
2 **cups raspberries**
5 **cups sugar**
2 **tablespoons lemon juice**
3/4 **cup water**
1 **package (1-3/4 ounces) powdered fruit pectin**

1 In a large bowl, mash the blueberries. Add the raspberries and mash. Stir in sugar and lemon juice. Let stand for 10 minutes. In a small saucepan, bring water and pectin to a boil. Boil for 1 minute, stirring constantly. Add to fruit mixture; stir for 3 minutes.

2 Pour into jars or freezer containers; cool to room temperature, about 30 minutes. Cover and let stand overnight or until set, but not longer than 24 hours. Refrigerate for up to 3 weeks or freeze for up to 1 year. **Yield:** 7 cups.

Raisin Bran Muffin Mix | *Darlene Brenden, Salem, Oregon*

My husband likes to take muffins to work. When I'm short on time, I just grab this mix from the freezer and have muffins ready in minutes.

2 **cups all-purpose flour**
1-1/4 **cups sugar**
1 **cup nonfat dry milk powder**
6 **teaspoons baking powder**
1 **teaspoon salt**
1/2 **teaspoon ground cinnamon**
1 **cup shortening**
1-1/2 **cups raisin bran cereal**
1 **cup chopped almonds**
ADDITIONAL INGREDIENTS (for each batch):
1 **egg**
1 **cup water**

1 In a large bowl, combine the flour, sugar, milk powder, baking powder, salt and cinnamon. Cut in shortening until crumbly. Stir in cereal and nuts. Store in an airtight container in a cool dry place or in the freezer for up to 2 months. **Yield:** 2 batches (8 cups total).

2 To prepare muffins: Place 4 cups of muffin mix in a bowl. Beat egg and water; stir into mix just until moistened.

3 Fill greased muffin cups two-thirds full. Bake at 400° for 15-17 minutes or until a toothpick inserted near the center comes out clean. Cool for 5 minutes before removing from pan to a wire rack. Serve warm. **Yield:** 1 dozen.

Editor's Note: Contents of muffin mix may settle during storage. When preparing recipe, spoon mix into measuring cup.

Rhubarb Coffee Cake | *Deb Quest, Saskatoon, Saskatchewan*

I adapted several coffee cake recipes to come up with this tender treat. It's so moist and yummy that even people who usually don't care for rhubarb (like me!) ask for seconds.

1/2 cup shortening
1-1/2 cups packed brown sugar
1 egg
2 cups all-purpose flour
1 teaspoon baking soda
1/2 teaspoon salt
1 cup (8 ounces) sour cream
2 cups diced fresh or frozen rhubarb, thawed

TOPPING:
1/2 cup packed brown sugar
1/2 cup chopped walnuts
1 tablespoon butter, melted
1 teaspoon ground cinnamon

1 In a large bowl, cream shortening and brown sugar until light and fluffy. Beat in egg. Combine the flour, baking soda and salt; add to the creamed mixture alternately with sour cream, beating well after each addition. Fold in rhubarb. Pour into two greased 8-in. square baking dishes.

2 Combine the topping ingredients; sprinkle over batter. Bake at 350° for 40-45 minutes or until a toothpick inserted near the center comes out clean. Cool on wire racks. Wrap and freeze for up to 6 months.

3 **To use frozen bread:** Thaw at room temperature. **Yield:** 2 coffee cakes (9 servings each).

Editor's Note: If using frozen rhubarb, measure rhubarb while still frozen, then thaw completely. Drain in a colander, but do not press liquid out.

Wild Berry Freezer Jam | *Barbara Hohmann, Petawawa, Ontario*

One summer, I wanted to make a wild berry jam but couldn't find a recipe. So I experimented with my favorite berries and invented my own recipe.

1 cup saskatoon berries
1 cup raspberries
1 cup strawberries
1 cup blackberries
1 cup blueberries
4 cups sugar
1 pouch (3 ounces) liquid fruit pectin
1 tablespoon lemon juice

1 In a large bowl, crush all of the berries. Stir in sugar; let stand for 10 minutes. Combine pectin and lemon juice; add to fruit, stirring constantly until sugar is dissolved, about 3 minutes.

2 Pour into jars or freezer containers, leaving 1/2-in. headspace. Cover tightly. Let stand at room temperature until set, up to 24 hours. Refrigerate for up to 3 weeks or freeze for up to 1 year. **Yield:** 6 half-pints.

Editor's Note: If saskatoon berries are not available in your area, add an extra cup of one of the other berries.

Jalapeno Cranberry Chutney | *Taste of Home Test Kitchen*

This crimson-colored chutney makes a tongue-tingling Christmas gift. Serve the chutney with crackers as an appetizer or with turkey or chicken as a condiment.

2-1/4	cups packed brown sugar
1-1/2	cups water
1/2	cup white vinegar
3/4	teaspoon curry powder
1/2	teaspoon ground ginger
1/2	teaspoon ground cinnamon
1/4	teaspoon ground cloves
1/4	teaspoon ground allspice
2	medium navel oranges
2	medium lemons
1	medium tart apple, peeled and chopped
1	jalapeno pepper, seeded and minced
6	cups fresh or frozen cranberries, divided
1/2	cup golden raisins
1/2	cup dried apricots, chopped
1/2	cup chopped walnuts

1 In a large saucepan, combine the brown sugar, water, vinegar and spices. Bring to a boil, stirring occasionally. Grate the peel from the oranges and lemons; add to sugar mixture. Peel off and discard the pith from oranges and lemons; chop the pulp and add to sugar mixture. Stir in apple and jalapeno. Bring to a boil. Reduce heat; simmer, uncovered, for 10 minutes.

2 Add 3 cups cranberries, raisins and apricots. Bring to a boil. Reduce heat; simmer, uncovered, for 30 minutes, stirring occasionally. Add the remaining cranberries. Bring to a boil. Reduce heat; simmer, uncovered, 15 minutes longer.

3 Stir in walnuts. Serve warm or chilled. Pour into refrigerator or freezer containers. Refrigerate for up to 3 weeks or freeze for up to 1 year. **Yield:** 4 pints.

Editor's Note: When cutting hot peppers, disposable gloves are recommended. Avoid touching your face.

Homemade Muffin Mix | *Audrey Thibodeau, Gilbert, Arizona*

Whether your family prefers sweet or savory muffins, you can satisfy them with this versatile muffin mix. The recipe makes plain, cheddar and cinnamon-raisin muffins.

8 cups all-purpose flour
1 cup sugar
1/3 cup baking powder
1 tablespoon salt
1 cup shortening

ADDITIONAL INGREDIENTS (for each batch):
1 egg
1 cup milk

FOR CHEDDAR MUFFINS:
3/4 cup shredded cheddar cheese
1/4 cup crumbled cooked bacon
2 tablespoons minced chives

FOR CINNAMON-RAISIN MUFFINS:
1/2 cup raisins
1/4 teaspoon ground cinnamon

1 In a large bowl, combine the flour, sugar, baking powder and salt. Cut in shortening until the mixture resembles coarse crumbs. Store in airtight containers in a cool dry place or in the freezer for up to 6 months. **Yield:** 4 batches (10 cups).

2 To prepare plain muffins: Place 2-1/2 cups muffin mix in a bowl. Whisk egg and milk; stir into flour mixture just until moistened. Fill greased or paper-lined muffin cups two-thirds full. Bake at 425° for 15-20 minutes or until a toothpick comes out clean. Let stand for 5 minutes before removing to a wire rack. **Yield:** 1 dozen per batch.

3 To prepare cheddar muffins: In a bowl, combine 2-1/2 cups muffin mix, cheese, bacon and chives. Whisk egg and milk; stir into cheese mixture just until moistened. Fill muffin cups and bake as directed for plain muffins. **Yield:** 1 dozen per batch.

4 To prepare cinnamon-raisin muffins: In a bowl, combine 2-1/2 cups muffin mix, raisins and cinnamon. Whisk egg and milk; stir into raisin mixture just until moistened. Fill muffin cups and bake as directed for plain muffins. **Yield:** 1 dozen per batch.

Editor's Note: Contents of muffin mix may settle during storage. When preparing recipe, spoon mix into measuring cup.

Orange Jelly | *Mary Rice, Maysville, Oklahoma*

For a change of pace, try this yummy jelly made from frozen orange juice. I've given it as gifts to friends and family—and many times the jars have been returned to me for refills!

2-1/3 cups water
1 can (12 ounces) frozen orange juice concentrate, thawed
1 package (1-3/4 ounces) powdered fruit pectin
4-1/2 cups sugar

1 In a Dutch oven, combine the water, orange juice concentrate and pectin. Cook and stir until mixture comes to a full rolling boil. Add sugar; return to a full rolling boil. Boil for 2 minutes, stirring constantly. Remove from the heat; skim off foam if necessary.

2 Pour into jars or freezer containers; cool to room temperature, about 1 hour. Cover and let stand overnight or until set. But not longer than 24 hours. Refrigerate for up to 3 weeks or freeze for up to 1 year. **Yield:** 6 cups.

Chocolate Pumpkin Bread | *Taste of Home Test Kitchen*

Save time during the holiday season with this moist pumpkin-flavored bread. Make a loaf or two in advance and store in the freezer, so you'll have one on hand for special events with just a few minutes of preparation.

3-1/3 cups all-purpose flour
3 cups sugar
4 teaspoons pumpkin pie spice
2 teaspoons baking soda
1 teaspoon salt
1/2 teaspoon baking powder
4 eggs
1 can (15 ounces) solid-pack pumpkin
2/3 cup water
2/3 cup canola oil
2 cups (12 ounces) semisweet chocolate chips
1 cup sliced almonds, toasted

1 In a large bowl, combine the flour, sugar, pumpkin pie spice, baking soda, salt and baking powder. In another bowl, combine the eggs, pumpkin, water and oil; stir into flour mixture just until moistened. Stir in chocolate chips and almonds.

2 Pour into two greased 9-in. x 5-in. loaf pans. Bake at 350° for 70-75 minutes or until a toothpick inserted near the center comes out clean. Cool for 10 minutes before removing from pans to wire racks to cool completely. Wrap and freeze for up to 3 months.

3 To use frozen bread: Thaw at room temperature. **Yield:** 2 loaves.

Orange Rhubarb Spread | *Betty Nyenhuis, Oostburg, Wisconsin*

This tangy spread is easy to make and tastes especially good on hot, buttered cinnamon toast. The recipe makes enough to have on hand well beyond the rhubarb growing season.

4   **cups diced fresh or frozen rhubarb**

2   **cups water**

1   **can (6 ounces) frozen orange juice concentrate, thawed**

1   **package (1-3/4 ounces) powdered fruit pectin**

4   **cups sugar**

1 In a large saucepan, bring rhubarb and water to a boil. Reduce heat; simmer, uncovered, for 7-8 minutes or until rhubarb is tender. Drain and reserve cooking liquid. Cool rhubarb and liquid to room temperature.

2 Place the rhubarb in a blender; cover and process until pureed. Transfer to a 4-cup measuring cup; add enough reserved cooking liquid to measure 2-1/3 cups. Return to the saucepan.

3 Add orange juice concentrate and pectin; bring to a full rolling boil, stirring constantly. Stir in sugar. Return to a full rolling boil; boil and stir for 1 minute. Remove from the heat; skim off foam.

4 Pour into jars or freezer containers; cool to room temperature, about 1 hour. Cover and let stand overnight or until set, but not longer than 24 hours. Refrigerate for up to 3 weeks or freeze for up to 1 year. **Yield:** 5 half-pints.

Whole Wheat Brownie Mix | *Roni Goodell, Spanish Fork, Utah*

Here's one way to get your kids to eat whole wheat—put it in your brownies! My mom baked these often when I was younger. They're so moist and scrumptious, they don't need frosting.

4 cups sugar
3 cups whole wheat flour
1 cup baking cocoa
2 teaspoons baking powder
2 teaspoons salt
1 cup shortening

ADDITIONAL INGREDIENTS (for each batch):

2 eggs
1 teaspoon vanilla extract
1/2 cup chopped walnuts, optional

1 In a large bowl, combine the sugar, flour, cocoa, baking and salt. Cut in shortening until the mixture resembles coarse crumbs. Store in an airtight container in the refrigerator or freezer for up to 3 months. **Yield:** about 4 batches (about 11 cups total).

2 To prepare brownies: In a large bowl, combine eggs, vanilla and 2-1/2 cups brownie mix until blended (batter will be stiff). Stir in nuts if desired.

3 Spread batter into a greased 8-in. square baking pan. Bake at 350° for 20-25 minutes or until a toothpick inserted near the center comes out clean. Cool on a wire rack. Cut into bars. **Yield:** 16 brownies per batch.

Editor's Note: Contents of brownie mix may settle during storage. When preparing recipe, spoon mix into measuring cup.

Apricot Pineapple Jam | *Carol Radil, New Britain, Connecticut*

Dried apricots, crushed pineapple and grapefruit juice combine to create a memorable jam. The juice adds a tart flavor that will wake up taste buds.

12 ounces dried apricots
1 cup water
1 can (20 ounces) crushed pineapple, undrained
1/2 cup grapefruit juice
3 cups sugar

1 In a large saucepan, bring apricots and water to a boil. Reduce heat; cover and simmer for 15 minutes or until apricots are very tender. Mash. Add pineapple, grapefruit juice and sugar. Simmer, uncovered, for 1 hour or until mixture is thick and translucent, stirring frequently.

2 Pour into jars or freezer containers; cool to room temperature, about 1 hour. Cover and let stand overnight or until set, but not longer than 24 hours. Refrigerate for up to 3 weeks or freeze for up to 1 year. **Yield:** 5 cups.

All-Day Apple Butter | *Betty Ruenholl, Syracuse, Nebraska*

I make several batches of this simple and delicious apple butter to freeze in jars. Depending on the sweetness of the apples, adjust the sugar to suit your taste.

5-1/2   **pounds apples, peeled and finely chopped**
4   **cups sugar**
2   **to 3 teaspoons ground cinnamon**
1/4   **teaspoon ground cloves**
1/4   **teaspoon salt**

1 Place apples in a 3-qt. slow cooker. Combine the sugar, cinnamon, cloves and salt; pour over apples and mix well. Cover and cook on high for 1 hour.

2 Reduce heat to low; cover and cook for 9-11 hours or until thickened and dark brown, stirring occasionally (stir more frequently as it thickens to prevent sticking).

3 Uncover; cook on low 1 hour longer. If desired, stir with a wire whisk until smooth. Cool; transfer to freezer containers, leaving 1/2-in. headspace. Cover and refrigerate up to 3 weeks or freeze for up to 8 months. **Yield:** 4 pints.

Peach Raspberry Jam | *Donn White, Wooster, Ohio*

Back when my children were young, I prepared about 100 jars of jams and jellies each summer, including this freezer version. Although I don't make that many now, I do stir up a batch or two to give as gifts.

1-1/4   **cups finely chopped peaches**
2   **cups fresh raspberries**
2   **tablespoons lemon juice**
4   **cups sugar**
3/4   **cup water**
1   **package (1-3/4 ounces) powdered fruit pectin**

1 Place peaches in a large bowl. In a small bowl, mash the raspberries; strain to remove seeds if desired. Add raspberries and lemon juice to peaches. Stir in sugar. Let stand for 10 minutes. In a small saucepan, bring water and pectin to a full rolling boil. Boil for 1 minute, stirring constantly. Add to fruit mixture; stir for 2-3 minutes or until sugar is dissolved.

2 Pour into jars or freezer containers; cool to room temperature, about 30 minutes. Cover and let stand overnight or until set, but not longer than 24 hours. Refrigerate for up to 3 weeks or freeze for up to 1 year. **Yield:** about 5 cups.

Apple Coffee Cake | *Dawn Fagerstrom, Warren, Minnesota*

Tart apples and sour cream flavor this moist coffee cake covered with brown sugar and crunchy nuts. The recipe makes two pans, so you can serve one and freeze the other for a busy morning or unexpected company.

1/2 **cup butter-flavored shortening**
1 **cup sugar**
2 **eggs**
1 **teaspoon vanilla extract**
2 **cups all-purpose flour**
1 **teaspoon baking powder**
1 **teaspoon baking soda**
1/2 **teaspoon salt**
1 **cup (8 ounces) sour cream**
1-3/4 **to 2 cups chopped peeled tart apples**
TOPPING:
3/4 **cup packed brown sugar**
1 **teaspoon ground cinnamon**
2 **tablespoons cold butter**
1/2 **cup chopped walnuts**

1 In a large bowl, cream shortening and sugar until light and fluffy. Beat in eggs and vanilla. Combine the flour, baking powder, baking soda and salt; gradually add to the creamed mixture alternately with sour cream, mixing well after each addition. Stir in apples. Transfer to two greased 8-in. square baking dishes.

2 For topping, combine brown sugar and cinnamon. Cut in butter until crumbly. Stir in nuts; sprinkle over batter. Bake at 350° for 30-35 minutes or until a toothpick inserted near the center comes out clean. Cool on a wire rack. Wrap and freeze for up to 6 months.

3 **To use frozen coffee cake:** Thaw overnight in the refrigerator. Warm in the oven or microwave. **Yield:** 2 coffee cakes (6-9 servings each).

Coconut Pumpkin Loaves | *Anne Smithson, Cary, North Carolina*

A friend gave me the recipe for this moist bread years ago. It yields three loaves, so I can give one loaf to a neighbor, enjoy one with my family and freeze one for later.

5	**eggs**
2	**cups sugar**
2	**cups canned pumpkin**
1-1/4	**cups canola oil**
3	**cups all-purpose flour**
2	**packages (3.4 ounces each) instant coconut pudding mix**
3	**teaspoons ground cinnamon**
2	**teaspoons baking soda**
1	**teaspoon ground nutmeg**
3/4	**cup chopped pecans**

1 In a large bowl, beat the eggs, sugar, pumpkin and oil until smooth. Combine the flour, dry pudding mixes, cinnamon, baking soda and nutmeg; add to the pumpkin mixture just until combined. Stir in the nuts.

2 Transfer to three greased and floured 8-in. x 4-in. loaf pans. Bake at 350° for 60-65 minutes or until a toothpick inserted near the center comes out clean.

3 Cool for 10 minutes before removing from pans to wire racks to cool completely. Wrap and freeze for up to 6 months.

4 To use frozen bread: Thaw at room temperature. **Yield:** 3 loaves.

Old-Fashioned Peach Butter | *Marilou Robinson, Portland, Oregon*

Cinnamon and ground cloves add down-home flavor to this spread perfect for toast or biscuits. Use a slow cooker to eliminate much of the stirring required when simmering fruit butter on the stovetop.

14 **cups coarsely chopped peeled fresh or frozen peaches (about 5-1/2 pounds)**
2-1/2 **cups sugar**
4-1/2 **teaspoons lemon juice**
1-1/2 **teaspoons ground cinnamon**
3/4 **teaspoon ground cloves**
1/2 **cup quick-cooking tapioca**

1 In a large bowl, combine the peaches, sugar, lemon juice, cinnamon and cloves. Transfer to a 5-qt. slow cooker. Cover and cook on low for 8-10 hours or until peaches are very soft, stirring occasionally.

2 Stir in tapioca. Cook, uncovered, on high for 1 hour or until thickened. Pour into jars or freezer containers; cool to room temperature, about 1 hour. Refrigerate for up to 3 weeks or freeze for up to 8 months. **Yield:** 4 pints.

Orange Pineapple Marmalade | *Stephanie Heise, Rochester, New York*

This sweet, citrusy marmalade is perfect for spreading on English muffins or biscuits. It also makes a delicious housewarming or hostess gift.

2 **medium oranges**
2 **cans (8 ounces each) crushed pineapple, drained**
4 **cups sugar**
2 **tablespoons lemon juice**

1 Grate outer peel from oranges and set aside. Peel off and discard white membrane from oranges and section the fruit, discard any seeds. In a food processor, combine orange peel and orange sections; cover and process until orange is in small pieces.

2 In a wide-bottomed 2-1/2-qt. microwave-safe bowl, combine the pineapple, sugar, lemon juice and orange mixture. Microwave, uncovered, on high for 2 to 2-1/2 minutes; stir. Heat 2 minutes longer (edges will be bubbly); stir. Microwave for 1-1/2 to 2 minutes or until mixture is bubbly in center; stir. Heat 2 minutes longer; stir. Cool for 10 minutes.

3 Carefully pour into jars or freezer containers; cool to room temperature, about 1 hour. Cover and let stand at room temperature for 4 hours. Refrigerate for up to 3 weeks or freeze for up to 1 year. **Yield:** 4 cups.

Editor's Note: This recipe does not use pectin and was tested in a 1,100-watt microwave.

Apple Pie Filling | *Laurie Mace, Los Osos, California*

My family is always delighted to see an oven-fresh apple pie cooling on the kitchen counter. It's such a convenience to have jars of this homemade pie filling on hand so I can treat them to pies year-round.

18	cups sliced peeled baking apples (about 6 pounds)
3	tablespoons lemon juice
4-1/2	cups sugar
1	cup cornstarch
2	teaspoons ground cinnamon
1	teaspoon salt
1/4	teaspoon ground nutmeg
10	cups water

1 In a large bowl, toss apples with lemon juice; set aside. In a Dutch oven, combine the sugar, cornstarch, cinnamon, salt and nutmeg. Add water; bring to a boil over medium heat. Boil for 2 minutes, stirring constantly. Add apples; return to a boil. Reduce heat; cover and simmer until the apples are tender, about 6-8 minutes. Cool for 30 minutes.

2 Cool mixture for no more than 1-1/2 hours. Divide mixture into 5 portions. Use one to make a pie. Ladle remaining four portions into freezer containers, leaving 1/2-in. headspace. Seal; may be frozen for up to 1 year. **Yield:** 5-1/2 quarts (enough for about five 9-inch pies).

Corn Bread Mix | *Donna Smith, Fairport, New York*

I always keep a batch of this corn bread mix in my freezer. All I have to do is add egg and milk for delicious, light-textured corn bread.

Editor's Note: Contents of corn bread mix may settle during storage. When preparing recipe, spoon mix into measuring cup.

4-1/4	cups all-purpose flour
4	cups cornmeal
3/4	cup sugar
1/4	cup baking powder
1	to 2 teaspoons salt
1	cup shortening

ADDITIONAL INGREDIENTS (for each batch):

1	egg
1	cup milk

1 In a large bowl, combine the flour, cornmeal, sugar, baking powder and salt; cut in shortening until crumbly. Store in an airtight container in a cool dry place or in the freezer for up to 6 months. **Yield:** 5 batches (11-2/3 cups total).

2 To prepare corn bread: In a large bowl, whisk egg and milk. Stir in 2-1/3 cups corn bread mix just until moistened (the batter will be lumpy). Pour into a greased 8-in. square baking pan. Bake at 425° for 20-25 minutes or until a toothpick inserted near the center comes out clean. Serve warm. **Yield:** 5 breads (9 servings each).

Freezer Salsa | *Cathy Mckenna, Summerside, Prince Edward Island*

I turn out 60 jars of salsa each fall to enjoy all winter long. I also give many jars as gifts and donate several for events sponsored by the schools in our community. This tasty salsa adds zip to everything from chips to meat loaf to fajitas.

3/4	cup chopped onion
1/2	cup finely chopped celery
1/3	cup finely chopped sweet red or green pepper
1	to 2 jalapeno peppers, seeded and finely chopped
3	garlic cloves, minced
1/4	cup olive oil
12	plum tomatoes, peeled, seeded and chopped (about 6 cups)
3	cans (6 ounces each) tomato paste
1/3	cup lime juice
1/3	cup white vinegar
1	tablespoon honey
1	tablespoon sugar
1-1/2	teaspoons salt
1	teaspoon dried basil

1 In a large saucepan, saute the onion, celery, peppers and garlic in oil for 5 minutes or until tender. Stir in the remaining ingredients; bring to a boil. Reduce heat; cover and simmer for 20 minutes, stirring occasionally. Cool completely.

2 Spoon into freezer containers. Cool. Cover and freeze for up to 3 months. Stir before serving. **Yield:** about 6 cups.

Editor's Note: When cutting hot peppers, disposable gloves are recommended. Avoid touching your face.

Chop to It!

A chef's knife can make short work of chopping veggies. Hold the knife handle with one hand, rest the fingers of your other hand on the top of the blade near the tip. Move knife in an arc across the food with a rocking motion until pieces of food are the desired size.

Quick Bread Mix | *Doris Barb, El Dorado, Kansas*

Looking for a speedy breakfast or take-along treat for the office? This mix is so convenient to have on hand to bake a batch of moist tropical muffins or a loaf of nutty banana bread.

10	cups all-purpose flour
1/3	cup baking powder
1/4	cup sugar
1	tablespoon salt
2	cups shortening

ADDITIONAL INGREDIENTS FOR MUFFINS:

1/4	cup sugar
1-1/2	teaspoons grated orange peel
1	egg
1	can (8 ounces) crushed pineapple, undrained
1/4	cup milk

ADDITIONAL INGREDIENTS FOR BREAD:

1	package (8 ounces) cream cheese, softened
1	cup sugar
2	eggs
3/4	cup mashed ripe banana (about 1 banana)
1/2	cup chopped pecans

1 In a large bowl, combine the flour, baking powder, sugar and salt. Cut in shortening until crumbly. Store in an airtight container in a cool dry place or in the freezer for up to 6 months. **Yield:** about 7 batches of muffins and about 5 batches of bread (13 cups total).

2 To prepare muffins: In a bowl, combine 1-3/4 cups quick bread mix, sugar and orange peel. In a small bowl, combine the egg, pineapple and milk; stir into dry ingredients just until moistened.

3 Fill greased or paper-lined muffin cups two-thirds full. Bake at 400° for 25 minutes or until a toothpick inserted near the center comes out clean. Cool for 5 minutes before removing from pan to a wire rack. **Yield:** 8 muffins.

4 To prepare bread: In a large bowl, beat cream cheese and sugar. Add eggs, one at a time, beating well after each addition. Beat in banana. Stir in 2-1/4 cups quick bread mix and pecans just until moistened.

5 Pour into a greased 9-in. x 5-in. loaf pan. Bake at 350° for 65-70 minutes or until a toothpick comes out clean. Cool for 10 minutes before removing from pan to wire rack to cool completely. **Yield:** 1 loaf (16 slices each).

Editor's Note: Contents of bread mix may settle during storage. When preparing recipe, spoon mix into measuring cup.

Rhubarb-Strawberry Sauce | *Earlene Ertelt, Woodburn, Oregon*

This pretty sauce perks up taste buds. It's good on hot muffins, waffles and pancakes.

1 pound fresh or frozen rhubarb, cut into 1-inch pieces
1 jar (12 ounces) currant jelly
2 cups sliced fresh or frozen strawberries
1/4 cup sugar

1 In a large saucepan over medium heat, bring rhubarb and jelly to a boil, stirring frequently. Reduce heat; cover and simmer for 8-10 minutes or until rhubarb is tender. Remove from the heat.

2 Mash mixture with a potato masher. Stir in the strawberries and sugar; bring to a boil. Cook and stir for 1 minute. Remove from the heat; cool. Pour into freezer containers. Refrigerate for up to a week or freeze up to 8 months. Serve as a side dish or over ice cream or waffles. **Yield:** 2 pints.

Strawberry Freezer Jam | *Mary Jean Ellis, Indianapolis, Indiana*

A dear friend gave me this recipe when I lived in Germany. My family loves it on toast, but it's also a delightful crowning touch to vanilla ice cream.

2 quarts fresh strawberries
5-1/2 cups sugar
1 cup light corn syrup
1/4 cup lemon juice
3/4 cup water
1 package (1-3/4 ounces) powdered fruit pectin

1 Wash and mash the berries, measuring out enough mashed berries to make 4 cups; place in a large bowl. Stir in the sugar, corn syrup and lemon juice. Let stand for 10 minutes.

2 In a kettle, combine strawberry mixture and water. Stir in pectin. Bring to a full rolling boil over high heat, stirring constantly. Boil for 1 minute, stirring constantly. Remove from the heat; skim off foam.

3 Pour into jars or freezer containers, leaving 1/2-in. headspace. Cover and let stand overnight or until set, but not longer than 24 hours. Refrigerate for up to 3 weeks or freeze for up to 1 year. **Yield:** 4-1/2 pints.

Pumpkin Chocolate Loaf | *Kathy Gardner, Rockville, Maryland*

These moist chocolate loaves, with a hint of pumpkin and spice, have been a favorite for years. They can be sliced to serve as snacks or dessert.

3-3/4   cups all-purpose flour
3-1/2   cups sugar
1-1/2   teaspoons salt
1-1/2   teaspoons baking powder
1-1/4   teaspoons baking soda
1-1/4   teaspoons ground cinnamon
    1   to 1-1/4 teaspoons ground cloves
  1/2   teaspoon ground nutmeg
    3   eggs
    1   can (29 ounces) solid-pack pumpkin
1-1/4   cups canola oil
    3   squares (1 ounce each) unsweetened chocolate, melted and cooled
1-1/2   teaspoons vanilla extract
    2   cups (12 ounces) semisweet chocolate chips

1 In a large bowl, combine the flour, sugar, salt, baking powder, baking soda, cinnamon, cloves and nutmeg. In another large bowl, whisk the eggs, pumpkin, oil, chocolate and vanilla. Stir into flour mixture just until moistened. Fold in chips.

2 Transfer to three greased 9-in. x 5-in. loaf pans. Bake at 350° for 55-65 minutes or until a toothpick inserted near the center comes out clean. Cool for 10 minutes before removing from pans to wire racks. Wrap and freeze for up to 6 months.

3 **To use frozen bread:** Thaw at room temperature. **Yield:** 3 loaves.

Pineapple Kiwi Jam | *Sondra Rogers, Columbus, Indiana*

Pineapple, kiwi and a hint of lime blend nicely in this unique combination. The jam is especially good spread on biscuits or English muffins.

    4   kiwifruit, peeled and thinly sliced
    3   cups sugar
    1   can (8 ounces) crushed pineapple, undrained
  1/4   cup lime juice
    1   pouch (3 ounces) liquid fruit pectin
    3   drops green food coloring, optional

1 In a 2-qt. microwave-safe bowl, combine the kiwi, sugar, pineapple and lime juice. Microwave, uncovered, on high for 7-10 minutes or until mixture comes to a full rolling boil, stirring every 2 minutes. Stir in pectin. Add food coloring if desired.

2 Pour into jars or freezer containers and cool to room temperature, about 1 hour. Cover and let stand overnight or until set, but not longer than 24 hours. Refrigerate for up to 3 weeks or freeze for up to 1 year. **Yield:** 4 cups.

Editor's Note: This recipe was tested in a 1,100-watt microwave.

MADE FOR LATER

Plan for the future with these **make-ahead** recipes. When time allows, whip up one of these dishes and **store it** in the freezer—you'll then have a great treat **at your fingertips.**

Potluck Lasagna, p. 83

Savory

Peanut Butter Cup Pie, p. 99

Sweet

Savory

Potluck Lasagna

Potluck Lasagna | *Colleen Wolfisberg, Everson, Washington*

This is a variation on a lasagna dish a co-worker made for a company potluck. When I was expecting our third son, I often prepared meals and froze them. It was so nice to have a substantial entree like this one to bake.

1 pound ground beef
1 can (14-1/2 ounces) Italian stewed tomatoes, cut up
1 can (6 ounces) tomato paste
1 tablespoon minced fresh parsley
1/2 teaspoon minced garlic
2 eggs
1-1/2 cups (12 ounces) 4% cottage cheese
1-1/2 cups ricotta cheese
1 cup grated Parmesan cheese
1 teaspoon salt
1 teaspoon pepper
6 lasagna noodles, cooked and drained
2 cups (8 ounces) shredded part-skim mozzarella cheese

1 In a large skillet, cook beef over medium heat until no longer pink; drain. Stir in the tomatoes, tomato paste, parsley and garlic; remove from the heat.

2 In a large bowl, combine the eggs, cheeses, salt and pepper. Layer three noodles in a greased 13-in. x 9-in. baking dish. Top with half of cottage cheese mixture, 1 cup mozzarella cheese and half of the meat sauce. Repeat layers. Cover; may be frozen for up to 3 months.

3 **To use frozen lasagna:** Thaw in refrigerator overnight. Cover and bake 375° for 30 minutes. Uncover; bake 25-30 minutes longer or until edges are bubbly. Let stand for 10 minutes before cutting. **Yield:** 12-15 servings.

Editor's Note: To use immediately, bake as directed.

Frozen Grapefruit-Avocado Salad | *Daphne York, Alford, Florida*

You might wonder about the unusual combination of ingredients, but you'll find it's a real taste treat.

1 package (8 ounces) cream cheese, softened
1 cup (8 ounces) sour cream
1/2 cup sugar
1/4 teaspoon salt
1 can (24 ounces) grapefruit sections, drained
1 medium ripe avocado, peeled and diced
1 cup green grapes, halved
1/2 cup chopped pecans

1 In a large bowl, beat cream cheese until smooth. Beat in the sour cream, sugar and salt until blended. Gently stir in the grapefruit, avocado, grapes and pecans.

2 Transfer to a 9-in. x 5-in. loaf pan lightly coated with cooking spray. Cover and freeze for 4 hours or until firm. May be frozen for up to 1 month.

3 **To use frozen salad:** Invert onto a cutting board; cut into slices. **Yield:** 10-12 servings.

Barbecued Meatballs | *Margery Bryan, Moses Lake, Washington*

Coated in a thick and luscious barbecue sauce, these tender meatballs taste like mini meat loaves with a little zip. I usually freeze them in small baking dishes that I cover tightly with foil. They can be quickly reheated in the microwave, or if you prefer, reheat them in the oven.

3/4	cup quick-cooking oats
1	can (5 ounces) evaporated milk
1/3	cup chopped onion
1	egg, lightly beaten
3/4	teaspoon salt
3/4	teaspoon chili powder
1/4	teaspoon garlic powder
1/4	teaspoon pepper
1-1/4	pounds lean ground beef

SAUCE:

1-1/2	cups ketchup
2/3	cup packed brown sugar
1/4	cup chopped onion
1/4	teaspoon garlic powder
2	drops Liquid Smoke, optional

1 In a large bowl, combine the oats, milk, onion, egg and seasonings. Crumble beef over mixture and mix well. Shape into 1-1/2-in. balls. Place 1 in. apart in ungreased 13-in. x 9-in. baking dishes. Combine the sauce ingredients; pour over meatballs.

2 Bake, uncovered, at 350° for 45-50 minutes or until the meat is no longer pink and a meat thermometer reads 160°. Cool. For each serving, place three meatballs with sauce in a small freezer container. Freeze for up to 3 months.

3 To use frozen meatballs: Thaw in the refrigerator or remove from the freezer 30 minutes before baking. Bake, uncovered, at 350° for 20-25 minutes or until heated through. **Yield:** 8 servings.

Cheesy Chili | *Codie Ray, Tallulah, Louisiana*

My grandchildren enjoy feasting on big bowls of this zesty chili. It's so creamy and delicious you can even serve it as a dip at parties.

- 2 **pounds ground beef**
- 2 **medium onions, chopped**
- 2 **garlic cloves, minced**
- 3 **cans (10 ounces each) diced tomatoes and green chilies, undrained**
- 1 **can (28 ounces) diced tomatoes, undrained**
- 2 **cans (4 ounces each) chopped green chilies**
- 1/2 **teaspoon pepper**
- 2 **pounds process cheese (Velveeta)**

1 In a large saucepan, cook the beef, onions and garlic until meat is no longer pink; drain. Stir in the tomatoes, chilies and pepper; bring to a boil. Reduce heat; simmer, uncovered, for 10-15 minutes. Stir in cheese until melted. Cool. Transfer to freezer containers. May be frozen for up to 3 months.

2 **To use frozen chili:** Thaw in the refrigerator; heat in a saucepan or microwave. **Yield:** 12 servings (about 3 quarts).

Sausage Pizza | *Taste of Home Test Kitchen*

Spicy sausage, onions, mushrooms and plenty of cheese make this pizza a real keeper. It beats the delivery variety every time! Substitute a combination of veggies and cheese to suit your family's taste.

- 1 **loaf (1 pound) frozen bread dough, thawed**
- 3/4 **pound bulk hot Italian sausage**
- 1/2 **cup sliced onion**
- 1/2 **cup sliced fresh mushrooms**
- 1/2 **cup chopped green pepper**
- 1/2 **cup pizza sauce**
- 2 **cups (8 ounces) shredded part-skim mozzarella cheese**

1 With greased fingers, pat the dough onto an ungreased 12-in. pizza pan. Prick the dough thoroughly with a fork. Bake at 400° for 10-12 minutes or until lightly browned. Meanwhile, in a large skillet, cook the sausage, onion, mushrooms and green pepper over medium heat until sausage is no longer pink; drain.

2 Spread pizza sauce over crust. Top with the sausage mixture; sprinkle with cheese. Wrap pizza; may be frozen for up to 2 months.

3 **To use frozen pizza:** Unwrap and place on a pizza pan; thaw in the refrigerator. Bake at 400° for 18-22 minutes or until golden brown. **Yield:** 8 slices.

Editor's Note: To use immediately, bake, uncovered, at 400° for 12-15 minutes or until golden brown.

Frosty Pineapple Salad | *Lillian Volf, Moncks Corner, South Carolina*

I serve this cool pineapple treat as a salad or dessert. The frozen fluff calls for only four ingredients, and it's particularly refreshing on a hot summer's day.

1-1/2   **cups buttermilk**
  3/4   **cup sugar**
    1   **can (20 ounces) unsweetened crushed pineapple, drained**
    1   **carton (8 ounces) frozen whipped topping, thawed**

1 In a small bowl, combine the buttermilk, sugar and pineapple. Fold in the whipped topping. Transfer to a 13-in. x 9-in. dish. Freeze for 4 hours or until firm. May be frozen up to 3 months.

2 To use frozen salad: Remove from the freezer 20 minutes before serving. **Yield:** 12 servings.

Zucchini Quiche | *Karen Howard, Lakeville, Massachusetts*

A few years ago, I found this zucchini recipe that's quick to prepare and freezes well, too. Just put it in the refrigerator to thaw in the morning and pop it into the oven when you get home!

  4   **cups thinly sliced zucchini**
  1   **large onion, thinly sliced**
  3   **tablespoons butter**
  2   **eggs**
  2   **teaspoons dried parsley flakes**
1/2   **teaspoon salt**
1/2   **teaspoon each garlic powder, dried basil and oregano**
1/4   **teaspoon pepper**
  2   **cups (8 ounces) part-skim shredded mozzarella cheese**
  2   **teaspoons prepared mustard**
  1   **pastry shell (9 inches)**

1 In a large skillet, saute the zucchini and onion in butter until tender; drain. In a large bowl, whisk the eggs, parsley, salt, garlic powder, basil, oregano and pepper. Stir in cheese and zucchini mixture. Spread mustard over pastry shell; add egg mixture. Cover; may be frozen for up to 2 months.

2 To use frozen quiche: Thaw in the refrigerator. Bake, uncovered, at 400° for 50-55 minutes or until a knife inserted near the center comes out clean and crust is golden brown (cover loosely with foil after 35 minutes if needed to prevent overbrowning). Let stand for 5 minutes before cutting. **Yield:** 6-8 servings.

Editor's Note: To use immediately, bake, uncovered, at 400° for 35-40 minutes or until a knife inserted near the center comes out clean and crust is golden brown (cover loosely with foil after 25 minutes if needed to prevent overbrowning). Let stand for 5 minutes before cutting.

Hearty Jambalaya | *Mel Miller, Perkins, Oklahoma*

It's a pleasure to serve this meaty, satisfying jambalaya. Since it freezes so nicely, I have a delicious meal at my fingertips when time is tight.

1   **pound smoked kielbasa or Polish sausage, cut into 1/2-inch slices**

1   **pound boneless skinless chicken breasts, cubed**

1   **large onion, chopped**

1/2 **cup chopped celery**

1/2 **cup chopped green pepper**

4   **garlic cloves, minced**

2   **tablespoons butter**

1   **can (14-1/2 ounces) diced tomatoes, undrained**

1   **can (6 ounces) tomato paste**

1/2 **teaspoon hot pepper sauce**

1/4 **to 1/2 teaspoon cayenne pepper**

1/8 **teaspoon garlic powder**

1/8 **teaspoon white pepper**

1/8 **teaspoon pepper**

1/2 **pound uncooked medium shrimp, peeled and deveined**

Hot cooked rice, optional

1 In a Dutch oven, saute the sausage, chicken, onion, celery, green pepper and garlic in butter until chicken is browned. Stir in the tomatoes, tomato paste and seasonings. Bring to a boil. Reduce heat; cover and simmer for 6-8 minutes or until chicken is no longer pink.

2 Stir in shrimp; cover and simmer for 4 minutes or until shrimp turn pink. Cool. Transfer to freezer containers. May be frozen for up to 2 months.

3 To use frozen jambalaya: Thaw in the refrigerator; heat in a saucepan or microwave. Serve over rice if desired. **Yield:** 8 servings.

Peeling Shrimp

To make light work of peeling shrimp, use frozen raw shrimp that is labeled easy peel and deveined. You'll just need to slip the shell off the shrimp.

Peachy Barbecue Chicken | *Laura Mahaffey, Annapolis, Maryland*

Barbecue sauce and peach preserves bring the perfect combination of sweet and savory flavors to this tender dish. It's a great meal if you have extra green peppers to use up.

1/2	cup all-purpose flour
1	teaspoon salt
1/8	teaspoon pepper
8	boneless skinless chicken breast halves (5 ounces each)
1/4	cup canola oil
2	cups peach preserves
1	cup chopped onion
1	cup barbecue sauce
1/4	cup soy sauce
2	medium green peppers, julienned
2	cans (8 ounces each) sliced water chestnuts, drained

Hot cooked rice

1 In a large resealable plastic bag, combine the flour, salt and pepper. Add chicken, a few pieces at a time, and shake to coat.

2 In a large skillet, brown chicken in oil in batches on both sides. Return all to skillet. In a large bowl, combine the preserves, onion, barbecue sauce and soy sauce; pour over chicken. Bring to a boil. Reduce heat; cover and simmer for 15 minutes.

3 Add green peppers and water chestnuts. Bring to a boil. Reduce heat; simmer, uncovered, for 5 minutes or until a meat thermometer reads 170°. Cool chicken. Transfer to a freezer containers. May be frozen for up to 3 months.

4 **To use frozen chicken:** Thaw in the refrigerator overnight. Remove from the refrigerator 30 minutes before reheating. Cover and bake at 350° for 50-60 minutes or until bubbly. Serve with rice. **Yield:** 8 servings.

Beef Mushroom Spaghetti | *Norene Wright, Manilla, Indiana*

You'll need just six simple ingredients to prepare this freezer-friendly spaghetti casserole. I often garnish it with a little Parmesan.

- 1 **pound ground beef**
- 1 **medium onion, chopped**
- 1 **can (15 ounces) tomato sauce**
- 1 **can (10-3/4 ounces) condensed cream of mushroom soup, undiluted**
- 1/4 **cup water**
- 1 **package (7 ounces) thin spaghetti, cooked and drained**

1 In a skillet, cook the beef and onion over medium heat until the meat is no longer pink; drain. Stir in the tomato sauce, soup and water. Add spaghetti; toss to coat. Place in a greased 8-in. square baking dish. Cover and freeze for up to 3 months.

2 **To use frozen casserole:** Thaw in the refrigerator. Cover and bake at 350° for 35-40 minutes or until heated through. **Yield:** 4 servings.

Crab Bisque | *Sherrie Manton, Folsom, Louisiana*

I love to try new recipes, and this soup is one of my prized finds. This hearty chowder has a rich creamy broth that's swimming with tasty chunks of crab and corn.

- 1 **celery rib, thinly sliced**
- 1 **small onion, chopped**
- 1/2 **cup chopped green pepper**
- 3 **tablespoons butter**
- 2 **cans (14-3/4 ounces each) cream-style corn**
- 2 **cans (10-3/4 ounces each) condensed cream of potato soup, undiluted**
- 1-1/2 **cups milk**
- 1-1/2 **cups half-and-half cream**
- 2 **bay leaves**
- 1 **teaspoon dried thyme**
- 1/2 **teaspoon garlic powder**
- 1/4 **teaspoon white pepper**
- 1/8 **teaspoon hot pepper sauce**
- 3 **cans (6 ounces each) crabmeat, drained, flaked and cartilage removed**

1 In a large saucepan or Dutch oven, saute the celery, onion and green pepper in butter until tender. Add the corn, soup, milk, cream and seasonings; mix well. Stir in crab; heat through. Discard bay leaves. Cool. Transfer to a freezer container. May be frozen for up to 3 months.

2 **To use frozen bisque:** Thaw in the refrigerator; heat in a saucepan or microwave. **Yield:** 10 servings.

Frozen Date Salad | *Margaret Dowdy, North Vassalboro, Maine*

Our family spent 15 years in Vermont, which is known for its delicious maple syrup, and that's where I found this recipe. Maine also has beautiful maple trees, so we continue to enjoy this salad made with locally produced syrup. Combined with cream cheese, dates and walnuts, the salad complements many meals.

1   package (8 ounces) cream cheese, softened
1   cup maple syrup
1   can (20 ounces) unsweetened crushed pineapple, drained
1   cup chopped dates
1   cup chopped walnuts
1   carton (8 ounces) frozen whipped topping, thawed

1 Line a 9-in. x 5-in. loaf pan with plastic wrap. In a small bowl, beat cream cheese and syrup until smooth. Fold in the pineapple, dates, walnuts and whipped topping. Spoon into prepared pan; cover with foil. Freeze for at least 8 hours or until firm. May be frozen for up to 3 months.

2 To use frozen salad: Remove from the freezer 20 minutes before serving. Invert onto a serving plate; cut into slices. **Yield:** 8 servings.

Freezer Coleslaw | *Donna Sasser Hinds, Milwaukie, Oregon*

Loaded with crunch, this sweet-tart slaw can be made ahead for a family gathering. There's no mayonnaise in the dressing, so it's perfect to take to a picnic.

1   medium head cabbage (about 2 pounds), shredded
1   teaspoon salt
2   cups sugar
1   cup cider vinegar
1/4   cup water
1   teaspoon celery seed
1   teaspoon mustard seed
1   large carrot, shredded
1/2   cup finely chopped green pepper

1 In a large bowl, combine cabbage and salt; let stand for 1 hour.

2 In a large saucepan, combine the sugar, vinegar, water, celery seed and mustard seed. Bring to a boil; boil for 1 minute. Remove from the heat; cool.

3 Add the carrot, green pepper and vinegar mixture to the cabbage mixture; stir. Transfer to large freezer bags; seal and freeze for up to 2 months.

4 To use frozen coleslaw: Remove from the freezer 2 hours before serving. Serve with a slotted spoon. **Yield:** 10 servings.

Peppery Pizza Loaves | *Lou Stasny, Poplarville, Mississippi*

I often take these French bread pizzas to church picnics or potluck suppers, and there is never any left. When I fix them for my spouse and me, I freeze the extra loaves in foil to enjoy later.

1-1/2   **pounds ground beef**
  1/2   **teaspoon salt**
  1/2   **teaspoon garlic powder**
    2   **loaves (8 ounces each) French bread, halved lengthwise**
    1   **jar (8 ounces) process cheese sauce**
    1   **can (4 ounces) mushroom stems and pieces, drained**
    1   **cup chopped green onions**
    1   **can (4 ounces) sliced jalapenos, drained**
    1   **can (8 ounces) tomato sauce**
  1/2   **cup grated Parmesan cheese**
    4   **cups (16 ounces) shredded part-skim mozzarella cheese**

1 In a large skillet, cook beef over medium heat until no longer pink; drain. Stir in salt and garlic powder. Place each bread half on a large piece of heavy-duty foil. Spread with cheese sauce. Top with the beef mixture, mushrooms, onions and jalapenos. Drizzle with tomato sauce. Top with Parmesan and mozzarella cheeses. Wrap and freeze. May be frozen for up to 3 months.

2 To bake: Unwrap loaves and thaw on baking sheets in the refrigerator. Bake at 350° for 18 minutes or until cheese is melted. **Yield:** 4 loaves (2-3 servings each).

Two-Meat Spaghetti Sauce | *Candi Johnsen, West Plains, Missouri*

This robust home-style pasta sauce tastes just as good as fresh even after it's been frozen.

  1   **pound ground beef**
  1   **pound Italian sausage links, cut into 3/4-inch slices**
  1   **large onion, chopped**
  2   **cans (15 ounces each) tomato sauce**
  1   **can (16 ounces) stewed tomatoes**
  1   **can (6 ounces) tomato paste**
3/4   **cup water**
  1   **can (4 ounces) mushroom stems and pieces, drained**
1/2   **cup sliced pimiento-stuffed olives, optional**
  2   **teaspoons Italian seasoning**
1-1/2 **teaspoons Worcestershire sauce**
  1   **teaspoon garlic powder**
  1   **teaspoon sugar**
1/2   **teaspoon chili powder**
1/4   **teaspoon dried oregano**
1/4   **teaspoon celery salt**
  1   **bay leaf**
Hot cooked spaghetti

1 In a Dutch oven, cook the beef, sausage and onion over medium heat until meat is no longer pink; drain. Add the tomato sauce, tomatoes, tomato paste, water, mushrooms, olives if desired and seasonings. Bring to a boil. Reduce heat; simmer, uncovered, for 45-60 minutes or until the sauce reaches desired thickness.

2 Discard the bay leaf. Cool. Transfer to freezer containers. May be frozen for up to 2 months.

3 To use frozen sauce: Thaw in the refrigerator; heat in a saucepan or microwave. Serve over spaghetti. **Yield:** 9 servings.

Cheese Frenchy Sandwiches | *Darlene Brenden, Salem, Oregon*

I remember enjoying these crispy golden sandwiches at a restaurant when I was a teenager. After it closed, I came up with this recipe. Now I make a batch and keep them in the freezer, ready to fry at any time. It's like reliving my teen years all over again!

1/4 **cup mayonnaise**

8 **slices bread**

8 **slices process American cheese**

1 **egg**

1/2 **cup milk**

1/4 **teaspoon salt**

1 **cup crushed saltines (about 25 crackers)**

Oil for frying

1 Spread mayonnaise on one side of each slice of bread. Top four slices with two cheese slices. Top with remaining bread, mayonnaise side down. Cut each sandwich into four triangles.

2 In a bowl, beat the egg, milk and salt. Dip sandwiches into egg mixture, then roll in cracker crumbs. Wrap in foil and freeze for up to 1 month.

3 To use frozen sandwiches: In a skillet, heat 1 in. of oil to 375°. Fry a few frozen sandwiches at a time for 2 minutes on each side or until golden brown. **Yield:** 4 servings.

Pineapple Mint Salad | *Dorothy Showalter, Broadway, Virginia*

This cool, refreshing salad goes with a variety of entrees. It has become our tradition during the Easter season.

1 **can (20 ounces) crushed pineapple**

1 **envelope unflavored gelatin**

1 **jar (10-1/2 ounces) mint jelly**

2 **to 3 drops food coloring, optional**

1 **cup heavy whipping cream**

1 **teaspoon confectioners' sugar**

1 Line the bottom and sides of an 8-in. x 4-in. loaf pan with foil, coat the foil with cooking spray. Set aside. Drain pineapple, reserving the juice; set pineapple aside. Sprinkle gelatin over 1/4 cup of the pineapple juice; set aside.

2 In a saucepan, combine the jelly and remaining pineapple juice. Cook and stir until mixture comes to a boil. Remove from the heat; stir in gelatin mixture until dissolved. Stir in pineapple and food coloring if desired. Refrigerate until syrupy.

3 In a small bowl, beat cream until soft peaks form. Add confectioners' sugar; beat until stiff peaks form. Fold into gelatin mixture. Pour into prepared pan. Cover and freeze until firm. May be frozen up to 3 months.

4 To use frozen salad: Remove from the freezer 10-15 minutes before serving. Using foil, remove loaf from pan. Carefully peal off foil and discard. Using a serrated knife, cut salad into slices. **Yield:** 8-10 servings.

Frozen Fruit Salad Ring | *Carol Heath, Fayetteville, Georgia*

This tasty, make-ahead salad is an appealing addition to any buffet table. For a pretty presentation, serve it on a bed of lettuce and garnish it with fresh strawberries.

1 package (8 ounces) cream cheese, softened
1 cup mayonnaise
1/3 cup sugar
1 teaspoon white vinegar
3 to 4 drops green food coloring, optional
1 can (30 ounces) fruit cocktail, drained
1-1/2 cups miniature marshmallows
1/2 cup chopped pecans
1 cup heavy whipping cream, whipped

1 In a bowl, beat the cream cheese, mayonnaise and sugar until smooth. Add vinegar and food coloring if desired and mix well. Fold in fruit cocktail, marshmallows, pecans and whipped cream.

2 Spoon into a 2-qt. ring mold or fluted tube pan coated with cooking spray. Cover and freeze for up to 2 months.

3 To use frozen salad: Just before serving, invert onto a platter. Cut into 1-in. slices. **Yield:** 12-14 servings.

Save-the-Day Soup | *Agnes Davis, Las Animas, Colorado*

I created this pureed vegetable soup from what was left in the refrigerator before we went on an extended vacation. I kept the mixture in the freezer of our RV, so it made supper a snap to prepare at the campground.

6 cups chopped fresh broccoli
6 cups chopped cauliflower
4 celery ribs with leaves, cut into 1-inch pieces
3 medium carrots, cut into chunks
1 medium onion, cut into chunks
2 cans (14-1/2 ounces each) chicken or vegetable broth
1/2 to 1 teaspoon seasoned salt or salt-free seasoning blend
1/2 to 1 teaspoon ground cumin
1/4 to 1/2 teaspoon garlic powder
1/4 to 1/2 teaspoon Cajun seasoning
1/4 to 1/2 teaspoon lemon-pepper seasoning
1/4 teaspoon crushed red pepper flakes
1/4 teaspoon pepper
1/4 teaspoon hot pepper sauce
ADDITIONAL INGREDIENTS (for each batch):
2 cups half-and-half cream or fat-free milk
Shredded cheddar cheese, optional

1 In a large saucepan or Dutch oven, combine the vegetables, broth and seasonings. Bring to a boil. Reduce heat; cover and simmer for 20 minutes or until vegetables are tender. Cool. Process in small batches in a blender until smooth.

2 Freeze in 2-cup portions in freezer containers. May be frozen up to 3 months.

3 To prepare frozen soup: Thaw soup base in the refrigerator. Transfer to a saucepan; stir in cream and heat through. Sprinkle with cheese if desired. **Yield:** 4 servings per batch.

Change the Flavor

Save-the-Day Soup has lots of spicy flavor. If you like the combination of vegetables, but would prefer a more traditional blend of flavors, omit the Cajun seasoning, red pepper flakes, hot pepper sauce and cumin. Instead, use some thyme, marjoram, parsley and bay leaf. Discard bay leaf before serving.

Six-Vegetable Juice | *Deborah Moyer, Liberty, Pennsylvania*

Our family and friends enjoy my vegetable garden by the glassfuls. My husband likes spicy foods, and after one sip, he proclaimed this juice perfect. For more delicate palates, you can leave out the hot peppers.

5 pounds ripe tomatoes, peeled and chopped
1/2 cup water
1/4 cup chopped green pepper
1/4 cup chopped carrot
1/4 cup chopped celery
1/4 cup lemon juice
2 tablespoons chopped onion
1 tablespoon salt
1 to 1-1/2 small serrano peppers

1 In a large Dutch oven, combine the tomatoes, water, green pepper, carrot, celery, lemon juice, onion and salt. Remove stems and seeds if desired from serranno peppers; add to tomato mixture. Bring to a boil; reduce heat. Cover and simmer for 30 minutes or until vegetables are tender.

2 Cool. Press mixture through a food mill or fine sieve. Transfer to freezer containers. May be frozen for up to 3 months.

3 To serve: Shake or stir juice well before serving. **Yield:** 2 quarts.

Editor's Note: When cutting hot peppers, disposable gloves are recommended. Avoid touching your face.

Garden Vegetable Soup | *Jennifer Black, San Jose, California*

Cooking with vegetables seems quick and healthy. I think this meatless soup makes a great dinner when you serve it with a salad or slice of bread.

1-1/2	teaspoons minced garlic
2	tablespoons olive oil
1/4	cup uncooked long grain rice
2	cans (14-1/2 ounces each) chicken broth
1	cup chopped sweet red pepper
1	cup chopped green pepper
1/2	cup thinly sliced fresh carrots
1	teaspoon salt
1/2	teaspoon dried basil
1/4	teaspoon dried rosemary, crushed

Dash pepper

2	medium zucchini, sliced
6	plum tomatoes, chopped

1 In a large saucepan, cook garlic in oil for 1 minute. Stir in rice; cook and stir for 1 minute. Add the broth, peppers, carrots and seasonings. Bring to a boil. Reduce heat; cover and simmer for 15-20 minutes or until rice is tender.

2 Stir in zucchini and tomatoes; cook for 3 minutes. Cool. Transfer to freezer containers. May be frozen for up to 3 months.

3 **To use frozen soup:** Thaw soup in the refrigerator overnight. Transfer to a saucepan. Cover and cook over medium heat until heated through. **Yield:** 8 servings (2 quarts).

Rich Mashed Potatoes | *Natalie Warf, Spring Lake, North Carolina*

These nicely seasoned potatoes are so fresh-tasting and creamy that there's no need for extra butter or gravy. I freeze them in individual and family servings for added convenience.

5 pounds potatoes, peeled and cubed
5 tablespoons butter, divided
1 package (8 ounces) cream cheese, cubed
1 cup (8 ounces) sour cream
2 teaspoons onion salt
1/4 teaspoon garlic powder
1/4 teaspoon pepper

1 Place potatoes in a large saucepan and cover with water. Bring to a boil. Reduce heat; cover and simmer for 15-20 minutes or until tender. Drain. Mash potatoes with 3 tablespoons butter. Stir in the cream cheese, sour cream, onion salt, garlic powder and pepper until smooth.

2 Spoon into a greased 13-in. x 9-in. baking dish. Melt remaining butter; drizzle over the top. Cover; may be frozen for up to 1 month.

3 To use frozen potatoes: Thaw in the refrigerator. Bake, uncovered, at 350° for 30-35 minutes or until heated through. **Yield:** 12-14 servings.

Editor's Note: To use immediately, bake as directed.

Cranberry Velvet Freeze | *Pat Seville, Hagerstown, Maryland*

Everyone in my family loves this dessert. I normally serve it at Thanksgiving and Christmas.

2 cans (16 ounces each) whole-berry cranberry sauce
2 cans (one 20 ounces, one 8 ounces) crushed pineapple, drained
1 package (10-1/2 ounces) miniature marshmallows
1 cup green maraschino cherries, quartered
1 cup red maraschino cherries, quartered
1 teaspoon lemon juice
3 cups heavy whipping cream, whipped

1 In a large bowl, combine the cranberry sauce, pineapple, marshmallows, cherries and lemon juice. Fold in whipped cream.

2 Spoon into an ungreased 13-in. x 9-in. dish. Cover and freeze overnight. May be frozen for up to 3 months.

3 To use frozen salad: Remove from the freezer 10 minutes before serving. **Yield:** 12-16 servings.

Sweet

Peanut Butter Cup Pie

Peanut Butter Cup Pie | *Tammy Casaletto, Goshen, Indiana*

I can whip up this pie in 10 minutes and then pull it out of the freezer when we're ready for a scrumptious dessert. Feel free to substitute different flavors of pudding mix and candy bars, such as butterscotch pudding and Butterfingers.

1-1/2 **cups cold milk**

1 **package (3.9 ounces) instant chocolate pudding mix**

1 **cup chopped peanut butter cups**

1 **carton (8 ounces) frozen whipped topping, thawed**

1 **chocolate crumb crust (8 or 9 inches)**

Additional peanut butter cups, chopped, optional

1 In a bowl, whisk the milk and pudding mix for 2 minutes. Let stand for 2 minutes or until soft-set. Fold in chopped peanut butter cups. Fold in whipped topping. Spoon into crust. Cover and freeze for at least 6 hours. May be frozen for up to 1 month.

2 To serve: Remove from the freezer 15-20 minutes before serving. Garnish with additional chopped peanut butter cups if desired. **Yield:** 6-8 servings.

Frappe Mocha | *Beverly Coyde, Gasport, New York*

Using coffee ice cubes adds body to this refreshing drink. It's a fabulous chilled treat that will "perk" up your taste buds.

1 **teaspoon instant coffee granules**

1/4 **cup boiling water**

1 **cup milk**

4-1/2 **teaspoons chocolate syrup**

1/2 **cup crushed ice**

Whipped topping and additional chocolate syrup, optional

1 In a small bowl, dissolve coffee granules in water. Pour into an ice cube tray; freeze. To keep, remove frozen cubes from ice cube tray and place in a resealable plastic freezer bag. May be frozen for up to 2 months.

2 To serve: In a blender, combine the milk, chocolate syrup and coffee ice cubes. Cover and process until smooth. Add crushed ice; blend. Pour into chilled glasses; serve immediately. Garnish with whipped topping and additional chocolate syrup if desired. **Yield:** 2 servings.

Raspberry Swirl Frozen Dessert | *Karen Suderman, Sugar Land, Texas*

Rich, creamy and delicious! That's how people describe this scrumptious raspberry treat. And it's worth the time it takes to prepare, because it's so fabulous!

2/3 **cup graham cracker crumbs**
2 **tablespoons butter, melted**
5 **teaspoons sugar**
FILLING:
3 **eggs, separated**
1/4 **cup plus 1 tablespoon water, divided**
1 **cup sugar, divided**
1/8 **teaspoon salt**
1/8 **teaspoon cream of tartar**
1 **package (8 ounces) reduced-fat cream cheese**
1-1/2 **cups reduced-fat whipped topping**
1 **package (10 ounces) frozen sweetened raspberries, thawed**

1 In a small bowl, combine the cracker crumbs, butter and sugar. Press into an 11-in. x 7-in. dish coated with cooking spray. Cover and refrigerate for at least 15 minutes.

2 Meanwhile, for filling, in a small heavy saucepan, combine the egg yolks, 1/4 cup water, 1/2 cup sugar and salt. Cook and stir over low heat until mixture reaches 160° or is thick enough to coat the back of a metal spoon.

3 Remove from the heat. Cool quickly by placing pan in a bowl of ice water; stir for 2 minutes. Set aside.

4 In a small heavy saucepan over low heat, combine the egg whites, cream of tartar and remaining water and sugar. With a portable mixer, beat on low speed until mixture reaches 160°. Transfer to a small bowl; beat on high until soft peaks form.

5 In a large bowl, beat cream cheese until smooth. Gradually beat in egg yolk mixture. Fold in whipped topping, then egg white mixture. Drain raspberries, reserving 3 tablespoons juice. In a small bowl, crush half of berries with 1 tablespoon juice. Set remaining berries and juice aside.

6 Spread a third of the cream cheese mixture over crust; spoon half of the crushed berry mixture over the top. Repeat layers. Cut through with a knife to swirl raspberries.

7 Top with remaining cream cheese mixture. Sprinkle with reserved berries and drizzle with remaining juice. Cover and freeze for 5 hours or until firm. Can be frozen for up to 1 month.

8 **To serve:** Remove from the freezer 15 minutes before cutting. **Yield:** 12 servings.

Frosty Key Lime Pie | *Lisa Feld, Grafton, Wisconsin*

Credit whipped cream for the fluffy, smooth texture and luscious flavor of this frozen refresher. I highly recommend this fabulous dessert to enjoy on a hot summer's day.

- 1 **can (14 ounces) sweetened condensed milk**
- 6 **tablespoons key lime juice**
- 1-3/4 **cups heavy whipping cream, whipped**
- 1 **graham cracker crust (9 inches)**

Additional whipped cream, optional

1 In a large bowl, combine milk and lime juice. Fold a fourth of the whipped cream into lime mixture; fold in remaining whipped cream. Spoon into crust. Cover and freeze overnight. May be frozen for up to 3 months.

2 **To serve:** Remove from the freezer 10-15 minutes before serving. Garnish with additional whipped cream if desired. **Yield:** 6-8 servings.

Strawberry Italian Ice | *Jaye Hansen, Winter Haven, Florida*

We discovered Italian ice about a year ago, and it has become a family favorite. The recipes I found, however, required a lot of sugar, so I developed my own version using fresh strawberries, fruit juice concentrate and a hint of lemon.

- 3/4 **cup unsweetened apple juice concentrate**
- 1 **to 3 tablespoons lemon juice**
- 2 **pints fresh strawberries, hulled and halved**

Fresh mint, optional

1 In a blender, combine the apple juice concentrate, lemon juice and strawberries; cover and process until blended. Pour into an ungreased 8-in. square dish. Cover and freeze for 1-1/2 to 2 hours or until partially set.

2 Spoon into a large bowl; beat on medium speed for 1-1/2 minutes. Return to dish; freeze for 2-3 hours or until firm. May be frozen for up to 2 months.

3 **To serve:** Remove from the freezer 10 minutes before serving. Garnish with mint if desired. **Yield:** 5 servings.

Dreamy Cherry Torte | *Valerie Putsey, Winamac, Indiana*

A purchased pound cake makes this showstopping dessert a breeze to prepare ahead of time. Cream cheese frosting gives this torte a rich taste that will have guests thinking you spent hours making it.

1 loaf (10-3/4 ounces) frozen pound cake, thawed
1 pint cherry ice cream, softened
2 packages (3 ounces each) cream cheese, softened
1/4 cup butter, softened
1 teaspoon almond extract
3 cups confectioners' sugar
1/4 cup chopped pecans
Maraschino cherries, optional

1 With a serrated knife, slice thawed pound cake horizontally into two layers. Place bottom layer on a freezer-safe serving platter; spread with ice cream. Replace cake top; cover and freeze for at least 3 hours.

2 For frosting, in a large bowl, beat the cream cheese, butter and extract until smooth. Gradually add sugar; beat until fluffy. Set aside 1/2 cup.

3 Remove torte from freezer; frost the top and sides. Cut a small hole in the corner of a plastic or pastry bag; insert a #20 star tip. Fill bag with reserved frosting; pipe around the bottom edge of torte. Cover and freeze for at least 1 hour. May be frozen for up to 3 months.

4 To serve: Remove from freezer 10 minutes before serving. Sprinkle with pecans. Garnish with cherries if desired. **Yield:** 8 servings.

Frozen Sandwich Cookies | *Mary Ann Gomez, Lombard, Illinois*

These cool, creamy treats are a snap to make! Calling for just three ingredients, the cute tasty cookies will be a hit with both young and old alike.

1/2 cup spreadable strawberry cream cheese
1/4 cup strawberry yogurt
16 chocolate wafers

1 In a small bowl, beat cream cheese and yogurt until smooth. Spread on the bottom of half of the chocolate wafers; top with remaining wafers. Place on a baking sheet. Cover and freeze for 25 minutes.

2 Wrap in plastic wrap. May be frozen for up to 1 month. **Yield:** 8 cookies.

Mocha Almond Dessert | *Taste of Home Test Kitchen*

Try this recipe for an easy, make-ahead dessert that's elegant and luscious. The perfect blend of mocha and chocolate is in each refreshing slice.

1	**cup cream-filled chocolate sandwich cookie crumbs**
1/4	**cup sugar**
1/4	**cup butter, melted**
1	**package (8 ounces) cream cheese, softened**
1	**can (14 ounces) sweetened condensed milk**
2/3	**cup chocolate syrup**
1/2	**teaspoon vanilla extract**
2	**tablespoons instant coffee granules**
1	**tablespoon hot water**
1	**cup whipped topping**
1/3	**cup chopped almonds, toasted**

Chocolate-covered coffee beans, optional

1 In a bowl, combine the cookie crumbs, sugar and butter. Press onto the bottom and 1 in. up the sides of a greased 9-in. springform pan; set aside.

2 In another bowl, beat the cream cheese, milk, chocolate syrup and vanilla until smooth. Dissolve coffee granules in hot water; beat into cream cheese mixture. Fold in the whipped topping and almonds. Pour over crust. Cover and freeze for 8 hours or overnight. May be frozen for up to 1 month.

3 To serve: Remove from the freezer 10-15 minutes before serving. Carefully run a knife around edge of pan to loosen. Remove sides of pan. Garnish with chocolate-covered coffee beans if desired. **Yield:** 10-12 servings.

Chocolate Chip Cookie Dessert | *Carol Marnach, Sioux Falls, South Dakota*

Drizzled with melted chocolate, this frosty favorite couldn't be much easier to prepare. My family loves it so much that we even use our grill to make it on camping trips or during the hot summer months when I don't like turning on the oven.

- 1 **tube (16-1/2 ounces) refrigerated chocolate chip cookie dough**
- 1/2 **cup caramel ice cream topping**
- 1/2 **cup cold milk**
- 1 **package (3.4 ounces) instant vanilla pudding mix**
- 1 **carton (8 ounces) frozen whipped topping, thawed**
- 3/4 **cup chopped nuts**
- 3/4 **cup English toffee bits or almond brickle chips**
- 3 **squares (1 ounce each) semisweet chocolate, chopped**
- 3 **tablespoons butter**

1 Let the dough stand at room temperature for 5-10 minutes to soften. Press into an ungreased 13-in. x 9-in. baking pan. Bake at 350° for 14-16 minutes or until golden brown. Cool completely on a wire rack.

2 Spread caramel topping over crust. In a bowl, whisk milk and pudding mix for 2 minutes. Let stand for 2 minutes or until soft-set. Fold in the whipped topping, nuts and toffee bits. Spread over caramel layer. Cover and freeze for 4 hours or until firm. May be frozen for up to 2 months.

3 To serve: In a microwave, melt chocolate and butter; stir until smooth. Drizzle over top. Cut into squares. **Yield:** 16 servings.

Fruity Banana Freeze | *Dixie Terry, Marion, Illinois*

It's easy to double or triple this refreshing recipe for a luncheon or shower. And the best part is it only takes minutes to assemble!

2 cups (16 ounces) sour cream
1-2/3 cups mashed ripe bananas (about 4 medium)
1 can (8 ounces) unsweetened crushed pineapple, undrained
3/4 cup sugar
1/2 cup chopped pecans
1/4 cup quartered maraschino cherries
1 tablespoon lemon juice
1/2 teaspoon salt

1 In a large bowl, combine all the ingredients. Pour into a 9-in. square pan. Freeze until firm. May be frozen for up to 3 months.

2 **To serve:** Remove from the freezer 15 minutes before serving. **Yield:** 12 servings.

Frozen Raspberry Cheesecake | *Donna Rear, Red Deer, Alberta*

I got this recipe from my sister years ago and like to fix it when times are rushed. It's fancy enough for the most special occasions, but so easy to prepare with ingredients always on hand. Try varying the juices and fruits for unique flavor twists.

1-1/2 cups cream-filled chocolate sandwich cookie crumbs (about 15 cookies)
1/4 cup butter, melted
1 package (8 ounces) cream cheese, softened
3/4 cup confectioners' sugar
1 package (10 ounces) frozen sweetened raspberries, thawed
3/4 cup cranberry-raspberry juice, divided
1 teaspoon lemon juice
2 cups heavy whipping cream, whipped

1 Combine cookie crumbs and butter; press onto the bottom of an ungreased 9-in. springform pan. In a large bowl, beat cream cheese and confectioners' sugar until smooth. Beat in the raspberries, 1/2 cup cranberry-raspberry juice and lemon juice until blended. Fold in whipped cream. Pour onto crust.

2 Spoon remaining juice over cheesecake; cut through batter with a knife to swirl. Cover and freeze overnight. May be frozen for up to 1 month.

3 **To serve:** Remove from the freezer 15 minutes before cutting into slices. **Yield:** 12 servings.

Peach Cheesecake Ice Cream | *Jenni Anderson, Bullhead City, Arizona*

I first tried this recipe to serve at my grandparents' 50th anniversary celebration—it was a wonderful way to top off an already delicious event. Everyone really appreciated the homemade treat.

1	**cup milk**
1-1/4	**cups plus 3 tablespoons sugar, divided**
3	**egg yolks, lightly beaten**
2	**cups heavy whipping cream**
2	**teaspoons vanilla extract**
2	**packages (8 ounces each) cream cheese, cubed**
1/2	**cup peach nectar**
4	**teaspoons lemon juice**
4	**medium peaches, peeled and chopped or 1-1/2 cups frozen sliced peaches, chopped**

1 In a small saucepan, heat milk to 175°; stir in 1-1/4 cups sugar until dissolved. Whisk a small amount into the egg yolks. Return all to the pan, whisking constantly. Cook and stir over low heat until mixture reaches at least 160° and coats the back of a metal spoon.

2 Remove from the heat. Cool quickly by placing pan in a bowl of ice water; stir for 2 minutes. Transfer to a large bowl.

3 In a blender, combine the cream, vanilla and cream cheese; cover and process until smooth. Add to cooled milk mixture. Stir in peach nectar and lemon juice. Refrigerate for several hours or overnight.

4 Fill cylinder of ice cream freezer two-thirds full; freeze according to manufacturer's directions. Refrigerate remaining ice cream mixture until ready to freeze. Place peaches in a bowl; sprinkle with remaining sugar. Set aside, stirring several times. Drain and discard juice from peaches. Add some of the peaches to each batch of ice cream during the last 5 minutes it is in the ice cream freezer.

5 Transfer ice cream to a freezer container; freeze for 2-4 hours before serving. May be frozen for up to 2 months. **Yield:** 2 quarts.

TIP

Peachy Pointers

If recipe calls for fresh peaches, purchase those that have an intense fragrance and that give slightly to palm pressure. Avoid ones that are hard or have soft spots. Store ripe peaches in a plastic bag in the refrigerator for up to 5 days. To ripen peaches, place in a brown paper bag and store at room temperature for about 2 days. A half pound will yield about 1 cup chopped peaches.

Lemon Baked Alaska | *Kevin Weeks, North Palm Beach, Florida*

This impressive dessert—piled high with vanilla ice cream, lemon sauce and meringue—won my mother the grand prize in a local cooking contest as a first-time entrant. It's the perfect finale to a special meal.

1 cup sugar
2 eggs
2 egg yolks, lightly beaten
1/3 cup lemon juice
1/8 teaspoon salt
6 tablespoons butter
1 teaspoon grated lemon peel
1-1/2 quarts vanilla ice cream, softened
1 pastry shell (9 inches), baked

MERINGUE:
5 egg whites
1/2 cup plus 2 tablespoons sugar
1/2 teaspoon cream of tartar
1 teaspoon vanilla extract

1 In a large saucepan, combine the sugar, eggs, egg yolks, lemon juice and salt. Cook and stir over medium heat until mixture reaches 160° or is thick enough to coat the back of a metal spoon. Stir in butter and lemon peel until blended. Cool completely. Refrigerate until chilled.

2 Spread half of the ice cream into pastry shell. Top with lemon mixture and remaining ice cream. Cover and freeze overnight. May be frozen up to 1 month.

3 **To serve:** In a small heavy saucepan, combine the egg whites, sugar and cream of tartar. With a hand mixer, beat on low speed for 1 minute. Continue beating over low heat until egg mixture reaches 160°, about 12 minutes.

4 Remove from the heat. Add vanilla; beat until stiff peaks form. Immediately spread over the frozen pie. Bake at 450° for 3-5 minutes or until lightly browned. Serve immediately. **Yield:** 8-10 servings.

Chocolate Peanut Butter Dessert | *Christine Montalvo, Windsor Heights, Iowa*

When I want to splurge on a rich dessert, I whip up this chocolate-glazed frozen peanut butter mousse. It's so luscious, even a thin slice will satisfy. It tastes just like a peanut butter cup.

1-1/4   cups packed dark brown sugar
1   cup heavy whipping cream, divided
3   egg yolks
1-1/4   cups creamy peanut butter
6   tablespoons butter, softened

GLAZE:
1-1/2   cups heavy whipping cream
2   tablespoons butter
4   teaspoons dark corn syrup
12   squares (1 ounce each) bittersweet chocolate, chopped
1/4   cup coarsely chopped dry roasted peanuts

1 In a small saucepan, combine brown sugar, 1/2 cup cream and yolks. Cook and stir over medium heat until mixture reaches 160° and is thick enough to coat the back of a metal spoon. Cover and refrigerate for 3 hours or until thickened.

2 Line an 8-in. x 4-in. loaf pan with plastic wrap; set aside. In a large bowl, cream peanut butter and butter until light and fluffy. Add brown sugar mixture; beat until smooth. In small bowl, beat remaining cream until stiff peaks form. Fold into peanut butter mixture. Spoon into prepared pan. Cover and refrigerate.

3 For glaze, in a large heavy saucepan, bring the cream, butter and corn syrup to a boil, stirring frequently. Remove from the heat. Add chocolate; whisk until smooth. Set aside 1/3 cup glaze to cool. Place remaining glaze in a microwave-safe bowl; cover and refrigerate overnight. Spread cooled glaze over loaf; cover and freeze overnight.

4 Using plastic wrap, lift loaf out of pan. Place chocolate side down in a waxed paper-lined 15-in. x 10-in. x 1-in. pan; place on a wire rack. Discard plastic wrap.

5 In microwave, warm refrigerated glaze; stir until smooth. Pour over loaf; spread with a metal spatula to completely cover top and sides. Sprinkle with peanuts. Freeze for 1 hour or until glaze is set. May be frozen for up to 3 months.

6 To serve: Remove from freezer 5-10 minutes before cutting into slices. **Yield:** 10-12 servings.

Iced Coffee Slush | *Iola Egle, Bella Vista, Arkansas*

We have a tradition of hosting a game night during the holidays with nine other couples. Our guests come for the camaraderie, but they sure love washing down delicious buffet items with this sweet slush. Even noncoffee drinkers enjoy it.

3 cups hot strong brewed coffee
1-1/2 to 2 cups sugar
4 cups milk
2 cups half-and-half cream
1-1/2 teaspoons vanilla extract

1 In a freezer-safe bowl, stir coffee and sugar until sugar is dissolved. Refrigerate until thoroughly chilled. Add the milk, cream and vanilla; freeze. May be frozen up to 2 months.

2 **To serve:** Remove from the freezer several hours before serving. Chop mixture until slushy; serve immediately. **Yield:** 12 servings (2-1/4 quarts).

Brownie Chunk Ice Cream | *Agnes Ward, Stratford, Ontario*

Each time I make brownies, half the batch goes to friends and the rest ends up in this ice cream. For a little crunch, I sometimes add a half cup of chopped nuts.

3 cups half-and-half cream
3/4 cup sugar, divided
3 tablespoons baking cocoa
6 egg yolks
6 squares (1 ounce each) semisweet chocolate, finely chopped
1 package fudge brownie mix (8-inch square pan size)

1 In a large saucepan, heat cream to 175°; stir in 1/2 cup sugar until dissolved. In a bowl, combine cocoa and remaining sugar; whisk in egg yolks until smooth. Whisk a small amount of hot cream mixture into the egg yolk mixture. Return all to the pan, whisking constantly. Cook and stir over low heat until mixture reaches at least 160° and coats the back of a metal spoon.

2 Remove from the heat; stir in chocolate until melted. Cool quickly by placing pan in a bowl of ice water; let stand for 30 minutes, stirring frequently.

3 Transfer to a bowl; press plastic wrap onto surface of custard. Refrigerate for several hours or overnight.

4 Prepare and bake brownies according to package directions. Cool on a wire rack; cut brownies into 1/2-in. cubes.

5 Fill cylinder of ice cream freezer two-thirds full with custard; freeze according to manufacturer's directions. Stir in half of the brownie cubes. Refrigerate remaining ice cream until ready to freeze. Add remaining brownies. When ice cream is frozen, transfer to a freezer container; freeze for 2-4 hours before serving. May be frozen for up to 2 months. **Yield:** about 1-1/2 quarts.

Pineapple Ice Cream | *Phyllis Schmalz, Kansas City, Kansas*

I rely on my ice cream maker when I whip up this easy frozen treat. The creamy concoction has just the right amount of pineapple to keep guests asking for more.

- 2 **cups milk**
- 1 **cup sugar**
- 3 **eggs, lightly beaten**
- 1-3/4 **cups heavy whipping cream**
- 1 **can (8 ounces) crushed pineapple, undrained**

1 In a large saucepan, heat milk to 175°; stir in sugar until dissolved. Whisk a small amount of the hot mixture into the eggs. Return all to the pan, whisking constantly. Cook and stir over low heat until mixture reaches at least 160° and coats the back of a metal spoon.

2 Remove from the heat. Cool quickly by placing pan in a bowl of ice water; stir for 2 minutes. Stir in whipping cream and pineapple. Press waxed paper onto surface of custard. Refrigerate for several hours or overnight.

3 Fill cylinder of ice cream freezer two-thirds full; freeze according to the manufacturer's directions. Refrigerate remaining mixture until ready to freeze. When ice cream is frozen, transfer to a freezer container; freeze for 2-4 hours before serving. May be frozen for up to 2 months. **Yield:** 6 servings.

Sherbet Cookie Delight | *Donna Carper, South Jordan, Utah*

Looking to save some time when preparing for a party? Throw together this creamy crowd-pleaser and freeze it a day or two before the event. The combination of raspberry and chocolate in this dessert is delightful, but it's also good made with lime sherbet, vanilla sandwich cookies and walnuts.

- 1/2 **gallon raspberry sherbet, softened**
- 2 **cups heavy whipping cream**
- 1/3 **cup confectioners' sugar**
- 15 **chocolate cream-filled sandwich cookies**
- 3/4 **to 1 cup chopped slivered almonds, toasted**

Additional chocolate cream-filled sandwich cookies, optional

1 Place sherbet in a 13-in. x 9-in. dish. Freeze for 10 minutes. Meanwhile, in a large bowl, beat cream until it begins to thicken. Add sugar; beat until stiff peaks form.

2 Break each cookie into six pieces; fold into cream mixture with almonds. Spoon over sherbet. Cover and freeze for up to 2 months.

3 To serve: Remove from the freezer 15 minutes before serving. Cut into squares. Garnish with additional cookies if desired. **Yield:** 16-20 servings.

Frosty Toffee Bits Pie | *LaDonna Reed, Ponca City, Oklahoma*

This dessert tastes oh-so-good on a hot summer day, as well as a wonderful finale to a meal any time of year.

- 1 **package (3 ounces) cream cheese, softened**
- 2 **tablespoons sugar**
- 1/2 **cup half-and-half cream**
- 1 **carton (8 ounces) frozen whipped topping, thawed**
- 1 **package (8 ounces) milk chocolate English toffee bits, divided**
- 1 **graham cracker crust (9 inches)**

1 In a large bowl, beat cream cheese and sugar until smooth. Beat in cream until blended. Fold in whipped topping and 1 cup toffee bits.

2 Spoon into crust; sprinkle with remaining toffee bits. Cover and freeze overnight. May be frozen up to 1 month.

3 To serve: Remove from the freezer 10 minutes before serving. **Yield:** 6-8 servings.

Make-Ahead Glazed Brownies | *Barbara Robbins, Chandler, Arizona*

I often rely on these moist brownies for last-minute treats. I've been making the sweet snacks for years, and they're high on everyone's list of favorites.

- 1/2 **cup butter, softened**
- 1 **cup sugar**
- 1 **egg**
- 1/4 **cup sour cream**
- 1 **cup all-purpose flour**
- 1/2 **cup baking cocoa**
- 1/2 **teaspoon baking powder**
- 1/4 **teaspoon salt**
- 1/2 **cup milk**

GLAZE:
- 1/4 **cup butter, softened**
- 1/2 **cup confectioners' sugar**
- 2 **tablespoons baking cocoa**
- 3 **tablespoons milk**
- 1/2 **cup chopped pecans**
- 1/2 **teaspoon vanilla extract**

1 In a large bowl, cream butter and sugar until light and fluffy. Beat in egg and sour cream. Combine the flour, cocoa, baking powder and salt; add to creamed mixture alternately with milk and mix well after each addition.

2 Spread into a greased 13-in. x 9-in. baking pan. Bake at 350° for 20-25 minutes or until a toothpick inserted near the center comes out clean.

3 In a small bowl, cream the butter, confectioners' sugar and cocoa until light and fluffy. Gradually beat in milk until smooth. Stir in pecans and vanilla. Spread over warm brownies. Cool on a wire rack. Cover and freeze for up to 1 month.

4 To serve: Thaw and cut into bars. **Yield:** 2 dozen.

Lemon Sorbet Torte | *Sarah Bradley, Athens, Texas*

Oohs and aahs are sure to be the reaction when you bring this elegant torte to the table. It all starts with the unique almond and cinnamon-flavored crust topped with a layer of strawberry jam, then filled with prepared lemon sorbet. The torte is served with a rhubarb-strawberry sauce and additional fresh strawberries.

3	cups slivered almonds, toasted
1/2	cup sugar
1/4	teaspoon ground cinnamon
5	tablespoons butter, melted
1/3	cup seedless strawberry jam
3	pints lemon sorbet, softened

STRAWBERRY-RHUBARB SAUCE:

1/2	cup sugar
1/4	cup water
2-1/2	cups sliced fresh or frozen rhubarb
2-1/2	cups frozen unsweetened strawberries, partially thawed and sliced
3/4	teaspoon vanilla extract
1	pint fresh strawberries, sliced

1 Place the almonds, sugar and cinnamon in a food processor; cover and process until finely chopped. Stir in the butter. Press onto the bottom and 2 in. up the sides of an ungreased 9-in. springform pan. Place pan on a baking sheet. Bake at 350° for 15-20 minutes or until lightly browned. Cool completely on a wire rack.

2 In a small saucepan over low heat, melt jam; spread over bottom of crust. Top with sorbet. Cover and freeze until firm. May be frozen for up to 2 months.

3 **To use frozen torte:** For sauce, combine sugar and water in a large saucepan. Bring to a boil. Add rhubarb; return to a boil. Reduce heat; cover and simmer for 5-8 minutes or until rhubarb is tender. Add thawed strawberries; bring to a boil. Remove from the heat; cool to room temperature. Stir in vanilla. Cover and refrigerate.

4 Remove sides of springform pan just before serving. Spoon 1/2 cup sauce onto center of torte; top with fresh strawberries. Serve with remaining sauce. **Yield:** 12 servings.

Banana Pineapple Slush | *Beth Myers, Lewisburg, West Virginia*

This sunny tropical slush refreshes on summer days and is also perfect for brunches, showers, weddings and neighborhood parties.

- 4 **cups sugar**
- 2 **cups water**
- 1 **can (46 ounces) pineapple juice**
- 3 **cups orange juice**
- 3/4 **cup lemon juice**
- 1/2 **cup orange juice concentrate**
- 8 **medium ripe bananas, mashed**
- 2 **bottles (2 liters each) cream soda**
- 3 **cans (12 ounces each) lemon-lime soda**

1 In a saucepan, bring sugar and water to a boil over medium heat; cool. Pour into a freezer container; add juices, orange juice concentrate and bananas. Cover; may be frozen for up to 2 months.

2 To serve: Thaw mixture until slushy; stir in cream soda and lemon-lime soda. **Yield:** about 9-1/2 quarts.

Frozen Strawberry Yogurt | *Teri Van Wey, Salina, Kansas*

After losing 60 pounds, I wanted a light version of the ice cream I made in my ice cream freezer. Everyone loves this recipe that uses reduced-fat ingredients.

- 2 **cups (16 ounces) fat-free plain yogurt**
- 2 **cups pureed fresh strawberries**
- 1 **can (14 ounces) fat-free sweetened condensed milk**
- 1 **cup fat-free milk**
- 3 **teaspoons vanilla extract**

1 In a large bowl, combine all the ingredients. Fill cylinder of ice cream freezer two-thirds full; freeze according to manufacturer's directions. Refrigerate remaining mixture until ready to freeze. When yogurt is frozen, transfer to a freezer container; freeze for 2-4 hours before serving. May be frozen for up to 2 months. **Yield:** 1-1/2 quarts.

Fudgy Ice Cream Dessert | *Jenny Haen, Red Wing, Minnesota*

For this frosty treat, a rich chocolate cookie crust is topped with vanilla ice cream, peanuts and hot fudge. Assemble it and keep it in the freezer to please a crowd any time of year.

1	**package (14 ounces) cream-filled chocolate sandwich cookies, crushed**
7	**tablespoons butter, melted**
1/2	**gallon vanilla ice cream, softened**
1-1/2	**cups finely chopped salted peanuts**
1	**carton (8 ounces) frozen whipped topping, thawed**
1	**jar (11-3/4 ounces) hot fudge ice cream topping, warmed**

1 In a bowl, combine cookie crumbs and butter until crumbly. Set aside 1/2 cup for topping. Press remaining crumb mixture into a greased 13-in. x 9-in. dish. Freeze for 30 minutes. Spread ice cream over crust. Cover and freeze for 2-1/2 hours.

2 Sprinkle peanuts over ice cream. Cover and freeze for 1 hour. Spread with whipped topping (pan will be very full). Sprinkle with reserved crumb mixture. Freeze for at least 8 hours. May be frozen for up to 2 months.

3 To serve: Remove from the freezer 15 minutes before serving. Cut into squares. Serve with hot fudge topping. **Yield:** 12-15 servings.

Apricot-Almond Antarctica | *Marcy McReynolds, Nixa, Missouri*

Almonds add a nutty crunch to the cookie crumb layers in this ice cream dessert. A friend brought us this special treat when she and her husband came over for dinner. The combination of almonds and apricots remains a family favorite.

1	**package (12 ounces) vanilla wafers, crushed**
1-1/3	**cups slivered almonds, toasted**
1/2	**cup butter, melted**
1	**tablespoon almond extract**
6	**cups vanilla ice cream, softened**
1	**jar (18 ounces) apricot preserves**

1 In a large bowl, combine the wafer crumbs, almonds, butter and extract. Pat a third into an ungreased 13-in. x 9-in. pan. Freeze for 15 minutes.

2 Carefully spread half of the ice cream over crust. Spoon half of the preserves over the ice cream. Sprinkle with half of the remaining crumb mixture. Freeze for 20-30 minutes. Repeat layers. Cover; may be frozen for up to 2 months.

3 To serve: Remove from freezer 5-10 minutes before cutting. **Yield:** 16-20 servings.

Tropical Fruit Slush | *Teresa Weikle, Morehead, Kentucky*

This recipe has been in my family for a long time. I have fond childhood memories of cooling off on many a scorching afternoon sipping this cold fruit treat.

3 cups water
1-1/2 cups sugar
6 medium ripe bananas, diced
2 cans (11 ounces each) mandarin oranges
1 can (20 ounces) crushed pineapple, undrained
1 can (12 ounces) frozen orange juice concentrate, thawed
1 jar (10 ounces) maraschino cherries, drained and halved
1/3 cup lemon juice

1 In a small saucepan, bring water and sugar to a boil; cook and stir for 5 minutes. Remove from the heat; cool completely. In a 4-qt. freezer container, combine the remaining ingredients. Pour sugar water over the fruit. Cover and freeze for at least 8 hours, stirring once or twice. May be frozen for up to 2 months.

2 To serve: Remove from the freezer 20 minutes before serving. **Yield:** 12-14 servings.

Gingered Pear Sorbet | *Donna Cline, Pensacola, Florida*

During the blistering summer here in Florida, we enjoy this refreshing sorbet. Sometimes I dress up servings with berries, mint leaves or crystallized ginger.

1 can (29 ounces) pear halves
1/4 cup sugar
2 tablespoons lemon juice
1/8 teaspoon ground ginger
Yellow food coloring, optional

1 Drain pears, reserving 1 cup syrup; set pears aside. In a saucepan, bring sugar and reserved syrup to a boil. Remove from the heat; cool.

2 In a blender, process the pears, lemon juice and ginger until smooth. Add cooled syrup and food coloring if desired; cover and process until pureed. Pour into an 11-in. x 7-in. dish. Cover and freeze for 1-1/2 to 2 hours or until partially frozen.

3 Return mixture to blender; cover and process until smooth. Place in a freezer container; cover and freeze for at least 3 hours. May be frozen for up to 3 months.

4 To serve: Remove from the freezer 20 minutes before serving. **Yield:** 3 cups.

Frozen Mocha Marbled Loaf | *Cheryl Martinetto, Grand Rapids, Minnesota*

This showstopping marbled dessert looks fancy, but it's really simple to prepare ahead of time. Frosty slices have a creamy blend of chocolate and coffee that's delightful anytime of year.

2   **cups finely crushed chocolate cream-filled sandwich cookies (about 22 cookies)**
3   **tablespoons butter, melted**
1   **package (8 ounces) cream cheese, softened**
1   **can (14 ounces) sweetened condensed milk**
1   **teaspoon vanilla extract**
2   **cups heavy whipping cream, whipped**
2   **tablespoons instant coffee granules**
1   **tablespoon hot water**
1/2 **cup chocolate syrup**

1 Line a 9-in. x 5-in. loaf pan with foil. In a bowl, combine the cookie crumbs and butter. Press firmly onto the bottom and 1-1/2 in. up the sides of prepared pan.

2 In a large bowl, beat cream cheese until light and fluffy. Add milk and vanilla and mix well. Fold in whipped cream. Spoon half of the mixture into another bowl and set aside. Dissolve coffee in hot water; fold into remaining cream cheese mixture. Fold in chocolate syrup.

3 Spoon half of the chocolate mixture over crust. Top with half of the reserved cream cheese mixture. Repeat layers. Cut through layers with a knife to swirl the chocolate (pan will be full). Cover and freeze for 6 hours or overnight. May be frozen up to 1 month.

4 **To serve:** Lift loaf out of the pan; remove foil. Cut into slices. **Yield:** 12 servings.

Refreshing Lime Slush | *Karen Bourne, Magrath, Alberta*

Nothing quenches my thirst on a hot summer day quite like this frozen slush featuring a subtle lime flavor. When warm weather arrives, a batch will be chilling in my freezer.

11 cups water
3 cups sugar
3/4 cup limeade concentrate
2 liters lemon-lime soda, chilled
Lime slices, optional

1 In a large bowl, combine the water, sugar and limeade concentrate until sugar is dissolved. Pour into a 4-qt. freezer container or several small freezer containers. May be frozen for up to 2 months.

2 To use frozen slush: Remove from the freezer several hours before serving. Chop mixture until slushy. Add soda just before serving. Garnish with lime slices if desired. **Yield:** 5-1/2 quarts (30 servings).

Strawberry Delight Torte | *Marianne Severson, West Allis, Wisconsin*

This festive torte looks fancy but is actually quite easy to make...and can be prepared ahead of time.

1 cup all-purpose flour
1/2 cup packed brown sugar
1/2 cup cold butter
2/3 cup finely chopped pecans
1 jar (7 ounces) marshmallow creme
2 tablespoons lemon juice
1 package (16 ounces) frozen sliced sweetened strawberries, thawed
1 cup heavy whipping cream, whipped
Fresh strawberries and mint sprigs, optional

1 In a large bowl, combine flour and brown sugar. Cut in butter until mixture resembles coarse crumbs. Stir in pecans. Press onto the bottom of an ungreased 9-in. springform pan. Bake at 350° for 15-18 minutes or until lightly browned. Cool to room temperature.

2 In a large bowl, combine marshmallow creme and lemon juice. Stir in berries. Fold in whipped cream. Pour over the crust. Cover and freeze overnight or until firm. May be frozen for up to 1 month.

3 To serve: Remove from the freezer 20 minutes before serving. Garnish with strawberries and mint if desired. **Yield:** 12-14 servings.

Tropical Slush | *Hollis Mattson, Brush Prairie, Washington*

I first tried this refreshing beverage—with its tasty combination of citrus juices and mashed banana—at a church reception. It's perfect for serving at birthday parties, wedding showers, anniversary dinners, barbecues and other special occasions.

6 cups water, divided
5 medium ripe bananas
2 cups sugar
2 cans (12 ounces each) frozen orange juice concentrate, thawed
1 can (12 ounces) frozen lemonade concentrate, thawed
1 can (46 ounces) unsweetened pineapple juice
3 bottles (2 liters each) lemon-lime soda

1 In a blender, combine 1 cup water, bananas and sugar; a large container; add the concentrates, pineapple juice and remaining water. Cover and freeze. May be frozen for up to 2 months.

2 To serve: Remove from freezer 2 hours before serving. Just before serving, stir until slushy. Stir in soda. Serve immediately. **Yield:** 40-50 servings (about 11 quarts).

Sherbet Angel Torte | *Amy Nichols, Brownville, Maine*

For a dramatic dessert, you can't go wrong with this sky-high torte. It's a wonderful make-ahead treat.

1 prepared angel food cake (16 ounces)
1 quart raspberry sherbet
1 carton (8 ounces) frozen reduced-fat whipped topping, thawed
1/2 cup reduced-sugar raspberry preserves, warmed
Fresh raspberries, optional

1 Freeze the cake for at least 2 hours or overnight.

2 Split cake horizontally into three layers. Place bottom layer on a freezer-safe serving plate; top with about 1 cup sherbet. Repeat layers. Top with remaining cake layer. Fill center with remaining sherbet. Frost top and sides with whipped topping. Gently spread preserves over top of cake.

3 Loosely cover and store in freezer. May be frozen for up to 1 week.

4 To serve: Thaw in the refrigerator for 30 minutes before slicing with a serrated knife. Garnish with raspberries if desired. **Yield:** 12 servings.

Frozen Strawberry Dessert | *Kate Murphy, Union Bay, British Columbia*

My grandpa gave me many of my grandmother's and great-grandmother's recipes, including this one, for a luscious strawberry delight.

1 cup all-purpose flour
1/4 cup packed brown sugar
1/2 cup butter, melted
1/2 cup chopped walnuts
2 egg whites
2/3 cup sugar, divided
2 teaspoons water
1/8 teaspoon cream of tartar
1 package (10 ounces) frozen sweetened sliced strawberries, thawed
2 tablespoons lemon juice
1 cup heavy whipping cream

1 In a small bowl, combine the flour, brown sugar, butter and walnuts. Place in a 15-in. x 10-in. x 1-in. baking pan. Bake at 350° for 18-20 minutes, stirring occasionally, until golden brown; cool on a wire rack. Reserve 1/3 cup for topping; sprinkle the remaining nut mixture into a lightly greased 13-in. x 9-in. dish.

2 In a large saucepan, combine the egg whites, 1 tablespoon sugar, water and cream of tartar over low heat. With a portable mixer, beat on low speed for 1 minute. Continue beating on low speed until mixture reaches 160°. Pour into a large bowl. Add strawberries, lemon juice and remaining sugar; beat on high for 8 minutes or until light and fluffy.

3 In another large bowl, beat cream until stiff peaks form. Fold into strawberry mixture. Transfer the mixture to prepared dish; sprinkle with the reserved nut mixture. Cover and freeze for at least 6 hours. May be frozen for up to 1 month. **Yield:** 8-10 servings.

Strawberry Lemonade Slush | *Sue Jorgensen, Rapid City, South Dakota*

This refreshing fruity slush really perks up the taste buds. I have made it for Christmas, Valentine's Day, summer potlucks and other occasions, and there is seldom any leftovers.

3/4　cup water

3/4　cup pink lemonade concentrate

1　package (10 ounces) frozen sweetened sliced strawberries, thawed

3/4　cup ice cubes

1　cup club soda

1 In a blender, combine the water, lemonade concentrate, strawberries and ice cubes. Cover and process until blended. Pour into a freezer container. Cover and freeze for at least 12 hours. May be frozen for up to 2 months.

2 To serve: Let stand at room temperature for 1 hour before serving. Stir in the club soda. Pour into chilled glasses and serve immediately. **Yield:** 4 servings.

Frozen Chocolate Cheesecake Tart | *Heather Bennett, Dunbar, West Virginia*

I first made this irresistible dessert for some dinner guests. They were impressed with its rich flavor and appearance. My husband commented that it was the best dessert he had ever eaten in his whole life.

2-1/4　cups crushed chocolate cream-filled sandwich cookies (about 22 cookies)

1/3　cup butter, melted

FILLING:

2　packages (8 ounces each) cream cheese, softened

1/3　cup confectioners' sugar

3　cups vanilla or white chips, melted and cooled

1/3　cup heavy whipping cream

1　teaspoon vanilla extract

1/2　cup miniature semisweet chocolate chips

Chocolate curls, optional

1 In a small bowl, combine cookie crumbs and butter. Press onto the bottom and up the sides of a greased 9-in. fluted tart pan with a removable bottom. Cover and freeze for at least 1 hour.

2 In a large bowl, beat cream cheese and sugar until smooth. Beat in the vanilla chips, cream, and vanilla until well combined. Stir in chocolate chips; pour over crust. Cover and freeze for 8 hours or overnight. May be frozen up to 1 month.

3 To serve: Uncover and refrigerate 3-4 hours before serving. Garnish with chocolate curls if desired. Refrigerate leftovers. **Yield:** 12 servings.

Frosty Mallow Fruit Dessert | *Patricia Swart, Bridgeton, New Jersey*

This fancy, frosty delight is as pretty as a picture...and goes together in just 10 minutes!

- 1 package (8 ounces) cream cheese, softened
- 1 cup (8 ounces) sour cream
- 1/4 cup sugar
- 1 can (15 ounces) apricot halves, drained and coarsely chopped
- 1 can (8 ounces) crushed pineapple, drained
- 1 cup miniature marshmallows
- 1 can (15 ounces) pitted dark sweet cherries, drained

1 In a bowl, beat the cream cheese, sour cream and sugar until smooth. Fold in the apricots, pineapple and marshmallows. Gently fold in cherries.

2 Spoon into a 5-cup ring mold coated with cooking spray. Cover and freeze for 4 hours or until firm. May be frozen for up to 1 month.

3 To serve: Invert onto a platter, just before serving. **Yield:** 8 servings.

Banana Split Freeze | *Shirley Buehler, Minnetonka, Minnesota*

Cut down on hostess duties by preparing this frosty sensation ahead of time. The pretty dessert features strawberry ice cream as well as a layer of rich chocolate. My children request this for their birthday cakes.

- 1 can (12 ounces) evaporated milk
- 1 cup (6 ounces) semisweet chocolate chips
- 1/2 cup plus 6 tablespoons butter, divided
- 2 cups confectioners' sugar
- 1-1/2 cups graham cracker crumbs
- 3 medium ripe bananas, cut into 1/4-inch slices
- 2 quarts strawberry ice cream, softened
- 2 cups chopped pecans
- 1 carton (8 ounces) frozen whipped topping, thawed

1 In a small saucepan, combine the milk, chocolate chips and 1/2 cup butter. Cook and stir over medium heat until melted and smooth. Stir in confectioners' sugar. Bring to a boil. Reduce heat; simmer, uncovered, for 12-15 minutes or until thickened, stirring frequently. Cool to room temperature.

2 Meanwhile, melt remaining butter; stir in cracker crumbs. Press into a greased 13-in. x 9-in. dish; freeze for 10 minutes. Top with bananas, ice cream and pecans. Spread cooled chocolate mixture over top. Freeze for 1 hour. Spread with whipped topping. Cover; may be frozen for up to 2 months.

3 To serve: Remove from the freezer 15 minutes before serving. **Yield:** 15-20 servings.

Chilly Coconut Pie | *Jeannette Mack, Rushville, New York*

Everyone loves this creamy coconut pie. It's so easy to make that I keep several in the freezer for those occasions when I need a quick dessert.

- 1 **package (3 ounces) cream cheese, softened**
- 2 **tablespoons sugar**
- 1/2 **cup milk**
- 1/4 **teaspoon almond extract**
- 1 **cup flaked coconut**
- 1 **carton (8 ounces) frozen whipped topping, thawed**
- 1 **graham cracker crust (9 inches)**

1 In a large bowl, beat cream cheese and sugar until smooth. Gradually beat in milk and extract. Fold in coconut and whipped topping. Spoon into crust. Cover and freeze for at least 4 hours. May be frozen for up to 1 month.

2 To serve: Remove from the freezer 30 minutes before serving. **Yield:** 6-8 servings.

Icy Holiday Punch | *Margaret Matson, Metamora, Illinois*

It's easy and convenient to prepare the base of this slushy punch in advance. The rosy color makes it pretty for the holidays. Try it with apricot gelatin for showers or any spring or summer occasion.

- 1 **package (6 ounces) cherry gelatin**
- 3/4 **cup sugar**
- 2 **cups boiling water**
- 1 **can (46 ounces) pineapple juice**
- 6 **cups cold water**
- 2 **liters ginger ale, chilled**

1 In a 4-qt. freezer container, dissolve gelatin and sugar in boiling water. Stir in pineapple juice and cold water. Cover and freeze overnight. May be frozen up to 2 months.

2 To serve: Remove from the freezer 2 hours before serving. Place in a punch bowl; stir in ginger ale just before serving. **Yield:** 32-36 servings (5-3/4 quarts).

Frosty Peppermint Dessert | *Carolyn Satterfield, Emporia, Kansas*

This creamy freeze with candy and a chocolate crust delivers make-ahead convenience and loads of minty flavor. It's a great dessert to serve after a hearty meal to cleanse the palate.

1-1/2 cups chocolate wafers
1/4 cup sugar
1/4 cup butter, melted
1 package (8 ounces) cream cheese, softened
1 can (14 ounces) sweetened condensed milk
1 cup crushed peppermint candies
3 drops red food coloring, optional
2 cups heavy whipping cream, whipped
10 to 14 peppermint candies

1 In a small bowl, combine the chocolate wafer crumbs, sugar and butter. Press onto the bottom and 2 in. up the sides of a greased 8-in. spring-form pan. Refrigerate the crust.

2 In a large bowl, beat cream cheese until smooth. Gradually add milk, beating until smooth. Beat in crushed candies and food coloring if desired. Fold in whipped cream. Spoon into crust. Cover and freeze for 8 hours or overnight. May be frozen up to 1 month.

3 To serve: Remove from the freezer 10 minutes before serving. Garnish with whole candies. **Yield:** 10-14 servings.

Black Forest Freezer Pie | *Angie Helms, Pontotoc, Mississippi*

A delightful dessert is never far off when you have this layered ice cream pie in the freezer. For variety, try strawberry pie filling and a chocolate crust.

1   pint chocolate or vanilla ice cream, softened
1   extra-servings-size graham cracker crust (9 ounces)
4   ounces cream cheese, softened
1   cup confectioners' sugar
1   carton (8 ounces) frozen whipped topping, thawed
1   can (21 ounces) cherry pie filling, chilled
3   tablespoons chocolate syrup

1 Spoon ice cream into pie crust; cover and freeze for 15 minutes.

2 Meanwhile, in a large bowl, beat cream cheese and confectioners' sugar until smooth; fold in whipped topping. Set aside 1-1/2 cups for garnish.

3 Spread remaining cream cheese mixture over ice cream. Using the back of a spoon, make an 8-in. diameter well in the center of the pie for the pie filling. Pipe reserved cream cheese mixture around pie. Cover and freeze for 3-4 hours or until firm. May be frozen for up to 2 months.

4 To serve: Spoon pie filling into the well just before serving; drizzle with chocolate syrup. Serve immediately. **Yield:** 6-8 servings.

Lime Fruit Slushies | *Linda Horst, Newville, Pennsylvania*

These frosty drinks have a bright green color and a refreshing flavor. Divide the mixture between two plastic containers before freezing.

3/4 cup sugar
1   package (3 ounces) lime gelatin
1   cup boiling water
3   cups cold water
3   cups unsweetened pineapple juice
1   can (6 ounces) frozen orange juice concentrate, thawed
1   liter ginger ale, chilled

1 In a large container, dissolve sugar and gelatin in boiling water. Stir in the cold water, pineapple juice and orange juice concentrate. May be frozen for up to 2 months.

2 To serve: Remove from the freezer 1-2 hours before serving. Transfer to a punch bowl; stir in the ginger ale. **Yield:** 12 servings.

SINGLE SERVINGS

Freeze dinners and treats in **single-serving** portions. It's so **convenient** to take one...or just the **right number** from the freezer.

Veggie Calzones, p. 127

Savory

Strawberry Mallow Pops, p. 155

Sweet

Savory

Veggie Calzones

Veggie Calzones | *Lee Ann Arey, Gray, Maine*

Bread dough makes it a breeze to assemble these savory turnovers. They freeze well, and once frozen, they can be heated in half an hour. Pizza dough also works for this recipe.

1/2	**pound fresh mushrooms, chopped**
1	**medium onion, chopped**
1	**medium green pepper, chopped**
2	**tablespoons canola oil**
3	**plum tomatoes, seeded and chopped**
1	**can (6 ounces) tomato paste**
1	**cup (4 ounces) shredded Monterey Jack cheese**
1	**cup (4 ounces) shredded part-skim mozzarella cheese**
1/2	**cup grated Parmesan cheese**
2	**loaves (1 pound each) frozen bread dough, thawed**
1	**egg**
1	**tablespoon water**

1 In a large skillet, saute the mushrooms, onion and green pepper in oil until tender. Add tomatoes; cook and stir for 3 minutes. Stir in tomato paste; set aside. Combine cheeses and set aside.

2 On a lightly floured surface, divide dough into eight pieces. Roll each piece into a 7-in. circle. Spoon a scant 1/2 cup vegetable mixture and 1/4 cup cheese mixture over one side of each circle. Brush edges of dough with water; fold dough over filling and press edges with a fork to seal. Place calzones 3 in. apart on greased baking sheets. Cover and let rise in a warm place for 20 minutes.

3 Whisk egg and water; brush over calzones. Bake at 375° for 15 minutes. Remove desired number of calzones from baking sheet and cool. Bake the remaining calzones 18-22 minutes longer or until golden brown. Serve immediately. Place cooled calzones in freezer bags. May be frozen for up to 3 months.

4 **To use frozen calzones:** Place 2 in. apart on a greased baking sheet. Bake at 350° for 30-35 minutes or until golden brown. **Yield:** 8 servings.

Caramelized Bacon Twists | *Jane Paschke, University Park, Florida*

A friend gave me this recipe to use at a bridal shower brunch, and the sweet chewy bacon strips were a big hit. Lining the pan with foil before baking helps cut down on cleanup.

1	**pound sliced bacon**
1/2	**cup packed brown sugar**
2	**teaspoons ground cinnamon**

1 Cut each bacon strip in half widthwise. Combine brown sugar and cinnamon. Dip bacon strips in sugar mixture; twist.

2 Place strips on a foil-lined 15-in. x 10-in. x 1-in. baking pan. Bake at 350° for 15-20 minutes or until crisp. Serve immediately or cool. Place in a freezer container and freeze for up to 1 month.

3 **To use frozen bacon twists:** Reheat in a microwave. **Yield:** 3 dozen.

Pizza Snacks | *Ruby Williams, Bogalusa, Louisiana*

Since pizza is a big favorite with my teenagers, I like to keep these crispy snacks on hand. Loaded with toppings, they go right from the freezer to the oven with little time and effort.

1/2　cup shredded cheddar cheese

1/2　cup shredded part-skim mozzarella cheese

1　jar (4-1/2 ounces) sliced mushrooms, drained

1/3　cup chopped pepperoni

1/3　cup mayonnaise

1/4　cup chopped onion

3　tablespoons chopped ripe olives

5　English muffins, split

1 In a large bowl, combine the cheeses, mushrooms, pepperoni, mayonnaise, onion and olives. Spread over cut side of each muffin half. Wrap each individually and place in a freezer bag. May be frozen for up to 2 months.

2 To use frozen snacks: Unwrap and place on an ungreased baking sheet. Bake at 350° for 20 minutes or until cheese is melted. **Yield:** 10 snacks.

Nutty Marmalade Sandwiches | *Iola Egle, Bella Vista, Arkansas*

I make batches of these fun-filled sandwiches to freeze for a few weeks' worth of brown-bag lunches. They taste so fresh you would never know they were ever frozen. The marmalade flavor in this hearty combination really shines through.

1/2　cup peanut butter

1/4　cup orange marmalade

1/4　cup shredded sharp cheddar cheese

1　to 2 teaspoons lemon juice

6　slices bread

1 In a small bowl, combine the peanut butter, marmalade, cheese and lemon juice. Spread over three slices of bread; top with remaining bread. Wrap individually and place in a freezer bag. May be frozen for up to 4 months.

2 To use frozen sandwiches: Remove from the freezer at least 4 hours before serving. **Yield:** 3 servings.

Italian Chicken Roll-Ups | *Barbara Wobser, Sandusky, Ohio*

Because I have a busy schedule, I like to keep a batch of these tender chicken rolls in the freezer. Coated with golden crumbs, they seem fancy enough for company.

8   **boneless skinless chicken breast halves (4 ounces each)**
8   **thin slices (4 ounces) deli ham**
4   **slices provolone cheese, halved**
2/3 **cup seasoned bread crumbs**
1/2 **cup grated Romano or Parmesan cheese**
1/4 **cup minced fresh parsley**
1/2 **cup milk**
Cooking spray

1 Flatten chicken to 1/4-in. thickness. Place a slice of ham and half slice of cheese on each piece of chicken. Roll up from a short side and tuck in ends; secure with a toothpick.

2 In a shallow bowl, combine crumbs, Romano cheese and parsley. Pour milk into another bowl. Dip chicken rolls in milk, then roll in crumb mixture.

3 Wrap each of four chicken roll-ups in plastic wrap; place in a large freezer bag. Seal and freeze for up to 2 months. Place the remaining roll-ups, seam side down, on a greased baking sheet. Spritz chicken with cooking spray. Bake, uncovered, at 425° for 25 minutes or until juices run clear. Remove toothpicks.

4 To use frozen chicken: Completely thaw in the refrigerator. Unwrap roll-ups and place on a greased baking sheet. Spritz with cooking spray. Bake, uncovered, at 425° for 30 minutes or until the juices run clear. **Yield:** 8 servings.

Potato Pancakes | *Otto Woltersdorf Jr., Chalfont, Pennsylvania*

I enjoy these crispy pancakes with steak, asparagus and a Caesar salad. With flavored cream cheese, Swiss cheese and a hint of cayenne pepper, they're sure to be popular at your house, too.

4 **medium uncooked baking potatoes**
1/2 **cup spreadable chive and onion cream cheese**
1 **tablespoon all-purpose flour**
1 **egg**
1/4 **cup heavy whipping cream**
1/2 **to 1 teaspoon onion salt**
1/8 **teaspoon cayenne pepper**
3/4 **cup shredded Swiss cheese**
1/4 **to 1/3 cup canola oil**

1 Peel and grate potatoes; drain on paper towels. Squeeze dry and set aside. In a large bowl, beat cream cheese and flour until smooth. Stir in the egg, cream, onion salt and cayenne until blended. Stir in potatoes and cheese.

2 In an electric skillet, heat 1/8 in. of oil to 375°. Drop batter by 1/3 cupfuls into skillet; press lightly to flatten. Fry for about 5 minutes on each side or until the potatoes are tender and golden brown. Drain on paper towels.

3 Arrange patties in a single layer on a waxed paper-lined baking sheet. Freeze overnight or until thoroughly frozen. Place in a resealable plastic bag. May be frozen for up to 2 months.

4 **To use frozen potato pancakes:** Place frozen pancakes on a lightly greased baking sheet. Bake at 400° for 10-12 minutes or until heated through. **Yield:** 16 pancakes.

Beef 'n' Bean Pockets | *Arlene Zerbst, Newcastle, Wyoming*

These tasty pockets are a whole meal wrapped up in one. Reheated in the microwave, they make a great dinner on the go.

2 **pounds ground beef**
1 **small onion, chopped**
1 **can (16 ounces) refried beans**
1 **can (8 ounces) tomato sauce**
2 **teaspoons chili powder**
1 **teaspoon garlic powder**
1 **teaspoon salt**
1/2 **teaspoon pepper**
1/2 **teaspoon paprika**
Dash cayenne pepper
2 **loaves (1 pound each) frozen white bread dough, thawed**
1 **cup (4 ounces) shredded cheddar cheese**

1 In a large skillet, cook beef and onion over medium heat until meat is no longer pink; drain. Add the bean, tomato sauce and seasonings; bring to a boil. Reduce heat; cover and simmer for 15 minutes. Cool.

2 Roll each loaf of dough into a 16-in. x 8-in. rectangle, about 1/4 in. thick. Cut each into eight 4-in. squares; top each with 1/4 cup filling and 1 tablespoon cheese. Bring the four corners together up over filling; pinch seams to seal.

3 Place on greased baking sheets. Cover and let rise for 15 minutes. Bake at 350° for 20-25 minutes or until browned. Serve immediately, or cool. Wrap cooled pockets. May be frozen for up to 3 months.

4 **To use frozen pockets:** Unwrap and reheat in microwave at 50% power for 1-1/2 minutes each. **Yield:** 16 servings.

Just Like Fresh Corn | *Denise Goedeken, Platte Center, Nebraska*

This recipe is a great way to extend the garden-fresh flavor of summer corn year-round. It remains crunchy, buttery and delicious, whether warmed in the microwave or on the stovetop.

  1 **pound butter**
 20 **cups fresh-cut sweet corn kernels**
       (about 24 large ears)
  2 **cups half-and-half cream**

1 In a roasting pan, melt butter in a 325° oven. Stir in corn and cream. Bake, uncovered, for 75 minutes or until the corn is tender, stirring occasionally. Immediately place the roaster in ice water to cool quickly, stirring frequently.

2 Transfer 1-cup portions of corn to freezer bags. May be frozen for up to 1 month.

3 **To use frozen corn:** Reheat in a microwave or on the stove. **Yield:** 16 cups.

Freezer Crescent Rolls | *Kristine Buck, Payson, Utah*

The recipe for these convenient, freezer-friendly crescent rolls was handed down to me from my aunt. I love having homemade rolls available anytime I want, especially during the holidays.

     3 **teaspoons active dry yeast**
     2 **cups warm water (110° to 115°)**
   1/2 **cup butter, softened**
   2/3 **cup nonfat dry milk powder**
   1/2 **cup sugar**
   1/2 **cup mashed potato flakes**
     2 **eggs**
 1-1/2 **teaspoons salt**
     6 **to 6-1/2 cups all-purpose flour**

1 In a large bowl, dissolve yeast in warm water. Add the butter, milk powder, sugar, potato flakes, eggs, salt and 3 cups flour. Beat until smooth. Stir in enough remaining flour to form a firm dough.

2 Turn onto a heavily floured surface; knead 8-10 times. Divide dough in half. Roll each portion into a 12-in. circle; cut each circle into 16 wedges. Roll up wedges from the wide ends and place point side down on waxed paper-lined baking sheets. Curve ends to form crescents.

3 Cover and freeze. When firm, transfer to a large freezer bags. May be frozen for up to 4 weeks.

4 **To use frozen rolls:** Arrange frozen rolls 2 in. apart on baking sheets coated with cooking spray. Cover and thaw in the refrigerator overnight.

5 Let rise in a warm place for 1 hour or until doubled. Bake at 350° for 15-17 minutes or until golden brown. Serve warm. **Yield:** 32 rolls.

Breaded Chicken Patties | *Brenda Martin, Lititz, Pennsylvania*

As a mother of three, I like to make a few batches of these patties at one time and freeze the extras for another meal. I remember helping my mother make big batches, too—there were 11 of us, so it took a lot of food to fill us up!

1/4 cup finely chopped onion
1/4 cup finely chopped celery
6 tablespoons butter, divided
3 tablespoons all-purpose flour
1-1/3 cups milk, divided
2 tablespoons minced fresh parsley
1 teaspoon salt
1 teaspoon onion salt
1/2 teaspoon celery salt
1/4 teaspoon pepper
2 cups finely chopped cooked chicken
1 cup dry bread crumbs
Sandwich rolls, split
Lettuce leaves and tomato slices, optional

1 In a large saucepan, saute onion and celery in 3 tablespoons butter until tender. Combine flour and 1 cup milk until smooth. Gradually add to pan. Bring to a boil; cook and stir for 2 minutes or until thickened. Add parsley, seasonings and chicken. Remove from the heat. Chill until completely cooled.

2 Shape chicken mixture into six patties, using about 1/3 cup mixture for each patty. Place crumbs and remaining milk in separate shallow bowls. Roll patties in crumbs, then dip into milk; roll again in the crumbs.

3 In a large skillet, cook patties in remaining butter for 3 minutes on each side or until golden brown. Serve desired amount on rolls with lettuce and tomato. Cool the remaining patties. Wrap patties individually and freeze for up to 3 months.

4 **To prepare frozen patties:** Cook in butter for 5-6 minutes on each side or until heated through. **Yield:** 6 servings.

TIP Freeze It Tip

To make cubed cooked chicken for recipes, simmer a few boneless, skinless chicken breasts in a little water seasoned with salt, pepper and your favorite herbs. Cool and dice; keep them in the freezer for later. Or, stop by the deli counter at your grocer's and have them cut a thick slice of cooked chicken breast sandwich meat, which you can cut up at home.

Meat Loaf Miniatures | *Joyce Wegmann, Burlington, Iowa*

I don't usually like meat loaf, but my family and I can't get enough of these mini loaves topped with a sweet ketchup sauce. This recipe requires no chopping, so it's quick and easy to make a double batch and have extras for another day.

1	cup ketchup
3	to 4 tablespoons packed brown sugar
1	teaspoon ground mustard
2	eggs, beaten
4	teaspoons Worcestershire sauce
3	cups Crispix cereal, crushed
3	teaspoons onion powder
1/2	to 1 teaspoon seasoned salt
1/2	teaspoon garlic powder
1/2	teaspoon pepper
3	pounds lean ground beef

1 In a large bowl, combine the ketchup, brown sugar and mustard. Remove 1/2 cup for topping; set aside. Add the eggs, Worcestershire sauce, cereal and seasonings to remaining ketchup mixture. Let stand for 5 minutes. Crumble beef over cereal mixture and mix well.

2 Press meat mixture into 18 muffin cups (about 1/3 cup each). Bake at 375° for 18-20 minutes. Drizzle with reserved ketchup mixture; bake 10 minutes longer or until meat is no longer pink and a meat thermometer reads 160°.

3 Serve desired number of meat loaves. Cool remaining loaves, then freeze. Once they are frozen, transfer to freezer bags; seal and freeze for up to 3 months.

4 To use frozen meat loaves: Completely thaw in the refrigerator. Place loaves in a greased baking dish. Bake at 350° for 30 minutes or until heated through, or cover and microwave on high for 1 minute or until heated through. **Yield:** 1-1/2 dozen.

Chocolate Chip Pancakes | *Taste of Home Test Kitchen*

Mornings will get off to a great start with these yummy double-chocolate pancakes. Whip up a batch on the weekend, and you'll have speedy breakfasts the whole family will rave about for days to come.

2 cups biscuit/baking mix
2 tablespoons instant chocolate drink mix
2 teaspoons baking powder
1 egg
1 cup milk
1/2 cup sour cream
1/4 cup miniature semisweet chocolate chips
Maple syrup and butter, optional

1 In a large bowl, combine the biscuit mix, drink mix and baking powder. Combine the egg, milk and sour cream; stir into dry ingredients just until moistened. Fold in chocolate chips.

2 Pour batter by 1/4 cupfuls onto a greased hot griddle. Turn when bubbles form on top; cook until second side is golden brown.

3 Serve desired amount with maple syrup and butter. Cool remaining pancakes; arrange in a single layer on baking sheets. Freeze overnight or until frozen. Transfer to a freezer bag. May be frozen for up to 2 months.

4 To use frozen pancakes: Place on a lightly greased baking sheet. Bake at 400° for 4-6 minutes or until heated through. Serve with maple syrup and butter if desired. **Yield:** 11 pancakes.

Veggie Tomato Juice | *Marge Hodel, Roanoke, Illinois*

Gather fresh vegetables from your garden and blend this thick and mellow beverage. It's wonderful as a relaxing sipper or for recipes that call for tomato juice.

16 cups quartered ripe tomatoes (about 7 pounds)
3 cups coarsely chopped celery
2 large onions, sliced
2 cups coarsely chopped cooked peeled beets
1-1/2 cups coarsely chopped carrots
1 cup chopped fresh spinach
1/2 cup minced fresh parsley
2 tablespoons sugar
1 tablespoon salt

1 In a Dutch oven or stockpot, combine all the ingredients; crush the tomatoes slightly. Bring to a boil. Reduced heat; cover and simmer for 1-1/2 hours or until the vegetables are tender, stirring frequently.

2 Cool. Press mixture through a food mill or fine sieve. Transfer mixture to refrigerator or freezer containers. May be refrigerated for 3 to 5 days or frozen for up to 3 months.

3 To serve: Shake or stir juice well before serving. **Yield:** 4-1/2 pints.

Parmesan Knots | *Cathy Adams, Parkersburg, West Virginia*

Refrigerated biscuits are the base for these buttery snacks. They're handy to keep in the freezer and a snap to reheat and serve with a meal.

1/2 cup canola oil
1/4 cup grated Parmesan cheese
1-1/2 teaspoons dried parsley flakes
1-1/2 teaspoons dried oregano
1 teaspoon garlic powder
Dash pepper
3 tubes (12 ounces each) refrigerated buttermilk biscuits

1 In a small bowl, combine the oil, cheese, parsley, oregano, garlic powder and pepper; set aside. Cut each biscuit in half. Roll each portion into a 6-in. rope; tie in a loose knot. Place on greased baking sheets.

2 Bake at 400° for 8-11 minutes or until golden brown; immediately brush with the Parmesan mixture. Serve desired amount warm. Cool remaining knots; transfer to a freezer container. May be frozen for up to 2 months.

3 To use frozen knots: Reheat, unthawed, at 350° for 15-20 minutes. **Yield:** 5 dozen.

Chicken Wonton Rolls | *Mary Dixson, Decatur, Alabama*

Guests will think you fussed over these warm golden bites. I sometimes turn the recipe into a main course by using egg roll wrappers and serving the rolls with chicken gravy.

1	package (3 ounces) cream cheese, softened
6	tablespoons butter, softened, divided
2	tablespoons minced chives
1/2	teaspoon lemon-pepper seasoning
1-1/2	cups finely chopped cooked chicken
1	can (4 ounces) mushroom stems and pieces, drained and chopped
1	package (12 ounces) wonton wrappers
2/3	cup crushed salad croutons

Sweet-and-sour sauce, optional

1 In a bowl, beat the cream cheese, 2 tablespoons butter, chives and lemon-pepper until blended. Stir in chicken and mushrooms.

2 Place a rounded teaspoonful in the center of a wonton wrapper. (Keep remaining wrappers covered with a damp paper towel until ready to use.) Fold bottom corner over filling; fold sides toward center. Moisten remaining corner with water; roll up tightly to seal.

3 Melt remaining butter; brush over wontons. Coat with croutons. Place on a baking sheet; freeze. Transfer to a large freezer bag. Seal bag and freeze for up to 3 months.

4 To use frozen wontons: Place wontons on greased baking sheets. Bake at 425° for 10 minutes. Turn; bake 5-10 minutes longer or until lightly browned. Serve warm with sweet-and-sour sauce if desired. **Yield:** about 4 dozen.

Broccoli Bites | *Laurie Todd, Columbus, Mississippi*

Herb stuffing and Parmesan cheese add nice flavor to the broccoli in these cute appetizers. The recipe makes several dozen, so you can just take out of the freezer as many as you need.

6	cups frozen chopped broccoli
2	cups crushed seasoned stuffing
1	cup grated Parmesan cheese
6	eggs, lightly beaten
1/2	cup butter, softened
1/2	teaspoon salt
1/4	teaspoon pepper

1 Cook broccoli according to package directions; drain and place in a bowl. Stir in the remaining ingredients. Shape into 1-in. balls.

2 Place in a greased 15-in. x 10-in. x 1-in. baking pan. Bake at 350° for 11-12 minutes or until golden brown. Or, place in a single layer in a freezer container; cover and freeze for up to 1 month.

3 To use frozen appetizers: Place in a greased 15-in. x 10-in. x 1-in. baking pan. Bake at 350° for 16-18 minutes or until golden brown. **Yield:** about 5 dozen.

Make-Ahead Burritos | *Jennifer Shafer, Durham, North Carolina*

We have two children who keep us busy, so I love meals I can just pull out of the freezer. The burritos are wrapped individually so it's easy to take out only the number you need. I serve them with canned refried beans and Spanish rice from a packaged mix.

3 cups shredded cooked chicken or beef

1 jar (16 ounces) salsa

1 can (16 ounces) refried beans

1 can (4 ounces) chopped green chilies, drained

1 envelope burrito seasoning

1/2 cup water

16 flour tortillas (8 inches), warmed

16 ounces Monterey Jack cheese, cut into 5-inch x 1/2-inch strips

1 In a large skillet or saucepan, combine meat, salsa, beans, chilies, seasoning and water. Bring to a boil. Reduce heat; simmer, uncovered, for 5 minutes or until heated through.

2 Spoon about 1/3 cup off-center on each tortilla; top with a cheese strip. Fold edge of tortilla nearest filling over to cover. Fold ends of tortilla over filling and roll up. Wrap individually in foil and freeze for up to 2 months.

3 **To use frozen burritos:** Place foil packets on a baking sheet. Bake at 350° for 50 minutes or until heated through. If thawed, bake for 25-30 minutes. **Yield:** 16 burritos.

Golden Knots | *Jayne Duce, Raymond, Alberta*

Prepare and partially bake these rolls on a day when you have plenty of time. The recipe makes enough for dinner and lots to freeze. The rolls reheat beautifully, so you'll have fresh-baked rolls whenever you want.

2 packages (1/4 ounce each) active dry yeast
1-1/2 cups warm water (110° to 115°)
2 teaspoons plus 1/2 cup sugar, divided
1-1/2 cups warm milk (110° to 115°)
1/4 cup canola oil
4 teaspoons salt
7-1/2 to 8-1/2 cups all-purpose flour
Melted butter

1 In a large bowl, dissolve yeast in warm water. Add 2 teaspoons sugar; let stand for 5 minutes. Add the milk, oil, salt and remaining sugar. Stir in enough flour to form a stiff dough.

2 Turn onto a floured surface; knead until smooth and elastic, about 6-8 minutes. Place in a greased bowl, turning once to grease top. Cover and let rise in a warm place until doubled, about 1-1/2 hours.

3 Punch dough down. Divide into four portions. Cover three pieces with plastic wrap. Shape one portion into 12 balls. To form knots, roll each ball into a 10-in. rope; tie into a knot. Tuck and pinch ends under. Repeat with remaining dough.

4 Place rolls on greased baking sheets; brush with butter. Cover and let rise until doubled, about 20-30 minutes. To serve immediately, bake at 375° for 15-18 minutes. To freeze for later use, partially bake at 300° for 15 minutes. Cool and transfer to freezer bags. May be frozen for up to 6 months.

5 **To use frozen rolls:** Place rolls 2 in. apart on greased baking sheets. Reheat frozen rolls at 375° for 12-15 minutes or until browned. **Yield:** 4 dozen.

Dilly Cheddar Cubes | *Lisa Lovitz, Lockport, New York*

This is a delicious crowd-pleasing appetizer, and I get requests for it every time I host a party. The cheese cubes are so easy to prepare ahead of time...just remove them from the freezer and pop them in the oven for a few minutes and you're done!

1 cup (4 ounces) shredded cheddar cheese
1/4 cup butter, cubed
1 package (3 ounces) cream cheese, cubed
2 teaspoons minced chives
1 teaspoon dill weed
2 egg whites
24 cubes French bread (1-inch cubes)

1 Line a baking pan with waxed paper; set aside. In a small saucepan, combine the cheddar cheese, butter, cream cheese, chives and dill. Cook and stir over medium-low heat until cheese is melted. Remove from the heat.

2 In a small bowl, beat the egg whites until stiff peaks form; fold into cheese mixture. Using a fork, dip bread cubes into cheese mixture and place on prepared pan. Freeze, uncovered, until firm. Transfer to a freezer bag. May be frozen for up to 3 months.

3 **To use frozen appetizers:** Arrange bread cubes 1 in. apart on greased baking sheets. Bake at 425° for 10-12 minutes or until lightly browned. Serve warm. **Yield:** 2 dozen.

Stuffed Sourdough Sandwiches | *Shannon Hansen, Oxnard, California*

These delectable stuffed sandwiches are easy to put together. Sometimes I use cubed sharp cheddar cheese instead of shredded cheese in these sandwiches.

1-1/2 **pounds ground beef**
1/2 **cup chopped onion**
1 **can (15 ounces) tomato sauce**
1 **can (4 ounces) chopped green chilies**
1/2 **cup chopped fresh mushrooms**
2 **tablespoons chili powder**
2 **tablespoons sliced ripe olives**
1/4 **teaspoon garlic salt**
1 **cup (4 ounces) shredded cheddar cheese**
8 **sourdough rolls**

1 In a large skillet, cook beef and onion over medium heat until meat is no longer pink; drain. Add the tomato sauce, chilies, mushrooms, chili powder, olives and garlic salt. Bring to a boil. Reduce heat; simmer, uncovered, for 10 minutes or until heated through. Add cheese; cook and stir until melted.

2 Cut 1/4 in. off the top of each roll; set aside. Carefully hollow out bottom of roll, leaving a 1/4-in. shell (discard removed bread or save for another use). Fill each roll with about 1/2 cup meat mixture. Replace bread tops.

3 Place desired number of sandwiches on a baking sheet. Bake rolls at 350° for 10-15 minutes or until heated through. Individually wrap remaining sandwiches tightly in foil. May be frozen for up to 3 months.

4 **To use frozen sandwiches:** Thaw in the refrigerator overnight. Place foil-wrapped sandwiches on baking sheets. Bake at 350° for 20-25 minutes or until heated through. **Yield:** 8 servings.

Breakfast Wraps | *Betty Kleberger, Florissant, Missouri*

We like quick and simple morning meals during the week—and these wraps are great when prepared ahead of time. With just a minute in the microwave, breakfast is ready.

6	**eggs**
2	**tablespoons milk**
1/4	**teaspoon pepper**
1	**tablespoon canola oil**
1	**cup (4 ounces) shredded cheddar cheese**
3/4	**cup diced fully cooked ham**
4	**flour tortillas (8 inches), warmed**

1 In a small bowl, whisk the eggs, milk and pepper. In a large skillet, heat oil. Add egg mixture; cook and stir over medium heat until eggs are completely set. Stir in cheese and ham.

2 Spoon egg mixture down the center of each tortilla; roll up. Serve immediately or cool. Wrap individually in plastic wrap and place in resealable plastic bag. May be frozen for up to 1 month.

3 To use frozen wraps: Thaw in the refrigerator overnight. Remove plastic wrap; wrap tortilla in a moist paper towel. Microwave on high for 30-60 seconds or until heated through. Serve immediately. **Yield:** 4 servings.

Onion Rye Appetizers | *Vicki Wolf, Aurora, Ohio*

I take these hearty appetizers to every party we attend and always bring home an empty tray. I also keep a supply in the freezer for a speedy snack that gets rave reviews—even from children.

- 1 can (2.8 ounces) french-fried onions, crushed
- 1 jar (2 ounces) crumbled bacon or 3/4 cup crumbled cooked bacon
- 1/2 cup mayonnaise
- 3 cups (12 ounces) shredded Swiss cheese
- 1 jar (14 ounces) pizza sauce
- 1 loaf (16 ounces) snack rye bread

1 In a bowl, combine the onions, bacon, mayonnaise and Swiss cheese. Spread about 1 teaspoon of pizza sauce on each slice of bread. Top with about 1 tablespoon of the cheese mixture.

2 Cover and freeze in a single layer for up to 2 months. To use immediately, bake appetizers on an ungreased baking sheet at 350° for 12-14 minutes or until heated and cheese is melted.

3 **To use frozen appetizers:** Place on an ungreased baking sheet. Bake at 350° for 14-16 minutes or until heated through and cheese is melted. **Yield:** 20 appetizers.

Editor's Note: Reduced-fat or fat-free mayonnaise is not recommended for this recipe.

Make-Ahead Sloppy Joes | *Alyne Fuller, Odessa, Texas*

When our children were growing up, I frequently made big batches of these stuffed beef-and-sausage buns.

- 1 pound bulk pork sausage
- 1 pound ground beef
- 1 medium onion, chopped
- 14 to 16 sandwich buns, split
- 2 cans (8 ounces each) tomato sauce
- 2 tablespoons prepared mustard
- 1 teaspoon dried parsley flakes
- 1 teaspoon garlic powder
- 1 teaspoon salt
- 1/4 teaspoon pepper
- 1/4 teaspoon dried oregano

1 In a large skillet, cook the sausage, beef and onion over medium heat until meat is no longer pink; drain. Remove the centers from the tops and bottoms of each bun. Tear removed bread into small pieces; add to skillet. Set buns aside.

2 Stir in remaining ingredients into sausage mixture. Spoon about 1/3 cupful onto the bottom of each bun; replace tops. Bake desired amount at 350° for 20 minutes or until heated through.

3 Cool remaining sandwiches. Wrap individually in heavy-duty foil. May be frozen for up to 3 months.

4 **To use frozen sandwiches:** Place foil packets on a baking sheet. Bake at 350° for 35 minutes or until heated through. **Yield:** 14-16 servings.

Miniature Meat Pies | *Gayle Lewis, Yucaipa, California*

My family loves these cute little bites of flaky dough stuffed with an easy-to-season ground beef mixture. They're filling and oh-so-good served with ketchup.

- 1 **pound ground beef**
- 1/2 **cup chili sauce**
- 2 **tablespoons onion soup mix**

DOUGH:
- 3 **cups all-purpose flour**
- 1 **to 2 tablespoons sesame seeds, optional**
- 1 **teaspoon salt**
- 1 **cup shortening**
- 3/4 **cup shredded cheddar cheese**
- 3/4 **cup evaporated milk**
- 1 **tablespoon cider vinegar**

1 In a large skillet, cook beef over medium heat until no longer pink; drain. Stir in chili sauce and soup mix; set aside.

2 In a large bowl, combine the flour, sesame seeds if desired and salt. Cut in shortening and cheese until crumbly. Combine milk and vinegar; gradually add to flour mixture, tossing with a fork until dough forms a ball.

3 Divide dough in half; roll out to 1/8-in. thickness. Cut with a lightly floured 2-1/2-in. round cutter. Place half of the circles 2 in. apart on ungreased baking sheets. Top each with a rounded tablespoonful of beef mixture; top with remaining circles. Moisten edges with water and press with a fork to seal. Cut a slit in the top of each.

4 Bake at 425° for 12-16 minutes or until golden brown. Serve meat pies immediately or cool. Wrap individually in plastic wrap and place in a freezer bag. May be frozen for up to 3 months.

5 **To use frozen meat pies:** Unwrap and place on an ungreased baking sheet. Bake at 425° for 14-16 minutes or until heated through. **Yield:** about 1-1/2 dozen.

Pizzawiches | *Jennifer Short, Omaha, Nebraska*

People of all ages like these pizza-flavored sandwiches, which can be made ahead of time and stored in the freezer. Frozen ones don't need to thaw before baking, so you'll have a meal in a flash.

- 2 **pounds ground beef**
- 1 **medium onion, chopped**
- 2 **cans (10-3/4 ounces each) condensed tomato soup, undiluted**
- 1 **teaspoon dried oregano**
- 1 **teaspoon chili powder**
- 1/2 **teaspoon garlic salt**
- 1 **cup (4 ounces) shredded cheddar cheese**
- 1 **cup (4 ounces) shredded part-skim mozzarella cheese**
- 12 **hamburger buns, split**
- 3 **to 4 tablespoons butter, melted**

1 In a large skillet, cook beef and onion over medium heat until meat is no longer pink; drain. Stir in the soup, oregano, chili powder and garlic salt. Bring to a boil. Remove from the heat; stir in cheeses. Place about 1/3 cup meat mixture on each bun. Brush tops of buns with butter.

2 Place desired amount of sandwiches on an ungreased baking sheet. Bake at 375° for 7-9 minutes or until cheese is melted. Individually wrap remaining sandwiches in foil and place in a freezer bag. May be frozen for up to 3 months.

3 **To use frozen sandwiches:** Place the foil packets on an ungreased baking sheet. Bake at 375° for 35-40 minutes or until heated through. **Yield:** 12 sandwiches.

Yogurt Pancakes | *Cheryll Baber, Homedale, Idaho*

Get your day off to a great start with these delicious yogurt pancakes. Simply whip up a quick batch on the weekend—varying the fillings—and pop them in your freezer for a no-fuss weekday breakfast. It's easy to alter the fillings because you just sprinkle them on the batter in the skillet.

2 cups all-purpose flour
2 tablespoons sugar
2 teaspoons baking powder
1 teaspoon baking soda
2 eggs
2 cups (16 ounces) plain yogurt
1/4 cup water
Semisweet chocolate chips, dried cranberries, sliced ripe bananas and coarsely chopped pecans, optional

1 In a small bowl, combine the flour, sugar, baking powder and baking soda. In another bowl, whisk the eggs, yogurt and water. Stir into the dry ingredients just until moistened.

2 Pour batter by 1/4 cupfuls onto a hot griddle coated with cooking spray. Sprinkle with chocolate chips or cranberries if desired. Turn when bubbles form on top; cook until the second side is golden brown. Serve with bananas or pecans if desired.

3 To freeze, arrange cooled pancakes in a single layer on baking sheets. Freeze overnight or until frozen. Transfer to a freezer bag. May be frozen for up to 2 months.

4 **To use frozen pancakes:** Place pancake on a microwave-safe plate; microwave on high for 40-50 seconds or until heated through. **Yield: 12 pancakes.**

Baked Pork Chimichangas | *LaDonna Reed, Ponca City, Oklahoma*

Lean shredded pork and pinto beans combine with south-of-the-border ingredients like green chilies and picante sauce in these from-scratch chimichangas.

1	pound dried pinto beans
1	boneless pork loin roast (3 pounds), trimmed
3	cans (4 ounces each) chopped green chilies
1	large onion, chopped
1/3	cup chili powder
1/2	cup reduced-sodium chicken broth
30	flour tortillas (6 inches)
4	cups (16 ounces) shredded reduced-fat cheddar cheese
2	cups picante sauce
1	egg white
2	teaspoons water

1 Place beans in a Dutch oven; add water to cover by 2 in. Bring to a boil; boil for 2 minutes. Remove from the heat; cover and let stand for 1 to 4 hours or until beans are softened. Drain and rinse beans, discarding liquid.

2 Place roast in a Dutch oven. In a bowl, combine the chilies, onion, chili powder and beans. Spoon over roast. Cover and bake at 325° for 1-1/2 hours. Stir in broth; cover and bake 30-45 minutes longer or until a meat thermometer reads 160°. Increase oven temperature to 350°.

3 Remove meat and shred with two forks; set aside. Mash bean mixture; stir in shredded pork. Spoon 1/3 cup mixture down the center of each tortilla; top with 2 tablespoons cheese and 1 tablespoon picante sauce. Fold sides and ends over filling and roll up. Place seam side down on two 15-in. x 10-in. x 1-in. baking pans coated with cooking spray.

4 In a bowl, whisk egg white and water; brush over top. Bake, uncovered, at 350° for 25-30 minutes or until heated through. Serve immediately or cool. Wrap cooled chimichangas. May be frozen for up to 3 months.

5 **To use frozen chimichangas:** Place chimichangas on a baking sheet coated with cooking spray. Bake at 400° for 10-15 minutes or until heated through. **Yield:** 2-1/2 dozen.

Time-to-Spare Spuds | *Dorothy Bateman, Carver, Massachusetts*

These creamy prefilled potato shells can be quickly thawed, then baked as a side dish to go with a steak or any entree of your choice.

6 large potatoes
1 cup (8 ounces) sour cream
1 cup (4 ounces) shredded cheddar cheese
1 green onion, chopped
1/4 cup milk
2 tablespoons butter, melted
1 tablespoon chopped fresh parsley
1 teaspoon salt
Additional butter

1 Scrub and pierce potatoes. Bake at 375° for 1 hour or until tender. When cool enough to handle, cut a thin slice off the top of each potato and discard. Cut each potato in half lengthwise. Scoop out the pulp, leaving a thin shell.

2 In a large bowl, mash pulp until smooth. Stir in the sour cream, cheese, onion, milk, butter, parsley and salt. Spoon into potato shells; brush with butter. Cover and refrigerate. Once cooled, wrap shells individually in plastic wrap; place in freezer bags. May be frozen for up to 1 month.

3 To use potato shells: Thaw in the refrigerator. Place shells in an ungreased shallow baking dish. Bake, uncovered, at 400° for 20-25 minutes or until golden and heated through. **Yield:** 12 servings.

Make-Ahead Sandwiches | *Marie Hass, Madison, Wisconsin*

I developed these fun buns many years ago when my children were little. Once they started high school, I'd keep some in the freezer for quick suppers on busy school nights.

1-1/2 pounds ground beef
3/4 cup chopped onion
3/4 cup ketchup
3/4 cup chopped dill or sweet pickles
1-1/2 teaspoons salt
1/4 to 1/2 teaspoon pepper
1/4 to 1/2 teaspoon garlic powder
1/8 teaspoon hot pepper sauce
1-1/2 cups (6 ounces) shredded part-skim mozzarella cheese
12 hot dog buns, split

1 In a large saucepan, cook the beef and onion over medium heat until meat is no longer pink; drain. Stir in the ketchup, pickles, salt, pepper, garlic powder and hot pepper sauce; heat through. Stir in cheese. Place about 1/3 cupful on six buns; serve immediately. Cool remaining meat mixture. Fill the remaining buns with cooled mixture; wrap individually in heavy-duty foil. May be frozen for up to 3 months.

2 To use frozen sandwiches: Place foil packets on a baking sheet. Bake at 400° for 30-35 minutes or until heated through. **Yield:** 1 dozen.

Cheesy Chive Crisps | *Eve McNew, St. Louis, Missouri*

These snack bites are great to keep on hand for guests. The recipe yields a good amount of cheese logs, so you can freeze some for future use.

1 cup butter, softened
3 cups (12 ounces) shredded sharp cheddar cheese
2 cups all-purpose flour
1/4 cup minced chives
1/2 teaspoon salt
1/2 teaspoon hot pepper sauce
Dash garlic salt
2 cups crisp rice cereal

1 In a large bowl, cream butter and cheese until light and fluffy. Beat in the flour, chives, salt, hot pepper sauce and garlic salt. Stir in cereal. Shape into four 6-1/2-in. x 1-1/2-in. logs. Wrap in plastic wrap. Refrigerate for 1 hour or until firm. For longer storage, transfer to freezer bags. May be frozen for up to 6 months.

2 To use refrigerated appetizers: Unwrap and cut into 1/4-in. slices. Place on ungreased baking sheets. Bake at 325° for 20-25 minutes or until edges are crisp and lightly browned. Remove to wire racks to cool. Store in the refrigerator.

3 To use frozen appetizers: Thaw in refrigerator for 2 to 3 hours before baking. Unwrap and cut into 1/4-in. slices. Place on ungreased baking sheets. Bake at 325° for 20-25 minutes or until edges are crisp and lightly browned. Remove to wire racks to cool. Refrigerate leftovers. **Yield:** about 9 dozen.

Twice-Baked Rolls | *Mary Jane Henderson, Salem, New Jersey*

Everyone appreciates being offered home-baked rolls at dinner, but time doesn't always allow...especially on busy weeknights. These rolls can be conveniently partially baked and frozen. Then you can remove and bake as many rolls as needed.

2 packages (1/4 ounce each) active dry yeast
1 cup warm water (110° to 115°)
1 teaspoon plus 1/4 cup sugar, divided
2 cups warm milk (110° to 115°)
1/2 cup shortening
5 teaspoons salt
10 cups all-purpose flour

1 In a large bowl, dissolve yeast in warm water. Add 1 teaspoon sugar; let stand for 5 minutes. Add the milk, shortening, salt, 2 cups flour and remaining sugar. Beat until smooth. Stir enough remaining flour to form a stiff dough.

2 Turn onto a floured surface; knead until smooth and elastic, about 6-8 minutes. Place in a greased bowl, turning once to grease top. Cover and let rise in a warm place until doubled, about 1-1/2 hours.

3 Punch dough down. Turn onto a lightly floured surface; divide into four pieces. Cover three with plastic wrap. Divide remaining piece into 12 balls. Shape into balls. Place 2 in. apart on greased baking sheets. Repeat with remaining dough. Cover and let rise until doubled, about 20 minutes.

4 To serve immediately, bake at 375° for 12-15 minutes or until golden brown. To freeze for later use, partially bake at 300° for 15 minutes. To freeze for later use, partially bake at 300° for 15 minutes. Cool and transfer to freezer bags. May be frozen for up to 6 months.

5 **To use frozen rolls:** Place rolls 2 in. apart on greased baking sheets. Bake at 375° for 12-15 minutes or until golden brown. **Yield:** 4 dozen.

Beef 'n' Olive Sandwiches | *Iola Egle, Bella Vista, Arkansas*

Dried beef, olives and walnuts are blended into a rich and creamy filling for these sandwiches. Cut into quarters, they're sophisticated enough to serve at parties.

1 package (8 ounces) cream cheese, softened
2 tablespoons heavy whipping cream
1/2 teaspoon white pepper
1/4 cup chopped dried beef
3 tablespoons sliced pimiento-stuffed olives
3 tablespoons chopped walnuts
8 slices bread

1 In a large bowl, beat the cream cheese, cream and pepper until smooth. Stir in the beef, olives and walnuts. Spread on each of four slices of bread; top with remaining bread slices. Wrap each sandwich individually and freeze for up to 2 months.

2 **To use frozen sandwiches:** Remove from the freezer at least 4 hours before serving. **Yield:** 4 servings.

Italian Chicken Strips | *Barbara Eberlein, Belleville, Illinois*

This moist chicken goes from stove to freezer to table without losing flavor or texture. I usually get two frying pans going and have four cookie sheets full of chicken when I'm done. The hardest part is keeping my fellas out of it till dinnertime.

1	package (15 ounces) dry bread crumbs
1	can (8 ounces) grated Parmesan cheese
2	tablespoons Italian seasoning
2	teaspoons garlic salt, divided
6	eggs
1/4	cup water
2-1/2	pounds boneless skinless chicken breasts, cut into 1/2-inch strips

Oil for deep-fat frying

1 In a large resealable plastic bag, combine the dry bread crumbs, Parmesan cheese, Italian seasoning and 1 teaspoon garlic salt. In a shallow bowl, beat eggs, water and remaining garlic salt. Dip chicken strips into egg mixture, then shake to coat in crumb mixture.

2 In an electric skillet or deep-fat fryer, heat 1 in. of oil to 375°. Fry chicken in batches until golden brown, about 4 minutes. Drain on paper towels. Serve immediately or cool. Wrap cooled chicken in single-serving portions. May be frozen for up to 3 months.

3 To use frozen chicken strips: Unwrap and reheat in the microwave. **Yield:** 10-12 servings.

Freezer Burritos | *Laura Winemiller, Delta, Pennsylvania*

I love burritos, but the frozen ones are so high in salt and chemicals. So I created these homemade ones filled with fresh ingredients. They're great to have on hand for quick dinners or late-night snacks.

1-1/4	pounds lean ground beef
1/4	cup finely chopped onion
1-1/4	cups salsa
2	tablespoons reduced-sodium taco seasoning
2	cans (15 ounces each) pinto beans, rinsed and drained
1/2	cup water
2	cups (8 ounces) shredded reduced-fat cheddar cheese
12	flour tortillas (8 inches), warmed

1 In a large skillet, cook beef and onion over medium heat until meat is no longer pink; drain. Stir in salsa and taco seasoning. Bring to a boil. Reduce heat; simmer, uncovered, for 2-3 minutes. Transfer to a large bowl; set aside.

2 In a food processor, combine pinto beans and water. Cover and process until almost smooth. Add to beef mixture. Stir in cheese.

3 Spoon 1/2 cup beef mixture down the center of each tortilla. Fold ends and sides over filling; roll up. Wrap each burrito in waxed paper, then in foil. Freeze for up to 1 month.

4 To use frozen burritos: Remove foil and waxed paper. Place one burrito on a microwave-safe plate. Microwave on high for 2-1/2 to 2-3/4 minutes or until a meat thermometer reads 165°, turning burrito over once. Let stand for 20 seconds. **Yield:** 12 servings.

Editor's Note: This recipe was tested in a 1,100-watt microwave.

Spinach Cheese Appetizers | *Marian Platt, Sequim, Washington*

Hosting a get-together is simple when you have these easy hors d'oeuvres stashed in the freezer. The rich squares are loaded with flavor.

1/2 cup butter, melted
1 cup all-purpose flour
1 teaspoon salt
1 teaspoon baking powder
3 eggs
1 cup milk
2 packages (10 ounces each) frozen chopped spinach, thawed and squeezed dry
4 cups (16 ounces) shredded Monterey Jack cheese

1 Pour butter into a 13-in. x 9-in. baking dish; tilt to coat. In a small bowl, combine the flour, salt and baking powder. Whisk eggs and milk; stir into dry ingredients just until blended. Fold in spinach and cheese. Pour into prepared dish.

2 Bake, uncovered, at 350° for 30-35 minutes or until a knife inserted near the center comes out clean. Cool for 5 minutes; cut into small squares. Serve immediately or transfer to a freezer container. May be frozen for up to 3 months.

3 **To use frozen appetizers:** Thaw in the refrigerator overnight. Place on baking sheet. Bake, uncovered, at 350° for 25-30 minutes or until heated through. Let stand 5 minutes before serving. **Yield:** about 6-1/2 dozen.

Potato Rosettes | *Florence Arbes, Courtland, Minnesota*

When I make these attractive mashed potato rosettes, I usually double or triple the recipe so I have more to freeze. It's easy to pull out only as many portions as I need for myself or for company.

2 medium potatoes, peeled and quartered
1/2 cup shredded cheddar cheese
1 egg, lightly beaten
2 tablespoons chopped green onion
3 tablespoons sour cream
1 teaspoon salt
1/4 to 1/2 teaspoon white pepper

1 Place potatoes in a large saucepan and cover with water; bring to a boil over medium-high heat. Cover and cook for 15-20 minutes or until tender; drain. Transfer to a large bowl; mash potatoes. Beat in the cheese, egg, onion, sour cream, salt and pepper.

2 Cut a hole in the corner of a pastry bag or heavy-duty plastic bag. Insert large star tip #409. Fill bag with potato mixture. Pipe potatoes into eight mounds on a greased baking sheet. Cover and freeze for up to 1 month.

3 **To use frozen potatoes:** Place on a microwave-safe plate. Cover with waxed paper; microwave on high for 6 minutes or until heated through. **Yield:** 8 servings.

Crescent Chicken Bundles | *Jo Groth, Plainfield, Iowa*

When I was expecting our third child, this was one of the meals I put in the freezer before my trip to the hospital. We now have four kids, and they all like these rich chicken pockets. I've also made them with ham or smoked turkey.

2 packages (3 ounces each) cream cheese, softened
4 tablespoons butter, melted, divided
2 tablespoons minced chives
2 tablespoons milk
1/2 teaspoon salt
1/4 teaspoon pepper
4 cups cubed cooked chicken
2 tubes (8 ounces each) refrigerated crescent rolls
1 cup crushed seasoned stuffing

1 In a small bowl, beat cream cheese, 2 tablespoons butter, chives, milk, salt and pepper until blended. Stir in chicken.

2 Unroll crescent roll dough and separate into eight rectangles; press perforations together. Spoon about 1/2 cup chicken mixture in the center of each rectangle. Bring edges up to the center and pinch to seal. Brush with remaining butter. Sprinkle with crushed croutons, lightly pressing down.

3 Divide squares between two ungreased baking sheets. Bake one baking sheet at 350° for 20-25 minutes or until golden brown. Serve warm. Cover second baking sheet and freeze until firm; transfer squares to a covered freezer container. May be frozen for up to 2 months.

4 To use frozen squares: Thaw in the refrigerator and bake as directed. **Yield:** 8 servings.

Mini Shepherd's Pies | *Ellen Osborne, Clarksville, Tennessee*

These fast mini pies are packed with meat-and-potato flavor. I'm as confident serving them to drop-in company as to my husband and three boys. If I'm not rushed for time, I'll sometimes make these with homemade biscuits and mashed potatoes.

1 pound ground beef
3 tablespoons chopped onion
1/2 teaspoon minced garlic
1/3 cup chili sauce or ketchup
1 tablespoon cider vinegar
1/2 teaspoon salt
1-1/4 cups water
3 tablespoons butter
1-1/4 cups mashed potato flakes
1 package (3 ounces) cream cheese, cubed
1 tube (12 ounces) refrigerated buttermilk biscuits
1/2 cup crushed potato chips
Paprika, optional

1 In a large skillet, cook the beef, onion and garlic over medium heat until meat is no longer pink; drain. Stir in the chili sauce, vinegar and salt; set aside.

2 In a small saucepan, bring water and butter to a boil. Pour into a small bowl. Whisk in potato flakes until blended. Beat in cream cheese until smooth.

3 Press biscuits onto the bottom and up the sides of 10 greased muffin cups. Fill with beef mixture. Spread potato mixture over beef. Sprinkle with potato chips; press down lightly.

4 Bake at 375° for 20-25 minutes or until golden brown. Sprinkle with paprika if desired. Serve desired amount immediately. Cool remaining pies before placing in a single layer in a freezer container. Cover and freeze for up to 2 months.

5 To use frozen pies: Thaw in the refrigerator for 8 hours. Place on a greased baking sheet. Bake at 375° for 15-18 minutes or until heated through. **Yield:** 5 servings.

French Toast Sticks | *Taste of Home Test Kitchen*

These French Toast Sticks are handy to have in the freezer for a hearty breakfast in an instant. They're great for buffets because they can be eaten on the go.

6   slices day-old Texas toast
4   eggs
1   cup milk
2   tablespoons sugar
1   teaspoon vanilla extract
1/4   to 1/2 teaspoon ground cinnamon
1   cup crushed cornflakes, optional
Confectioners' sugar, optional
Maple syrup

1 Cut each piece of bread into thirds; place in an ungreased 13-in. x 9-in. dish. In a large bowl, whisk eggs, milk, sugar, vanilla and cinnamon. Pour over bread; soak for 2 minutes; turn once. Coat bread with cornflake crumbs on all sides if desired.

2 Place in a greased 15-in. x 10-in. x 1-in. baking pan. Freeze until firm, about 45 minutes. Transfer to an airtight container or freezer bag. May be frozen for up to 3 months.

3 **To use frozen French Toast Sticks:** Place desired number of sticks on a greased baking sheet. Bake at 425° for 8 minutes. Turn and bake 10-12 minutes longer or until golden brown. Sprinkle with the confectioners' sugar if desired. Serve with syrup. **Yield:** 1-1/2 dozen.

Party Pinwheels | *Taste of Home Test Kitchen*

It's nice to have these tasty little appetizers on hand for after-school snacks or as a treat when watching TV.

- 6 **packages (8 ounces each) cream cheese, softened, divided**
- 2 **jars (5-3/4 ounces each) pimiento-stuffed olives, drained and finely chopped**
- 12 **flour tortillas (10 inches), divided**
- 1 **package (6 ounces) thinly sliced cooked turkey**
- 1 **cup finely chopped dill pickles**
- 2 **tablespoons Dijon mustard**
- 1 **package (6 ounces) thinly sliced fully cooked ham**
- 3/4 **cup finely chopped celery**
- 1/2 **cup hickory-flavored barbecue sauce**
- 1 **package (6 ounces) thinly sliced cooked roast beef**

1 In a large bowl, beat two packages of cream cheese until smooth. Add olives. Spread about 3/4 cup each on four tortillas; top with four slices of turkey. Roll up tightly; wrap in plastic wrap.

2 In another large bowl, beat two packages of cream cheese with pickles and mustard until blended. Spread on each of four tortillas; top with ham. Roll up and wrap in plastic wrap.

3 In a large bowl, beat remaining cream cheese; add celery and barbecue sauce. Spread on remaining tortillas; top with beef. Roll up and wrap in plastic wrap. Refrigerate for at least 2 hours before cutting into 1/2-in. slices. Or place in freezer bags. May be frozen for up to 2 months.

4 **To use frozen pinwheels:** Thaw for 10 minutes before cutting. **Yield:** about 50 appetizers.

Baked Ham Sandwiches | *Charlotte Rowe, Alto, New Mexico*

Minced onion and prepared mustard put a flavorful spin on these ham and cheese sandwiches. I simply take a few foil-wrapped favorites from the freezer and warm them in the oven for effortless lunches.

1/3	cup butter, softened
1/2	cup dried minced onion
1/3	to 1/2 cup prepared mustard
2	tablespoons poppy seeds
8	hamburger buns, split
16	slices deli ham
8	slices Swiss cheese

1 In a bowl, combine the butter, onion, mustard and poppy seeds; spread about 2 tablespoons on each bun. Layer with ham and cheese; replace tops. Wrap each sandwich in foil.

2 Bake desired amount of sandwiches at 350° for 6-10 minutes or until cheese is melted. Freeze the remaining sandwiches for up to 2 months.

3 **To use frozen sandwiches:** Bake at 350° for 30-35 minutes or until cheese is melted. **Yield:** 8 servings.

Pizza Meat Loaf Cups | *Susan Wollin, Marshall, Wisconsin*

These little pizza-flavored loaves are convenient to reheat as a quick snack or an easy dinner. Drizzle some pizza sauce on top for a little extra pizzazz.

1	egg, lightly beaten
1/2	cup pizza sauce
1/4	cup seasoned bread crumbs
1/2	teaspoon Italian seasoning
1-1/2	pounds ground beef
1-1/2	cups (6 ounces each) shredded part-skim mozzarella cheese

Additional pizza sauce, optional

1 In a large bowl, combine the egg, pizza sauce, bread crumbs and Italian seasoning. Crumble beef over mixture and mix well. Divide among 12 greased muffin cups; press onto the bottom and up the sides. Fill center with cheese.

2 Bake at 375° for 15-18 minutes or until meat is no longer pink. Serve desired amount immediately with additional pizza sauce if desired. Cool remaining cups and place in freezer bags. May be frozen for up to 3 months.

3 **To use frozen pizza cups:** Thaw in the refrigerator for 24 hours. Microwave on a microwave-safe plate on high for 2-3 minutes or until heated through. Serve with additional pizza sauce if desired. **Yield:** 1 dozen.

Sweet

Strawberry Mallow Pops

Strawberry Mallow Pops | *Arlene Pickard, Redvers, Saskatchewan*

These strawberry pops are popular with our family on hot summer days. It's so much fun taking a big bite into the yummy bits of fruit and marshmallow.

1 **package (8 ounces) cream cheese, softened**
1/4 **cup honey**
1 **package (16 ounces) frozen sweetened sliced strawberries, thawed**
3 **cups miniature marshmallows**
1 **cup heavy whipping cream, whipped**
24 **Popsicle molds or paper cups (3 ounces each)**
24 **Popsicle sticks**

1 In a small bowl, beat cream cheese and honey until smooth. Add strawberries with juice; beat until blended. Fold in marshmallows and whipped cream.

2 Fill each mold or cup with 1/4 cup strawberry mixture. Top molds with holders or insert sticks into cups, then cover. Freeze until firm. May be frozen for up to 2 months. **Yield:** 2 dozen.

Frozen Almond-Cream Desserts | *Eva Wright, Grant, Alabama*

These little frozen cheesecakes are a surefire crowd-pleaser, particularly when served with the peach puree. They're even great when made with a sugar substitute.

3/4 **cup ground almonds**
1 **tablespoon butter, melted**
1 **envelope unflavored gelatin**
1/4 **cup cold water**
12 **ounces reduced-fat cream cheese**
1/3 **cup sugar**
3/4 **cup fat-free milk**
1/4 **teaspoon almond extract**
PEACH SAUCE:
3 **cups sliced peeled peaches**
2 **tablespoons sugar**
1/8 **teaspoon salt**

1 In a small bowl, combine almonds and butter. Press onto the bottom of 12 paper- or foil-lined muffin cups. Cover and freeze for 10 minutes.

2 Meanwhile, in a small saucepan, sprinkle gelatin over cold water; let stand for 1 minute. Cook over low heat, stirring until gelatin is completely dissolved; set aside.

3 In a small bowl, beat cream cheese and sugar until smooth. Gradually beat in milk and extract. Stir in gelatin mixture. Spoon into muffin cups; freeze until firm. Remove from muffins cups and transfer to freezer bags. May be frozen for up to 2 months.

4 **To use frozen dessert:** Remove from the freezer 10 minutes before serving. Place the sauce ingredients in a blender; cover and process until pureed. Spoon onto dessert plates. Peel liners off desserts; invert onto peach sauce. Extra peach sauce may be frozen for up to 2 months. **Yield:** 12 servings.

Frozen Mocha Cheesecakes | *Wendy Nuis, Stokes Bay, Ontario*

Enjoy multiple desserts in one with this luscious, no-bake cheesecake. Turn it into a whole new creation by using different flavored chips or mini chips, replacing the coffee with another flavor stir-in or adding in crushed toffee or peppermints. Be sure to add in only 1 tablespoon to prevent overwhelming your taste buds.

1	egg
1/3	cup sugar
1/4	cup all-purpose flour
2	tablespoons baking cocoa
1/4	teaspoon vanilla extract
3	tablespoons butter, melted

FILLING:

2/3	cup milk chocolate chips
4	to 6 teaspoons instant coffee granules
2	teaspoons hot water
1	package (8 ounces) cream cheese, softened
1	can (14 ounces) sweetened condensed milk

Whipped cream, optional

1 In a small bowl, combine the egg, sugar, flour, cocoa and vanilla; stir in butter. Press onto the bottom of four 4-in. springform pans coated with cooking spray.

2 Place pans on a baking sheet. Bake at 350° for 12 minutes. Cool on a wire rack.

3 In a microwave, melt chips; stir until smooth. Cool. In a small bowl, combine coffee granules and water. In a large bowl, beat the cream cheese, milk, chocolate and coffee mixture until smooth. Pour into crusts. Cover and freeze for at least 6 hours or until firm. Cheesecakes may be frozen for up to 2 months.

4 To use frozen cheesecakes: Remove from the freezer 15 minutes before serving. Remove sides of pan. Garnish with whipped cream if desired. **Yield:** 8 servings.

Chocolate Peanut Butter Bombes | *Taste of Home Test Kitchen*

Kids of all ages are sure to love these creamy frozen bombes with the peanut butter surprise inside!

1   **package (8 ounces) fat-free cream cheese**

3   **tablespoons chocolate syrup**

1/2 **cup confectioners' sugar**

1   **carton (12 ounces) frozen reduced-fat whipped topping, thawed**

8   **miniature peanut butter cups**

ADDITIONAL INGREDIENTS:

Fat-free hot fudge ice cream topping, warmed

Chopped salted peanuts

1 Line eight 6-oz. ramekins or custard cups with plastic wrap; set aside. In a large bowl, beat cream cheese and chocolate syrup until smooth. Beat in the confectioners' sugar; fold in the whipped topping.

2 Spoon into prepared cups; insert a peanut butter cup into the center of each. Cover and freeze for 4-5 hours or until firm. For longer freezer storage, wrap bombes securely with foil. May be frozen for up to 2 months.

3 **To use frozen bombes:** Remove wrapping. Invert bombes into dessert dishes; remove cups. Drizzle with hot fudge topping and sprinkle with peanuts. **Yield:** 8 servings.

Striped Fruit Pops | *Taste of Home Test Kitchen*

These frosty favorites are thrice as nice, lusciously layered with fresh strawberries, kiwifruit and peaches. A touch of honey adds to their natural sweetness. Plus, the pops' bright stripes are sure to light up kids' eyes!

- 3/4 **cup honey, divided**
- 2 **cups sliced fresh strawberries**
- 12 **plastic or paper cups (3 ounces each)**
- 6 **kiwifruit, peeled and sliced**
- 12 **Popsicle sticks**
- 1-1/3 **cups sliced fresh ripe peaches**

1 In a blender, combine 1/4 cup honey and strawberries; cover and process until blended. Pour into cups. Freeze for 30 minutes or until firm.

2 In a blender, combine 1/4 cup honey and kiwi; cover and process until blended. Pour over frozen strawberry layer; insert sticks into cups. Freeze until firm.

3 Repeat with peaches and remaining honey; pour over kiwi layer. Cover and freeze until firm. May be frozen for up to 2 months. **Yield:** 1 dozen.

Golden Fruit Punch | *Margaret Wagner Allen, Abingdon, Virginia*

This light, fruity punch is a breeze to serve—I make it ahead and store it in the freezer. Since it calls for canned fruit, there's no time wasted peeling or chopping.

- 1 **can (30 ounces) fruit cocktail, undrained**
- 1 **can (29 ounces) peaches, undrained**
- 1 **can (20 ounces) crushed pineapple, undrained**
- 4 **medium bananas**
- 2 **cups sugar**
- 2 **cups water**
- 1 **can (12 ounces) frozen orange juice concentrate, thawed**
- 2 **tablespoons lemon juice**

ADDITIONAL INGREDIENT (for each serving):
- 3/4 **cup lemon-lime soda, chilled**

1 Place fruit cocktail in a blender; cover and process until smooth. Pour into a large freezer container. Repeat with peaches and pineapple.

2 Place bananas, sugar and water in the blender; cover and process until smooth. Add to pureed fruit along with orange juice concentrate and lemon juice; mix well. Pour into a large or several small freezer containers. May be frozen up to 2 months.

3 To use frozen punch: Remove from the freezer 2 hours before serving. Just before serving, break apart with a large spoon. For each serving, in a chilled glass, combine 1/4 cup fruit slush with 3/4 cup soda. **Yield:** 64 (1-cup) servings.

Melon Fruit Slush | *Jane Walker, Dewey, Arizona*

This pretty pink drink is packed with fruit flavor. It features fresh honeydew and cantaloupe as well as sweet pineapple, strawberries and bananas.

- 1 **can (20 ounces) crushed pineapple, undrained**
- 1 **container (10 ounces) frozen sweetened sliced strawberries**
- 4 **medium ripe bananas, cut into chunks**
- 1 **cup cubed cantaloupe**
- 1 **cup cubed honeydew**
- 2-1/2 **cups water**
- 3/4 **cup orange juice concentrate**
- 3/4 **cup lemonade concentrate**

ADDITIONAL INGREDIENT (for each serving):
- 1 **cup lemon-lime soda, chilled**

1 In a blender, process the fruit in batches until smooth. Pour into a large bowl. Stir in the water and concentrates. Pour into a large or several small freezer containers. Cover and freeze until icy. May be frozen for up to 2 months.

2 To use frozen slush: Let stand at room temperature until icy. Spoon 1/2 cup into a glass; add about 1 cup soda. **Yield:** 20-25 servings.

Chunky Oatmeal Cookies | *Sandra Castillo, Janesville, Wisconsin*

I keep balls of this cookie dough in the freezer, so home-baked cookies are just minutes away. This way you can make as many as you would like...just a couple for an afternoon treat or the entire batch.

3/4　cup butter, softened
1　cup packed brown sugar
1/2　cup sugar
2　eggs
1　teaspoon vanilla extract
3　cups quick-cooking oats
1-1/2　cups all-purpose flour
1/2　teaspoon baking soda
1/4　teaspoon salt
3/4　cup raisins
3/4　cup Reese's Pieces or M&M's

1 In a large bowl, cream butter and sugar until light and fluffy. Beat in eggs and vanilla. Combine the oats, flour, baking soda and salt; gradually add to creamed mixture and mix well. Stir in raisins and candy. Drop by tablespoonfuls onto ungreased baking sheets. Cover and freeze.

2 Transfer frozen cookie dough balls to a large resealable plastic freezer bag. May be frozen for up to 6 months.

3 **To use frozen cookie dough:** Place dough balls 2 in. apart on greased baking sheets. Bake at 350° for 18-22 minutes or until golden brown. Remove to wire racks to cool. **Yield:** about 3-1/2 dozen.

Citrus Ice | *Taste of Home Test Kitchen*

It's hard to resist the refreshing flavor of lemon and lime in this delightful, frosty treat.

1-1/4　cups water
1/3　cup sugar
1/4　cup orange juice
2　tablespoons lemon juice
2　tablespoons lime juice

1 In a small saucepan, combine all the ingredients. Bring to a boil. Reduce heat; cook and stir over medium heat until sugar is dissolved, about 2 minutes. Cool.

2 Pour into a 13-in. x 9-in. dish; cover and freeze for 45 minutes or until edges begin to firm. Stir and return to the freezer. Repeat every 20 minutes or until slushy, about 1 hour. If desired, divide into two small freezer containers. May be frozen for up to 2 months.

3 **To use frozen ice:** Let stand at room temperature until slushy. **Yield:** 2 servings.

Editor's Note: This recipe can easily be doubled. Be sure to use two 13-in. x 9-in. dishes.

Frosty Peanut Butter Cups | *Kimberly Rendino, Cicero, New York*

With their creamy smooth texture and peanut butter flavor, these cups are addictive! Graham cracker crumbs make up the simple crust. They freeze well in muffin cups for cute individual servings.

1 **cup reduced-fat graham cracker crumbs (about 5 whole crackers)**

2 **tablespoons reduced-fat spreadable margarine**

1 **cup cold 1% milk**

1/2 **cup reduced-fat creamy peanut butter**

1 **package (3.4 ounces) instant vanilla pudding mix**

2 **cups fat-free whipped topping**

1 In a small bowl, combine cracker crumbs and margarine. Press about 1 tablespoon each into 12 paper-lined muffin cups.

2 In a large bowl, whisk milk and peanut butter until blended. Whisk in pudding mix until smooth. Let stand for 2 minutes or until soft-set. Fold in whipped topping. Spoon into cups. Freeze until firm. Remove from muffin cups and transfer to freezer bags. May be frozen for up to 2 months.

3 To use frozen cups: Remove from paper liners and let stand at room temperature for 5 minutes before serving. **Yield:** 1 dozen.

Editor's Note: This recipe was tested with Parkay reduced-fat tub margarine.

Honey Peach Freeze | *Dorothy Smith, El Dorado, Arkansas*

Want a cool and refreshing dessert? This slightly sweet delight, which is big on peach flavor, will be the perfect answer.

1/4	cup honey
2	tablespoons orange juice
1	tablespoon lemon juice
1	package (20 ounces) frozen sliced peaches, partially thawed

Additional sliced peaches for garnish, optional

1 In a blender, combine the honey, juices and peaches; cover and process until smooth. Pour into four dishes. Cover and freeze. May be frozen for up to 2 months.

2 To use frozen dessert: Remove from the freezer 5 minutes before serving. Garnish with additional peaches if desired. **Yield:** 4 servings.

Frosty Strawberry Slims | *Patricia Schroedl, Jefferson, Wisconsin*

I've been serving tall glasses of this delicious fruity beverage for years. I once won first place with this recipe in the low-calorie division of a state strawberry contest.

1	package (16 ounces) frozen unsweetened whole strawberries
1	pint fat-free frozen vanilla yogurt, softened
1	package (.3 ounce) sugar-free strawberry gelatin
1/2	cup boiling water
2	teaspoons lemon juice

ADDITIONAL INGREDIENT (for each serving):

1	cup diet lemon-lime soda

1 In a large bowl, mash strawberries. Stir in yogurt. In a small bowl, dissolve gelatin in boiling water; add lemon juice. Stir into strawberry mixture.

2 Pour mixture into a large or several small freezer containers. Cover and freeze for 4 hours or until firm. May be frozen for up to 2 months.

3 To use frozen slush: Remove from the freezer 15 minutes before serving. To serve, scoop 1/2 cup frozen mixture into a glass; fill with 1 cup soda. **Yield:** 9 servings.

Coconut Pineapple Pops | *Taste of Home Test Kitchen*

There's a taste of the tropics in these shivery sensations that pair pineapple with coconut pudding. With these sunny color and creamy texture, these pops just might be your hottest fresh-from-the-freezer treat.

1-1/2 cups cold 2% milk

1 can (6 ounces) unsweetened pineapple juice

1 can (8 ounces) unsweetened crushed pineapple

1 package (3.4 ounces) instant coconut cream pudding mix

14 Popsicle molds or paper cups (3 ounces each)

14 Popsicle sticks

1 In a blender, combine the milk, pineapple juice and pineapple; cover and process until smooth. Pour into a bowl; whisk in pudding mix for 2 minutes. Let stand for 2 minutes.

2 Fill each mold or cup with 1/4 cup pineapple mixture; top mold with holders or insert sticks into cups, then cover. Freeze until firm. May be frozen for up to 2 months. **Yield:** 14 servings.

Granola Banana Sticks | *Diane Toomey, Allentown, Pennsylvania*

My daughter and I won an award at our local fair for these healthy snacks. I like to assemble the ingredients ahead for my kids to whip up when they get home from school. Sometimes we substitute rice cereal as a crunchy alternative to the granola bars.

1/4 cup peanut butter

2 tablespoons plus 1-1/2 teaspoons honey

4-1/2 teaspoons brown sugar

2 teaspoons milk

3 medium firm bananas

6 Popsicle sticks

2 crunchy oat and honey granola bars, crushed

1 In a small saucepan, combine the peanut butter, honey, brown sugar and milk; cook until heated through, stirring occasionally.

2 Peel bananas and cut in half widthwise; insert a Popsicle stick into one end of each banana half. Spoon peanut butter mixture over bananas to coat completely. Sprinkle with crushed granola. Serve immediately or place on a waxed paper-lined baking sheet and freeze. Once frozen, transfer to freezer bags. May be frozen for up to 2 months. **Yield:** 6 servings.

Orange Pops | *JoAnn Skarivoda, Manitowoc, Wisconsin*

Five ingredients are all you'll need for these fruity frozen pops. When my sister and I were raising our families, we looked for budget-friendly recipes—our kids loved making and eating these tasty treats.

1 package (3 ounces) orange gelatin
1 envelope (.15 ounce) unsweetened orange soft drink mix
1 cup sugar
2 cups boiling water
2 cups cold water
16 to 18 Popsicle molds or paper cups (3 ounces each)
16 to 18 Popsicle sticks

1 In a bowl, dissolve the gelatin, soft drink mix and sugar in boiling water. Stir in cold water.

2 Pour into molds or cups. Top mold with holders or insert sticks into cups, then cover. Freeze until firm. May be frozen for up to 2 months. **Yield:** 16-18 servings.

Fruity Cooler | *Debra Cornelius, Grant, Nebraska*

This yummy fruit-filled slush sports a tangy citrus flavor. It's especially refreshing on a warm day, but I make it year-round as an after-school snack.

2   cans (8 ounces each) crushed pineapple, drained

1   can (11 ounces) mandarin oranges, drained

5   large ripe bananas, sliced

2   cups sliced fresh strawberries

2   cups water

1   can (12 ounces) frozen lemonade concentrate, thawed

1   can (12 ounces) frozen orange juice concentrate, thawed

1   cup diet lemon-lime soda

1 In a blender, place half of the pineapple, oranges, bananas and strawberries; cover and process until smooth. Pour into a large bowl. Repeat. Stir in the remaining ingredients. Pour or spoon 1/2 cup into each of 24 glasses or plastic cups. Cover and freeze for at least 2 hours. May be frozen for up to 1 month.

2 To use frozen cooler: Remove from the freezer 15 minutes before serving. **Yield:** 24 servings.

Chocolate Mousse Balls | *Michael Nye, Upper Sandusky, Ohio*

It's such a joy to be creative in the kitchen with my grandkids. The key is using recipes like this one that allow them to get involved and yield such yummy results.

6   milk chocolate candy bars (1.55 ounces each)

1   container (12 ounces) frozen whipped topping, thawed

1   cup crushed vanilla wafers (about 30 wafers)

1 In a saucepan over low heat, melt candy bars. Cool for 10 minutes. Fold into the whipped topping. Cover and chill for 3 hours.

2 Shape into 1-in. balls and roll in wafer crumbs. Refrigerate or freeze. To freeze, arrange on a waxed paper-lined baking sheet. Store in the freezer until frozen. Transfer to freezer bags. May be frozen for up to 3 months. **Yield:** about 3 dozen.

Pina Colada Slush | *Alisa Allred, Vernal, Utah*

For a special treat on a steamy day, try this fruity cooler. I first had it when I was pregnant, and it really hit the spot that summer—and ever since! I'm asked to bring it to family gatherings all year long, so I always keep a batch or two in my freezer...just to be prepared.

3 cans (6 ounces each) unsweetened pineapple juice
2 cups water
1 can (10 ounces) frozen nonalcoholic pina colada mix
1 tablespoon lime juice
1 tub sugar-free lemonade soft drink mix
ADDITIONAL INGREDIENT (for each serving):
1/2 cup lemon-lime soda, chilled

1 In a large bowl, combine the pineapple juice, water, pina colada mix, lime juice and soft drink mix; stir until drink mix is dissolved. Transfer to a 2-qt. freezer container or several small freezer containters. Freeze for at least 6 hours. May be frozen for up to 2 months.

2 **To use frozen slush:** Remove from the freezer 45 minutes before serving. For each serving, combine 1/2 cup slush mixture with 1/2 cup lemon-lime soda. **Yield:** 12 servings (3 quarts).

Editor's Note: This recipe was tested with Crystal Light lemonade soft drink mix.

Dipped Fruit on a Stick | *Paula Marchese, Rocky Point, New York*

This quick and easy dessert has been a staple in my family for as long as I can remember. Our five grown sons loved these when they were tots. Nowadays, it's our two grandchildren who request the flavorful snacks.

2 cups (12 ounces) semisweet chocolate chips
2 tablespoons shortening
3 medium firm ripe bananas
3 medium apples
10 Popsicle sticks
1 cup finely chopped walnuts
1 cup flaked coconut

1 In a microwave, melt chocolate and shortening; stir until smooth. Cut bananas in half widthwise. Cut apples in half lengthwise; remove cores. Insert sticks into fruit; dip into chocolate, coating fruit completely. Roll in nuts or coconut.

2 Place on a waxed paper-lined baking sheet. Freeze for at least 20 minutes or until frozen. Transfer to freezer bags. May be frozen for up to 2 months.

3 **To use frozen fruit:** Remove from freezer 10 minutes before serving.

Peanutty Pops | *Lynn Lehman, Superior, Wisconsin*

When my two sons were young, these pops were a favorite treat, and they still enjoy them. They're fast and easy to make and don't melt as quickly as some frozen treats. For a variety, you can add mint chocolate chips, mini marshmallows or chopped banana.

1   **envelope unflavored gelatin**
1   **cup cold water**
1/2   **cup sugar**
1   **cup creamy peanut butter**
1   **cup chocolate milk**
10   **plastic cups (3 ounces each)**
10   **Popsicle sticks**

1 In a small saucepan, sprinkle gelatin over cold water; let stand for 1 minute. Stir in sugar. Cook and stir over medium heat until gelatin and sugar are dissolved. Transfer to a large bowl; beat in the peanut butter and milk until smooth. Pour mixture into cups.

2 Cover each cup with heavy-duty foil; insert sticks through foil. Place in a 9-in. square pan. Freeze until firm. May be frozen for up to 2 months. **Yield:** 10 servings.

Icy Indulgences

For a refreshing summer treat and a frosty delight, push a Popsicle stick through the foil cover of a small yogurt cup. Pop it in the freezer until it's frozen, then remove the plastic container and enjoy your pop!

Frozen Cheesecake Bites | *Frank Millard, Janesville, Wisconsin*

It only takes one of these delicious nibbles to cure your cheesecake cravings. But your guests are sure to ask to sample a few more.

3 packages (8 ounces each) cream cheese, softened
1-1/4 cups sugar, divided
1-1/2 teaspoons vanilla extract
1/2 teaspoon salt
4 eggs, lightly beaten
9 squares (1 ounce each) semisweet chocolate, chopped
3/4 cup heavy whipping cream
1/2 cup graham cracker crumbs
1/2 cup English toffee bits or almond brickle chips, crushed

1 Line the bottom of a 9-in. springform pan with parchment paper; coat paper and sides of pan with cooking spray. Set aside. In a large bowl, beat the cream cheese, 1 cup sugar, vanilla and salt until smooth. Add eggs; beat on low speed just until combined. Pour into prepared pan.

2 Place on a baking sheet. Bake at 325° for 40-45 minutes or until center is almost set. Cool on a wire rack for 10 minutes. Carefully run a knife around edge of pan to loosen; cool 1 hour longer. Cover and freeze overnight.

3 Remove from the freezer and let stand for 30 minutes or until easy to handle. Meanwhile, in a small saucepan over low heat, melt chocolate with cream; stir until blended. Remove from the heat. Transfer to a bowl; cover and refrigerate until mixture reaches spreading consistency, stirring occasionally.

4 In a small bowl, combine cracker crumbs and remaining sugar. Using a melon baller, scoop out 1-in. balls of cheesecake; place on parchment paper-lined baking sheets. Top each with a heaping teaspoonful of chocolate mixture. Sprinkle crumb mixture over half of the balls and toffee bits over the remaining balls. Cover and freeze for 2 hours or until firm. May be frozen for up to 2 months. **Yield:** 5-1/2 dozen.

Peanut Butter Snack Cups | *Nancy Clark, Cochranton, Pennsylvania*

When our kids were little, they loved this cool and creamy summertime treat. We'd keep several batches in the freezer so there were plenty when their neighborhood friends came over to play.

12 vanilla wafers
1 carton (8 ounces) frozen whipped topping, thawed, divided
1 cup cold milk
1/2 cup peanut butter
1 package (3.9 ounces) instant chocolate pudding mix

1 Place wafers in paper or foil-lined muffin cups. Top each with 1 tablespoon whipped topping. In a large bowl, combine milk and peanut butter. Add pudding mix; whisk for 2 minutes. Let stand for 2 minutes or until soft-set. Fold in the remaining whipped topping. Spoon into prepared cups. Cover and freeze for up to 2 months.

2 To use frozen cups: Remove from the freezer 10 minutes before serving. **Yield:** 12 servings.

Frosty Raspberry Parfaits | *Clare Hafferman, Kalispell, Montana*

This layered dessert looks so elegant and pretty. It gets compliments every time I serve it. Parfaits are a traditional part of our Fourth of July buffet.

4 cups fresh or frozen raspberries, thawed, divided
4 egg yolks, lightly beaten
1/2 cup sugar
1 teaspoon vanilla extract
1 cup heavy whipping cream, whipped
Additional fresh raspberries, optional

1 Place 2 cups raspberries in a food processor; cover and process until blended. Press through a fine mesh strainer; discard seeds and pulp.

2 In a small saucepan, combine egg yolks and sugar; stir in raspberry puree until smooth. Cook and stir over medium heat until mixture reaches at least 160° and coats the back of a metal spoon. Remove from the heat; stir in vanilla. Transfer to a bowl. Refrigerate until chilled.

3 Fold in whipped cream. Coarsely mash remaining raspberries. In six parfait glasses, layer 1 tablespoon mashed berries and 1/4 cup cream mixture. Repeat layers. Cover and freeze for 6 hours or overnight. May be frozen for up to 2 months.

4 To use frozen parfaits: Remove from the freezer 10 minutes before serving. Garnish with additional raspberries if desired. **Yield:** 6 servings.

Strawberry Crumble Parfaits | *Carol Anderson, Salt Lake City, Utah*

Time to take out those parfaits glasses! This is one of those elegant, but effortless recipes perfect for simple summer entertaining. You'll love the texture contrast between the smooth, creamy berry mixture and the buttery, crunchy topping.

1   **cup all-purpose flour**
1/4 **cup packed brown sugar**
1/2 **cup chopped pecans**
1/2 **cup cold butter**
1   **can (14 ounces) sweetened condensed milk**
3   **tablespoons lemon juice**
3   **tablespoons orange juice**
2   **cups chopped fresh strawberries**
1   **cup heavy whipping cream, whipped**

1 In a large bowl, combine the flour, brown sugar and pecans; cut in butter until mixture resembles coarse crumbs. Spread into an ungreased 15-in. x 10-in. x 1-in. baking pan. Bake at 350° for 15-18 minutes or until golden brown.

2 In another large bowl, combine the milk, lemon juice and orange juice. Add strawberries. Fold in whipped cream.

3 Spoon 1 tablespoon of crumb mixture into each parfait glass; top with a scant 3 tablespoonfuls of berry mixture. Repeat layers. Sprinkle with the remaining crumb mixture. Freeze until firm. May be frozen covered for up to 1 month.

4 To use frozen parfaits: Remove from the freezer 20-30 minutes before serving. **Yield:** 10 servings.

Apricot Coconut Balls | *Barbara Strohbehn, Gladbrook, Iowa*

I appreciate that these fruity candies are easy to prepare and can be made ahead of time. They're a nice alternative to chocolate sweets.

1-1/2 **cups dried apricots**
2   **cups flaked coconut**
2/3 **cup sweetened condensed milk**
Confectioners' sugar

1 Place apricots in a food processor; cover and pulse until chopped. Transfer to a large bowl; add coconut and milk. Shape into 1-in. balls; roll balls in sugar.

2 Place on a baking sheet. Refrigerate until firm. Store in an airtight container in the freezer or refrigerator. **Yield:** 3 dozen.

Ice Cream Crunchies | *Sady Craig, Lapeer, Michigan*

Four ingredients are all you need for these frosty bars. Kids have so much fun putting these together.

1/2 cup light corn syrup
1/2 cup peanut butter
  3 cups crisp rice cereal
2-1/2 cups vanilla ice cream, softened

1 In a large bowl, combine corn syrup and peanut butter; stir in cereal. With buttered hands, press the mixture into a greased 13-in. x 9-in. pan. Refrigerate for 15 minutes.

2 Cut cereal mixture into 12 rectangles; remove from the pan. Place 1/2 cup ice cream on six rectangles; top with remaining rectangles. Wrap each in plastic wrap and freeze until firm. May be frozen for up to 2 months.

3 To use frozen dessert: Cut in half before serving. **Yield:** 1 dozen.

Creamy Frozen Fruit Cups | *Karen Hatcher, St. Amant, Louisiana*

I love to prepare these cool, fluffy fruit cups to give a refreshing boost to many meals. They've been well received at family gatherings and summer barbecues. There's no last-minute fuss since you make them well in advance.

  1 package (8 ounces) cream cheese, softened
1/2 cup sugar
  1 jar (10 ounces) maraschino cherries, drained
  1 can (11 ounces) mandarin oranges, drained
  1 can (8 ounces) crushed pineapple, drained
1/2 cup chopped pecans
  1 carton (8 ounces) frozen whipped topping, thawed
Fresh mint, optional

1 In a large bowl, beat the cream cheese and sugar until fluffy. Halve 9 cherries; chop the remaining cherries. Set aside halved cherries and 18 oranges for garnish. Add the pineapple, pecans and chopped cherries to cream cheese mixture. Fold in whipped topping and remaining oranges.

2 Line muffin cups with paper or foil liners. Spoon fruit mixture into cups; garnish with reserved cherries and oranges. Freeze until firm. Remove from muffin cups and transfer to freezer bags. May be frozen up to 2 months.

3 To use frozen cups: Remove from the freezer 10 minutes before serving. Top with mint if desired. **Yield:** 1-1/2 dozen.

Refrigerator Cookies | *Dottie Gray, Bartlett, Tennessee*

During the holidays, I usually keep at least two rolls of this cookie dough in my freezer in case I need to whip up something special in a hurry.

1	cup butter, softened
1	cup sugar
2	tablespoons milk
1	teaspoon vanilla extract
2-1/2	cups all-purpose flour
3/4	cup chopped red and green candied cherries
1/2	cup finely chopped pecans

1 In a large bowl, cream butter and sugar until light and fluffy. Add milk and vanilla. Gradually add flour and mix well. Fold in the cherries and pecans. Shape dough into two 8-in. x 2-in. rolls; wrap in plastic wrap and freeze. For longer storage, transfer logs to freezer bags. May be frozen up to 6 months.

2 To use frozen dough: Unwrap and let stand at room temperature for about 10 minutes. Cut into 1/4-in. slices. Place 2 in. apart on ungreased baking sheets. Bake at 375° for 10-12 minutes or until lightly browned. Cool on wire racks. **Yield:** about 7 dozen.

Tutti-Frutti Cups | *Holly Keithley, Lowell, Indiana*

Scooping up spoonfuls of this tangy slush is a tongue-tingling treat! The convenient single-serving cups burst with wholesome chunks of strawberries, bananas and more. Mix in diet pop instead of regular to reduce the calorie count.

1	can (11 ounces) mandarin oranges, undrained
1	can (8 ounces) unsweetened crushed pineapple, undrained
2	medium firm bananas, thinly sliced
3/4	cup fresh or frozen sliced strawberries
3/4	cup fresh or frozen blueberries
3/4	cup lemon-lime soda
1/2	cup water
6	tablespoons frozen lemonade concentrate, thawed
1/4	cup sugar

1 In a large bowl, combine all ingredients. Fill 8-oz. plastic cups three-fourths full; cover and freeze for about 4 hours or until frozen. May be frozen for up to 2 months.

2 To use frozen cups: Remove from the freezer 30 minutes before serving. **Yield:** 10 servings.

Rocky Road Fudge Pops | *Karen Grant, Tulare, California*

These sweet frozen treats are simple to prepare and guaranteed to bring out the kid in anyone. The creamy pops feature a special chocolate and peanut topping.

  1   **package (3.4 ounces) cook-and-serve chocolate pudding mix**
2-1/2   **cups milk**
1/2   **cup chopped peanuts**
1/2   **cup miniature semisweet chocolate chips**
 12   **plastic or paper cups (3 ounces each)**
1/2   **cup marshmallow creme**
 12   **Popsicle sticks**

1 In a large microwave-safe bowl, combine pudding mix and milk. Microwave, uncovered, on high for 4-6 minutes or until bubbly and slightly thickened, stirring every 2 minutes. Cool for 20 minutes, stirring several times.

2 Meanwhile, combine peanuts and chocolate chips; place about 2 tablespoons in each cup. Stir marshmallow cream into pudding; spoon into cups. Insert Popsicle sticks; cover and freeze until firm. Pops may be frozen for up to 2 months. **Yield:** 12 servings.

Editor's Note: This recipe was tested in a 1,100-watt microwave.

Peanut Butter Cookies | *Maria Regakis, Somerville, Massachusetts*

These classic peanut butter cookies bake up in a jiffy and are guaranteed to please. They taste so yummy no one will ever know they're made with reduced-fat peanut butter.

3 tablespoons butter
2 tablespoons reduced-fat peanut butter
1/2 cup packed brown sugar
1/4 cup sugar
1 egg white
1 teaspoon vanilla extract
1 cup all-purpose flour
1/4 teaspoon baking soda
1/8 teaspoon salt

1 In a large bowl, cream the butter, peanut butter and sugars until light and fluffy. Add egg white; beat until blended. Beat in vanilla. Combine the flour, baking soda and salt; gradually add to the creamed mixture and mix well. Shape into an 8-in. roll; wrap in plastic wrap. Freeze for 2 hours or until firm. For longer storage, transfer to a freezer bag. May be frozen for up to 6 months.

2 To use frozen cookie dough: Unwrap and cut into 1/4-in. slices. Place 2 in. apart on baking sheets coated with cooking spray. Flatten with a fork. Bake at 350° for 6-8 minutes for chewy cookies or 8-10 minutes for crisp cookies. Cool for 1-2 minutes before removing to wire racks; cool completely. **Yield:** 2 dozen.

Caramel Marshmallow Buttons | *Mrs. Terry Dorale, Cody, Wyoming*

Kids of all ages dive into these sweet, fluffy treats. The chewy marshmallow, gooey caramel and crisp coating set off an appetizing explosion of textures.

50 to 54 large marshmallows
1 package (14 ounces) caramels
1 can (14 ounces) sweetened condensed milk
1 cup butter, cubed
5 to 6 cups crisp rice cereal

1 Place a toothpick in each marshmallow. Place on waxed paper-lined baking sheets. Freeze until firm, about 1 hour.

2 In a heavy saucepan over medium-low heat, combine the caramels, milk and butter. Cook and stir until caramels are melted and mixture is smooth. Dip marshmallows in caramel mixture; roll in cereal. Return to prepared baking sheet. Freeze until firm, at least 1 hour. Transfer to a freezer container. May be frozen for up 2 months. **Yield:** 50-54 pieces.

3 **To use frozen candy:** Remove from the freezer 45 minutes before serving, discard toothpicks.

Strawberry Slush | *Patricia Schroedl, Jefferson, Wisconsin*

This make-ahead slush is really refreshing on hot summer days. Pour lemon-lime soda over scoops of the strawberry blend for a fast fruity treat that's so thick, you'll have to eat it with a spoon.

4 cups fresh strawberries
2 cups fat-free vanilla ice cream, softened
1 package (.3 ounces) sugar-free strawberry gelatin
1/2 cup boiling water
2 teaspoons lemon juice
ADDITIONAL INGREDIENTS (for each serving):
3/4 cup diet lemon-lime soda, chilled
Additional fresh strawberries, optional

1 In a large bowl, mash strawberries; add ice cream. In a small bowl, dissolve gelatin in water; stir in lemon juice. Add to the strawberry mixture; mix well. Pour into a 1-1/2-qt. freezer container or several small containers; cover and freeze overnight. May be frozen for up to 2 months.

2 **To use frozen slush:** Remove from the freezer 15 minutes before serving. Spoon about 1/2 cup into glasses; add about 1/2 to 3/4 cup soda. Garnish with strawberries if desired. **Yield:** 10 servings.

Puddingwiches | *Joanne Zimmerman, Ephrata, Pennsylvania*

Our daughter loves these fun chocolate and peanut butter snacks. I often defrost them in the microwave so they're a bit softer.

1-1/2 cups cold milk
1/4 to 1/2 cup peanut butter
1 package (3.9 ounces) instant chocolate pudding mix
15 whole graham crackers

1 In a large bowl, combine the milk and peanut butter. Whisk in the pudding mix for 2 minutes. Let stand for 5 minutes or until thickened. Break or cut graham crackers in half.

2 Spread pudding mixture over half of the crackers; top with the remaining crackers. Wrap and freeze until firm. May be frozen for up to 1 month. **Yield:** 15 servings.

Raspberry Swirls | *Marcia Hostetter, Canton, New York*

My mother-in-law shared the recipe for these old-fashioned cookies. Swirls of raspberry jam give them a yummy flavor twist.

1 cup butter, softened
2 cups sugar
2 eggs
1 teaspoon vanilla extract
1/2 teaspoon lemon extract
3-3/4 cups all-purpose flour
2 teaspoons baking powder
1 teaspoon salt
1 jar (12 ounces) seedless raspberry jam
1 cup flaked coconut
1/2 cup chopped pecans

1 In a large bowl, cream butter and sugar until light and fluffy. Beat in the eggs and extracts. Combine flour, baking powder and salt; add to creamed mixture and mix well. Cover and chill dough for at least 2 hours.

2 Divide dough in half. On a lightly floured surface, roll each half into a 12-in. x 9-in. rectangle. Combine the jam, coconut and pecans; spread over rectangles. Carefully roll up, starting with the long end, into a tight jelly roll. Wrap in plastic wrap. Refrigerate overnight or freeze for 2-3 hours. For longer storage, transfer to freezer bags. May be frozen for up to 3 months.

3 To use refrigerated cookie dough: Cut into 1/4-in. slices; place on greased baking sheets. Bake at 375° for 10-12 minutes or until lightly browned. Cool cookies on wire racks.

4 To use frozen cookie dough: Unwrap and let stand at room temperature for about 10 minutes. Cut and bake as directed. **Yield:** 8 dozen.

Sensational Slush | *Connie Friesen, Altona, Manitoba*

Colorful and refreshing, this sweet-tart slush has become a family favorite. I freeze the mix in 2- and 4-cup containers so it can be served in small portions for individuals or the whole family. I also freeze crushed strawberries to make preparation simpler.

1/2 cup sugar

1 package (3 ounces) strawberry gelatin

2 cups boiling water

1 cup unsweetened pineapple juice

2 cups sliced fresh strawberries

1 can (12 ounces) frozen lemonade concentrate, thawed

1 can (12 ounces) frozen limeade concentrate, thawed

2 cups cold water

ADDITIONAL INGREDIENT (for each serving):

1/2 cup lemon-lime soda, chilled

1 In a large bowl, dissolve sugar and gelatin in boiling water. In a blender, combine the pineapple juice and strawberries; cover and process until blended. Add to gelatin mixture. Stir in the concentrates and cold water. Transfer to a large freezer container or several small freezer containers. Cover and freeze for 8 hours or overnight. May be frozen up to 2 months.

2 **To use frozen slush:** Remove from the freezer 45 minutes before serving. For each serving, combine 1/2 cup slush mixture with 1/2 cup lemon-lime soda; stir well. **Yield:** 20 servings.

Holiday Cookie Dough | *Taste of Home Test Kitchen*

Whip up this make-ahead dough and store it in your freezer. You'll have a head start when holiday baking time rolls around.

2 **cups butter, softened**
1 **cup sugar**
1/4 **cup sweetened condensed milk**
1 **teaspoon vanilla extract**
4 **cups all-purpose flour**
1/8 **teaspoon salt**
Sprinkles, jimmies or colored sugar, optional

1 In a large bowl, cream the butter and sugar until it is light and fluffy. Beat in milk and vanilla. Combine flour and salt; gradually add to creamed mixture and mix well.

2 Divide dough into five 1-cup portions; shape each into a 10-in.-long roll. Wrap individually in plastic wrap. Refrigerate for 1 hour or until easy to handle. Or, place in a freezer bag. May be frozen for up to 6 months. **Yield:** 5 portions (1 cup each).

3 **To use refrigerated cookie dough:** Cut roll into 1/4-in. slices. Place 2 in. apart on ungreased baking sheets. Decorate with sprinkles, jimmies or colored sugar if desired. Bake at 350° for 7-9 minutes or until lightly browned. Cool for 2 minutes before removing to wire racks. Decorate with sprinkles if desired.

4 **To use frozen cookie dough:** Thaw in the refrigerator overnight. Bake according to recipe directions. **Yield:** 200 slice-and-bake cookies.

178

Versatile Slice 'n' Bake Cookies | *Taste of Home Test Kitchen*

When you crave a sweet treat or want something fun and festive to make with the grandkids, just pull a cookie dough log from the freezer, slice and pop in the oven. The cookies will keep for a week...but they'll probably disappear much faster!

1 **cup butter, softened**
1 **cup sugar**
1/4 **teaspoon vanilla extract**
1-3/4 **cups all-purpose flour**
3/4 **teaspoon baking soda**
1/4 **teaspoon salt**
2 **tablespoons chopped mixed candied fruit, optional**
Nonpareils, jimmies, melted semisweet chocolate chips and chopped nuts, optional

1 In a small bowl, cream butter and sugar until light and fluffy. Beat in vanilla. Combine the flour, baking soda and salt; gradually add to creamed mixture and mix well.

2 Divide into three portions. If desired, add candied fruit to one portion. Shape each into a 5-in. roll; Wrap in plastic wrap. Place in a freezer bag. May be frozen for up to 6 months.

3 To use frozen dough: Remove from the freezer 1 hour before baking. Unwrap and cut into 1/4-in. slices. Place 2 in. apart on baking sheets coated with cooking spray. Sprinkle with nonpareils and jimmies if desired.

4 Bake at 350° for 12-14 minutes or until set. Remove to wire racks to cool. Frost with melted chocolate chips and sprinkle with nuts if desired. **Yield:** 4-1/2 dozen.

Raspberry Lime Slush | *Taste of Home Test Kitchen*

For a cool ending to a meal, scoop this bright pink slush into stemmed glasses, then drizzle it with ginger ale. The lime adds a little zing for a sweet-tart taste that's especially refreshing.

3/4 **cup sugar**
2 **cups water, divided**
1 **cup fresh or frozen raspberries, thawed**
1/2 **cup lime juice**
ADDITIONAL INGREDIENT (for each serving):
1/2 **cup ginger ale, chilled**

1 In a small saucepan, combine sugar and 1/2 cup water. Cook and stir over high heat until sugar is completely dissolved. Remove from the heat. Press raspberries through a sieve; discard seeds.

2 In a large bowl, combine the raspberry puree, sugar syrup, lime juice and remaining water. Transfer to a 1-qt. freezer container. Cover and freeze for 12 hours, stirring occasionally. May be frozen for up to 2 months.

3 To use frozen raspberry mixture: For one serving, combine 1/2 cup raspberry mixture and 1/2 cup ginger ale in a glass. **Yield:** 6 servings.

Chocolate Coconut Neapolitans | *Lena Marie Brownell, Rockland, Massachusetts*

These yummy striped cookies with a chocolaty twist are easy and fun to make, and are sure to satisfy hungry tummies.

Editor's Note: For the entire batch of cookies use 1/2 cup chocolate chips and 1-1/2 teaspoons shortening. For one 9-in. log, use 1/4 cup chocolate chips and 3/4 teaspoon shortening, and for a fourth of the cookies use 2 tablespoons chocolate chips and 1/4 teaspoon shortening.

Don't Forget to Floss

TIP If you're looking for a quick and easy way to slice logs of cookie dough, try dental floss. Slide a piece of floss (about 1 foot long) under the roll of dough, crisscross the ends above the dough and pull until you've cut through the dough.

1	cup butter, softened
1-1/2	cups sugar
1	egg
1	teaspoon vanilla extract
2-1/2	cups all-purpose flour
1-1/2	teaspoons baking powder
1/2	teaspoon salt
1	teaspoon almond extract
4	drops red food coloring
1/2	cup flaked coconut, finely chopped
4-1/2	teaspoons chocolate syrup

ADDITIONAL INGREDIENTS:
Semisweet chocolate chips
Shortening

1 Line a 9-in. x 5-in. loaf pan with waxed paper; set aside. In a large bowl, cream butter and sugar until light and fluffy. Beat in egg and vanilla. Combine the flour, baking powder and salt; gradually add to creamed mixture and mix well.

2 Divide dough into thirds. Add almond extract and red food coloring to one portion; spread evenly into prepared pan. Add coconut to second portion; spread evenly over first layer. Add chocolate syrup to third portion; spread over second layer. Cover with foil; freeze for 4 hours or overnight.

3 To freeze, unwrap the loaf; cut in half lengthwise. Leave as two 9-in. logs or cut into smaller logs if desired. Wrap logs in plastic wrap and transfer to a freezer bag. May be frozen for up to 6 months.

4 To use frozen cookies: Cut each portion widthwise into 1/4-in. slices. Place 2 in. apart on ungreased baking sheets. Bake at 350° for 12-14 minutes or until edges are lightly browned. Remove to wire racks to cool.

5 In a microwave, melt the chocolate chips and shortening; stir until smooth. Dip one end of each cookie into chocolate; allow excess to drip off. Place cookies on waxed paper; let stand until set. **Yield:** 5-1/2 dozen.

Coconut Parfaits | *Merval Harvey, Glennie, Michigan*

Every time I serve this simple but elegant dessert to guests, I have to give them the recipe, too. I found this dessert recipe many years ago and since then, it has earned a place in my tried-and-true file. I had to make adjustments to prepare it for two people, but it can be easily increased to serve any number.

6	tablespoons water
3	tablespoons sugar
1/2	cup flaked coconut
1-1/2	teaspoons vanilla extract
1/2	cup heavy whipping cream
1	tablespoon sliced almonds, toasted
1	tablespoon flaked coconut, toasted

1 In a large saucepan, combine water and sugar. Bring to a boil over medium heat; boil for 5 minutes. Remove from the heat; cool for 10 minutes. Stir in coconut and vanilla. Cool to room temperature.

2 In a small bowl, beat cream until soft peaks form; fold into coconut mixture. Pour into dishes. Cover and freeze 1 hour or overnight. May be frozen for up to 2 months.

3 To use frozen parfaits: Sprinkle with almonds and coconut just before serving. **Yield:** 2 servings.

Two-Tone Butter Cookies | *Kathy Kittell, Lenexa, Kansas*

During the hectic holiday season, you'll appreciate the ease of these irresistible butter cookies. It's wonderful to pull the two-tone dough from the freezer and bake a festive batch in no time.

1 **cup butter, softened**
1 **cup confectioners' sugar**
1 **teaspoon vanilla extract**
2 **cups all-purpose flour**
Red and green liquid or paste food coloring
Red colored sugar, optional

1 In a large bowl, cream butter and confectioners' sugar until light and fluffy. Beat in vanilla. Gradually add flour and mix well. Divide dough in half. With food coloring, tint half red and half green. Shape each portion into an 8-in. log. Wrap in plastic wrap and refrigerate for at least 1 hour.

2 Cut each log in half lengthwise. Press red and green halves together. Tightly wrap each roll in plastic wrap. Place rolls in a freezer bag. May be frozen for up to 6 months.

3 To use frozen dough: Let dough stand at room temperature for 15 minutes. Unwrap; cut into 1/4-in. slices. Place 2 in. apart on ungreased baking sheets. Sprinkle with colored sugar if desired. Bake at 350° for 12-14 minutes or until set. Cool on wire racks. **Yield:** about 5 dozen.

Homemade Ladyfingers | *Peggy Bailey, Covington, Kentucky*

Having a difficult time finding ladyfingers in the grocery store? Try baking your own! I keep a few dozen of these light sponge cookies in my freezer to serve with fresh fruit or to use in trifles and other desserts.

> 3   **eggs, separated**
> 1/4 **teaspoon cream of tartar**
> 1/4 **cup plus 1/3 cup sugar, divided**
> 3   **tablespoons water**
> 1/2 **teaspoon vanilla extract**
> 1/4 **teaspoon lemon extract**
> 3/4 **cup all-purpose flour**
> 1/4 **teaspoon baking powder**
> 1/8 **teaspoon salt**
> **Confectioners' sugar**

1 In a small bowl, beat egg whites and cream of tartar until foamy. Gradually add 1/4 cup sugar, 1 tablespoon at a time, beating on high until stiff glossy peaks form and sugar is dissolved, about 6 minutes; set aside.

2 In another bowl, beat egg yolks with remaining sugar for 3 minutes or until thick and lemon colored; add water and extracts. Combine the flour, baking powder and salt; stir into yolk mixture. Fold in egg white mixture.

3 Cut a small hole in the corner of a pastry or plastic bag; insert #12 round tip. Spoon batter into bag. Pipe 3-1/2-in.-long lines 2 in. apart onto a greased and floured baking sheet.

4 Bake at 350° for 10-12 minutes or until lightly browned. Remove to a wire rack; cool completely. Cover and freeze for up to 1 month.

5 To use frozen ladyfingers: Thaw in the refrigerator; dust with confectioners' sugar. Serve as a cookie or use in desserts. **Yield:** about 2-1/2 dozen.

Hot Buttered Rum Mix | *Carol Beyerl, East Wenatchee, Washington*

I offered this comforting hot drink to guests, and everyone wanted the recipe. I like to keep a batch in the freezer for easy entertaining.

> 1   **cup butter, softened**
> 2   **cups confectioners' sugar**
> 1   **cup plus 2 tablespoons packed brown sugar**
> 2   **cups vanilla ice cream, softened**
> 1-1/2 **teaspoons ground cinnamon**
> 1/2 **teaspoon ground nutmeg**
> 1   **teaspoon rum extract**
> **ADDITIONAL INGREDIENT (for each serving):**
> 3/4 **cup boiling water**

1 In a large bowl, cream butter and sugars until light and fluffy. Add the ice cream, cinnamon, nutmeg and extract. Transfer to a freezer container; freeze overnight. The mix may be frozen for up to 2 months. **Yield:** 3-1/2 cups.

2 To prepare hot drink: Dissolve 3-4 tablespoons of rum mix in boiling water; stir well. **Yield:** 14-18 servings.

Cranberry Slush | *Sharen Christensen, Salem, Utah*

One sip of this sweet icy treat leads to another...and another. My mother-in-law makes it for parties, and it never lasts long. Often, my family requests it as a snack or dessert.

- 1 **pound fresh or frozen cranberries**
- 2-1/2 **cups cold water, divided**
- 3-1/2 **cups fresh or frozen unsweetened raspberries**
- 1 **envelope unflavored gelatin**
- 2 **cups sugar**
- 2 **cups ginger ale**

ADDITIONAL INGREDIENT (for each serving):
- 1/4 **cup raspberry ginger ale or additional ginger ale**

1 In a large saucepan, cook the cranberries and 1-1/2 cups water over medium heat until the berries pop, about 15 minutes. Stir in raspberries. Cool slightly.

2 Transfer to a blender; cover and process until smooth. Strain and discard seeds, reserving juice. Pour the juice into a large bowl; set aside.

3 In a small saucepan, sprinkle the gelatin over remaining water. Let stand for 1 minute. Stir in sugar. Cook and stir over medium heat until gelatin and sugar are dissolved. Add to berry juice. Stir in ginger ale. Pour into a large or several small freezer containers. Cover and freeze for 8 hours or overnight. May be frozen for up to 2 months.

4 **To use frozen slush:** Remove from the freezer 1 hour before serving. For each serving, combine 1 cup cranberry slush with 1/4 cup raspberry ginger ale in a glass; stir well. **Yield:** 7 servings.

Icy Fruit Pops | *Le Ann Kane, Forsyth, Illinois*

My grandmother made these pineapple treats for my brother and I when we were little. Today, the pops remain a cool and simple snack that delights kids of all ages.

- 1 **can (20 ounces) crushed pineapple, undrained**
- 1 **cup water**
- 3/4 **cup orange juice concentrate**
- 3/4 **cup lemonade concentrate**
- **Sugar substitute equivalent to 1/2 cup sugar**
- 5 **medium firm bananas, cut into 1/4-inch slices and quartered**
- 1 **can (12 ounces) diet ginger ale**
- 24 **maraschino cherries or fresh strawberries**
- 24 **paper cups (3 ounces each)**
- 24 **Popsicle sticks**

1 In a large bowl, combine the pineapple, water, orange juice concentrate, lemonade concentrate and sugar substitute. Stir in the bananas and ginger ale.

2 Place a cherry in each cup; fill with pineapple mixture. Insert sticks into cups. Cover and freeze until firm. May be frozen for up to 2 months. **Yield:** 2 dozen.

Editor's Note: This recipe was tested with Splenda no-calorie sweetener.

CREATIVE LEFTOVERS

Say **no** to the same old leftovers. Change leftovers into **fabulous** **new creations** with the addition of a **few ingredients**.

Steak Tortillas, p. 187

Savory

Praline-Peach Brownie Sundaes, p. 237

Sweet

Savory

Steak Tortillas

Steak Tortillas | *Kris Wells, Hereford, Arizona*

When I fix steak, I always grill one extra so I have leftovers to make these delicious filled tortillas. The steak strips are seasoned with salsa, chili powder and cumin, then tucked inside soft flour tortillas with tasty toppings.

2 cups thinly sliced cooked beef rib eye steak (about 3/4 pound, see Grilled Rib Eye Steaks below)
1 small onion, chopped
1/4 cup salsa
1/2 teaspoon ground cumin
1/2 teaspoon chili powder
1/4 teaspoon garlic powder
1-1/2 teaspoons all-purpose flour
1/2 cup cold water
6 flour tortillas (8 inches), warmed
Shredded cheese, chopped lettuce and tomatoes and additional salsa, optional

1 In a large nonstick skillet, saute steak and onion until meat is no longer pink; drain. Stir in the salsa, cumin, chili powder and garlic powder.

2 In a small bowl, combine flour and water until smooth; gradually add to the skillet. Bring to a boil; cook and stir for 1-2 minutes or until thickened. Place steak slices on tortillas; top with cheese, lettuce, tomatoes and additional salsa if desired. Fold in sides. **Yield:** 6 servings.

Grilled Rib Eye Steaks | *Tim Hanchon, Muncie, Indiana*

In summer, I love to marinate these steaks overnight, then grill them for family and friends. Leftovers freeze nicely and can be used for two tasty recipes.

1/2 cup soy sauce
1/2 cup sliced green onions
1/4 cup packed brown sugar
2 garlic cloves, minced
1/4 teaspoon ground ginger
1/4 teaspoon pepper
2-1/2 pounds beef rib eye steaks

1 In a large resealable plastic bag, combine the soy sauce, onions, brown sugar, garlic, ginger and pepper. Add the steaks. Seal bag and turn to coat; refrigerate for 8 hours or overnight.

2 Drain and discard marinade. Grill steaks, uncovered, over medium-hot heat for 8-10 minutes or until the meat reaches desired doneness (for medium-rare, a meat thermometer should read 145°; medium, 160°; well-done, 170°). Freeze leftovers in 3/4-pound or 1/2-pound portions. May be frozen for up to 3 months. **Yield:** 2-4 servings and about 1-1/2 pounds leftover steak.

Pepper Steak Salad | *Amanda Prestigiacomo, Seabrook, Texas*

This hearty luncheon salad is a great way to use up leftover steak. Pepper strips give the chilled medley color while store-bought Italian dressing makes assembly a breeze.

1-1/2   **cups thinly sliced cooked beef rib eye steak (1/2 pound, see Grilled Rib Eye Steaks, p. 187)**

1   **small green pepper, julienned**

1   **small sweet yellow pepper, julienned**

1   **small sweet orange pepper, julienned**

1   **small sweet red pepper, julienned**

1   **can (6 ounces) pitted ripe olives, drained**

1/3   **cup prepared Italian salad dressing**

1 In a large bowl, combine the steak, peppers and olives. Drizzle with salad dressing; toss to coat. **Yield:** 7 servings.

Speedy Sliced Peppers

Here's a time-saving technique for slicing sweet peppers. Holding the pepper by the stem, use a chef's knife to slice straight down from the top of the pepper to the bottom. Continue around the pepper, slicing around the seeds. Discard the stem, center and seeds, then slice the pepper pieces into strips or chop as desired.

Versatile Beef Mix | *Joanne Rocchetti, New London, Connecticut*

This quick-and-easy mix uses only 1 pound of ground beef, yet it can be used to prepare the three recipes that follow, which are suitable for single serving meals.

1 **egg**
1/2 **cup dry bread crumbs**
2 **tablespoons 2% milk**
1 **teaspoon salt**
1 **teaspoon dried thyme**
1/4 **teaspoon pepper**
1 **pound lean ground beef**

1 In a large bowl, combine the egg, bread crumbs, milk, salt, thyme and pepper; crumble beef over mixture and mix well. Divide into four portions; place in freezer containers. May be frozen for up to 3 months. Thaw in the refrigerator before using. **Yield:** 4 portions.

Bacon Salisbury Steak | *Joanne Rocchetti, New London, Connecticut*

Bacon gives this saucy steak a satisfying, smoky flavor. Using one portion of the beef mix makes an ideal dinner for one, but just double the recipe to serve two.

1 **bacon strip, cut into 2-inch pieces**
1 **portion Versatile Beef Mix (see recipe above), thawed**
1 **teaspoon dried parsley flakes**
1 **teaspoon dried minced onion**
2 **tablespoons all-purpose flour**
1/3 **cup beef gravy**
2 **tablespoons water**

1 In a small skillet, cook bacon over medium heat until crisp. Meanwhile, place beef mix in a small bowl; stir in parsley and onion. Shape into a patty; coat with flour. Using a slotted spoon, remove bacon to paper towel to drain.

2 In the drippings, brown the patty on both sides. Add gravy and water. Bring to a boil. Reduce heat; cover and simmer for 15-20 minutes or until meat is no longer pink. Top with bacon. **Yield:** 1 serving.

Meatball Stew | *Joanne Rocchetti, New London, Connecticut*

This hearty stew is sure to warm you both up on a cool night, so double the recipe to use two portions of the beef mix. It's great served with a crusty bread.

1   portion Versatile Beef Mix (see recipe, p. 189), thawed
2   tablespoons all-purpose flour
2   teaspoons canola oil
1   small potato, peeled and quartered
1   small carrot, cut into 1-inch pieces
1/2 cup beef gravy
1/3 cup water
1/3 cup sliced celery
1/4 cup chopped onion
1   teaspoon Worcestershire sauce
1   garlic clove, minced
1/8 teaspoon paprika
Dash dried thyme

1 Shape beef mix into three meatballs; coat with flour. In a large skillet, brown meatballs in oil on all sides. Remove and keep warm.

2 Add the remaining ingredients to the skillet. Bring to a boil. Reduce heat; cover and simmer for 20 minutes.

3 Stir in meatballs. Bring to a boil. Reduce heat; cover and simmer 15 minutes longer or until meat is no longer pink. **Yield:** 1 serving.

Microwave Meat Loaf | *Joanne Rocchetti, New London, Connecticut*

Tomato sauce drapes this well-seasoned mini loaf that's a snap to fix with my Versatile Beef Mix. Since this is cooked in the microwave, you'll have your dinner for one on the table in no time.

1 portion Versatile Beef Mix (see recipe, p. 189), thawed
1/4 cup tomato sauce or meatless spaghetti sauce, divided
2 tablespoons chopped onion
1/4 teaspoon Italian seasoning

1 Place beef mix in a small bowl; add 2 tablespoons tomato sauce, onion and Italian seasoning. Mix well; shape into a loaf.

2 Place in a microwave-safe shallow baking dish coated with cooking spray. Cover and microwave on high for 3-4 minutes or until a meat thermometer reads 165°.

3 Place remaining tomato sauce in a small microwave-safe bowl. Cover and microwave on high for 15 seconds or until heated through. Pour over meat loaf. **Yield:** 1 serving.

Editor's Note: This recipe was tested in a 1,100-watt microwave.

Stew Turned into Chili | *Don Trumbly, Paola, Kansas*

A big pot of this tasty blend can be enjoyed two ways—as a satisfying stew or a zippy chili.

5 pounds beef stew meat, cut into 3/4-inch cubes
5 garlic cloves, minced
3 tablespoons canola oil
4 cans (14-1/2 ounces each) diced tomatoes with green peppers and onions, undrained
2 teaspoons salt
1 teaspoon pepper
2 cans (16 ounces each) kidney beans, rinsed and drained
2 cans (15-1/2 ounces each) great northern beans, rinsed and drained
ADDITIONAL INGREDIENTS (for each batch of chili):
1 jar (16 ounces) picante sauce
1 to 2 teaspoons chili powder
Sour cream and chopped green onions, optional

1 In a Dutch oven, brown beef and garlic in oil until meat is no longer pink; drain. Add tomatoes, salt and pepper. Bring to a boil. Reduce heat; cover and simmer for 1-1/4 hours.

2 Stir in the beans. Cover and simmer 30-45 minutes longer or until meat is tender. Serve desired amount. Cool remaining stew; transfer in 4-cup portions to freezer containers. May be frozen for up to 3 months.

3 For each batch of chili: Thaw in the refrigerator overnight. Stir picante sauce and chili powder into the meat mixture. Bring to a boil. Reduce heat; cook until heated through, stirring occasionally. Serve with sour cream and green onions if desired. **Yield:** 4 batches of stew (16 cups total).

Three-Meat Sauce | *Lillian Di Senso, Lake Havasu City, Arizona*

This authentic Italian spaghetti sauce recipe makes a big batch. Very robust with lots of meat and a zippy flavor, it's wonderful over your favorite pasta and in the two recipes that follow.

1   **boneless chuck roast (2-1/2 to 3 pounds), trimmed and cut into 1-inch cubes**

1   **pork shoulder roast (2 to 2-1/2 pounds), trimmed and cut into 1-inch cubes**

1   **pound Italian sausage links, cut into 1-inch slices**

3   **tablespoons olive oil**

3   **large onions, chopped**

5   **cans (15 ounces each) tomato sauce**

3   **cans (6 ounces each) tomato paste**

1   **cup water**

1/2   **cup minced fresh parsley or 3 tablespoons dried parsley flakes**

1/2   **cup minced fresh oregano or 3 tablespoons dried oregano**

5   **teaspoons salt**

2   **teaspoons pepper**

1 In a large Dutch oven or stockpot, brown beef, pork and sausage in oil; drain. Add onions; cook until tender. Add the tomato sauce and paste, water, parsley, oregano, salt and pepper. Bring to a boil. Reduce heat; cover and simmer for 2-1/2 to 3 hours or until beef and pork are tender.

2 For 4-6 people, serve 4 cups of the meat sauce over 1 pound of cooked and drained spaghetti. Refrigerate or freeze remaining sauce for up to 3 months. **Yield:** 18 cups.

Quick Calzones | *Taste of Home Test Kitchen*

Here's a winning way to use up leftover meat sauce—hearty calzones that taste like they're made from scratch. Frozen bread dough makes them a snap to assemble and creates a tasty crust, thanks to the Parmesan topping.

- 1 loaf (1 pound) frozen bread dough, thawed
- 1 cup Three-Meat Sauce (see recipe, p. 192), thawed
- 1/4 cup shredded part-skim mozzarella cheese
- 1 to 2 tablespoons milk
- 1 tablespoon grated Parmesan cheese
- 1/2 teaspoon Italian seasoning

1 Divide the bread dough into four portions; roll each into a 6-in. circle. Spoon 1/4 cup of meat sauce on half of each circle to within 1/2 in. of edges. Sprinkle each with 1 tablespoon mozzarella cheese.

2 Fold dough over filling and press edges firmly to seal. Brush with milk. Combine Parmesan cheese and Italian seasoning; sprinkle over the calzones.

3 Place calzones on a greased baking sheet. Bake at 350° for 20 minutes or until golden brown. **Yield:** 4 servings.

Easy Lasagna | *Pam Beerens, Evart, Michigan*

For a supper to please a crowd, layer lasagna noodles with the homemade meat sauce and a delicious cottage cheese mixture to create this speedy version of a traditional favorite.

- 1-1/2 cups (12 ounces) 4% cottage cheese
- 1 egg
- 1/4 cup grated Parmesan cheese
- 1 tablespoon minced fresh parsley
- 1/2 teaspoon dried oregano
- 1/4 teaspoon dried basil
- 9 lasagna noodles, cooked, rinsed and drained
- 4 cups Three-Meat Sauce (see recipe, p. 192), thawed
- 2 cups (8 ounces) shredded part-skim mozzarella cheese

1 In a large bowl, combine the cottage cheese, egg, Parmesan cheese, parsley, oregano and basil. In a greased 13-in. x 9-in. baking dish, layer a third of the noodles, meat sauce, cottage cheese mixture and mozzarella. Repeat layers twice.

2 Cover and bake at 350° for 30 minutes. Uncover; bake 15-20 minutes longer or until bubbly. Let stand for 15 minutes. **Yield:** 12 servings.

Beef 'n' Bean Starter | *Nancy Ware, Enon, Ohio*

My slow cooker does most of the work when I prepare this hearty beef and bean mixture. Once it's done, I divide it into two freezer bags. When you're racing against the clock, pull a bag of starter from the freezer to fix a warming chili or soup.

2-1/2 **pounds beef stew meat, cut into 1-inch cubes**

2 **cans (14-1/2 ounces each) diced tomatoes with garlic and onions, undrained**

1 **can (16 ounces) kidney beans, rinsed and drained**

1 **can (15-1/2 ounces) great northern beans, rinsed and drained**

1 **teaspoon salt**

1/2 **teaspoon pepper**

1 In a 3-qt. slow cooker, combine all of the ingredients. Cover and cook on low for 8-9 hours or until beef is tender. Cool.

2 Transfer 4 cups to each of two freezer bags or freezer-safe containers. May be frozen for up to 3 months. **Yield:** 8 cups.

Beef 'n' Bean Chili | *Nancy Ware, Enon, Ohio*

Picante sauce, green onions and a little seasoning go a long way when combined with my beef and bean mixture. Warm up a winter night with this tangy change-of-pace chili. Your family will enjoy the flavor, and you'll appreciate the time you saved.

4 **cups Beef 'n' Bean Starter (see recipe above), thawed**

1 **jar (16 ounces) picante sauce**

1/2 **cup sliced green onions**

2 **teaspoons chili powder**

Sour cream, optional

1 In a large saucepan, combine the Beef 'n' Bean Starter, picante sauce, onions and chili powder. Cook, uncovered, over medium heat until heated through. Serve with sour cream if desired. **Yield:** 5 servings.

Tasty Chili Toppers

A dollop of sour cream brings cool contrast to a warm bowl of nicely seasoned chili. But there are plenty of other garnishes that can add interest. Sprinkle on shredded cheddar or Monterey Jack for a savory touch. For crunch, toss on a few oyster crackers, salad croutons or fried tortilla strips. For color, add chopped green onions or sweet red pepper. Serve a selection of toppings in small bowls and let your family choose their favorites.

Beef 'n' Bean Tortellini Soup | *Nancy Ware, Enon, Ohio*

Chock-full of vegetables, beans and tortellini, this sensational soup is a fast fix when you have the easy-to-make starter mix on hand. Simply stir in four ingredients and simmer. Then slice a loaf of crusty bread, and dinner is served.

4 cups Beef 'n' Bean Starter (see recipe, p. 194), thawed

2 cans (14-1/2 ounces each) beef broth

2 cups frozen broccoli stir-fry vegetable blend

1 cup frozen cheese tortellini

3/4 teaspoon Italian seasoning

Shredded Parmesan cheese, optional

1 In a large saucepan, combine the Beef 'n' Bean Starter, broth, vegetables, tortellini and Italian seasoning. Bring to a boil. Reduce heat; cook and stir for 6-8 minutes or until vegetables and tortellini are tender. Garnish with Parmesan cheese if desired. **Yield:** 8 servings.

Turkey with Cranberry Sauce | *Marie Ramsden, Fairgrove, Michigan*

This is a very tasty and easy way to cook turkey breast in the slow cooker. The sweet cranberry sauce complements the turkey nicely. It makes a lot, so it's ideal for holiday potlucks, or you can use the leftovers in the two recipes that follow.

> 2 **boneless skinless turkey breast halves (4 pounds each)**
> 1 **can (14 ounces) jellied cranberry sauce**
> 1/2 **cup plus 2 tablespoons water, divided**
> 1 **envelope onion soup mix**
> 2 **tablespoons cornstarch**

1 Cut each turkey breast in half; place in two 5-qt. slow cookers. In a large bowl, combine the cranberry sauce, 1/2 cup water and soup mix. Pour half over each turkey. Cover and cook on low for 4-6 hours or until turkey is no longer pink and meat thermometer reads 170°. Remove turkey and keep warm.

2 Transfer both cranberry mixtures to a large saucepan. Combine the cornstarch and remaining water until smooth. Bring cranberry mixture to a boil; gradually stir in cornstarch mixture until smooth. Cook and stir for 2 minutes or until thickened. Slice turkey; serve with cranberry sauce. Leftover turkey may be frozen for up to 3 months. **Yield:** 20-25 servings.

Curried Turkey Salad | *Jo Crouch, East Alton, Illinois*

Leftover turkey gets a face-lift with grapes, peanuts and celery, then the ingredients are tied together with a creamy curry dressing. The colorful combination's great for a light lunch or dinner.

3	cups cubed cooked turkey (see Turkey with Cranberry Sauce, p. 196)
1-1/2	cups seedless red grapes, halved
4	celery ribs, chopped
2/3	cup mayonnaise
2	tablespoons lemon juice
1	to 2 teaspoons curry powder
1/2	to 1 teaspoon salt
1	to 2 teaspoons sugar, optional
1/2	cup salted peanuts

1 In a large bowl, combine the turkey, grapes and celery. In a small bowl, combine the mayonnaise, lemon juice, curry powder, salt and sugar if desired. Pour over turkey mixture and toss to coat. Cover and refrigerate for 1 hour. Just before serving, stir in the peanuts. **Yield:** 6-8 servings.

Crunchy Turkey Casserole | *Lois Koogler, Sidney, Ohio*

This comforting casserole, which makes the most of extra turkey, is perfect for a family supper or potluck. With its appealing crunch from water chestnuts, almonds and chow mein noodles, it's enjoyed by all.

2	cans (10-3/4 ounces each) condensed cream of mushroom soup, undiluted
1/2	cup milk or chicken broth
4	cups cubed cooked turkey (see Turkey with Cranberry Sauce, p. 196)
2	celery ribs, thinly sliced
1	small onion, chopped
1	can (8 ounces) sliced water chestnuts, drained and halved
1	tablespoon soy sauce
1	can (3 ounces) chow mein noodles
1/2	cup slivered almonds

1 In a large bowl, combine soup and milk. Stir in the turkey, celery, onion, water chestnuts and soy sauce.

2 Transfer to a greased shallow 2-qt. baking dish. Sprinkle with noodles and almonds. Bake, uncovered, at 350° for 30 minutes or until heated through. **Yield:** 6-8 servings.

Basic Beef Starter | *Amie Wollgast, Florissant, Missouri*

I store this savory combination of ground beef, onions and garlic in my freezer. It gives me a head start on the two easy entrees that follow and saves me many hours in the kitchen.

5 pounds ground beef
4 medium onions, chopped
3 garlic cloves, minced
1 bottle (12 ounces) chili sauce
1 envelope brown gravy mix
1 envelope onion soup mix
1 teaspoon salt

1 In a Dutch oven, cook the beef, onions and garlic over medium heat until meat is no longer pink; drain. Stir in the remaining ingredients. Cook for 10 minutes or until heated through. Cool.

2 Place about 2-3/4 cups each in four freezer containers. May be frozen for up to 3 months. **Yield:** 4 portions (11-1/2 cups).

Start-Ahead Stroganoff | *Amie Wollgast, Florissant, Missouri*

It only takes a few moments to stir up this hearty Stroganoff when you have a portion of my basic beef mix on hand. Simply combine it with canned mushrooms and a few other items and simmer gently. Then ladle servings over cooked noodles for a sensational supper in no time.

1 portion Basic Beef Starter (see recipe above), thawed
1 can (4 ounces) mushroom stems and pieces, drained
1 teaspoon beef bouillon granules
1 teaspoon Worcestershire sauce
3 tablespoons all-purpose flour
1/2 cup cold water
1 package (8 ounces) cream cheese, cubed
Hot cooked noodles

1 In a large skillet over medium heat, combine the beef starter and mushrooms. Add the bouillon and Worcestershire sauce. Combine flour and water until smooth; stir into the beef mixture. Bring to a boil. Reduce heat; simmer, uncovered, for 5 minutes. Stir in cream cheese until melted. Serve with noodles. **Yield:** 4 servings.

Beef-Stuffed Peppers | *Amie Wollgast, Florissant, Missouri*

This dish takes just minutes in the microwave when you start with my tasty beef mix. Green peppers are stuffed with the ground beef blend, tomato sauce, rice and seasonings.

1	portion Basic Beef Starter (see recipe, p. 198), thawed
1-1/4	cups cooked rice
1	can (8 ounces) tomato sauce
1/2	teaspoon dried basil
1/8	teaspoon pepper
4	medium green peppers
1/3	cup shredded cheddar cheese

1 In a bowl, combine the beef starter, rice, tomato sauce, basil and pepper. Cut tops off green peppers and remove seeds. Spoon 1 cup of beef mixture into each pepper.

2 Place in a 10-in. round microwave-safe dish. Cover loosely; cook on high for 7-9 minutes or until peppers are tender, rotating a half turn once. Let stand, covered, for 3 minutes. Sprinkle with cheese. **Yield:** 4 servings.

Editor's Note: This recipe was tested in a 1,100-watt microwave.

Pork with Apricot Sauce | *Kris Wells, Hereford, Arizona*

Pork tenderloin gets dressed up with a sweet apricot sauce mildly seasoned with ginger. It makes an impressive entree, yet leaves plenty of extra pork that can be frozen for the two recipes that follow. The sauce is also good on baked ham.

4	pork tenderloins (1 pound each)
1	jar (12 ounces) apricot preserves
1/3	cup lemon juice
1/3	cup ketchup
1/4	cup sherry or chicken broth
3	tablespoons honey
1	tablespoon soy sauce
1/8	to 1/4 teaspoon ground ginger

1 Place tenderloins on a rack in a shallow roasting pan. Bake, uncovered, at 450° for 30-35 minutes or until a meat thermometer reads 160°. Cover; let stand for 10 minutes. Meanwhile, in a saucepan, combine the remaining ingredients. Cook and stir until heated through.

2 Slice the pork; serve 1-1/2 pounds with the apricot sauce. Refrigerate or freeze remaining pork for up to 3 months. **Yield:** 4-6 servings (2 cups sauce) plus 2-1/2 pounds leftover pork.

Chili Verde | *Jo Oliverius, Alpine, California*

Leftover pork adds heartiness to this zippy chili. It's great on a cool night with a stack of tortillas. I've taken it to many gatherings, and it's always gone when the party's over.

2 cups cubed cooked pork (about 1 pound, see Pork with Apricot Sauce, p. 200)
1 can (16 ounces) kidney beans, rinsed and drained
1 can (15 ounces) pinto beans, rinsed and drained
1 can (15 ounces) chili with beans, undrained
1 can (14-1/2 ounces) stewed tomatoes
1-1/2 to 2 cups green salsa
1 large onion, chopped
2 cans (4 ounces each) chopped green chilies
2 garlic cloves, minced
1 tablespoon minced fresh cilantro
2 teaspoons ground cumin

1 In a saucepan, combine all the ingredients. Bring to a boil. Reduce heat; simmer, uncovered, for 10 minutes or until heated through. **Yield:** 8 servings.

Freeze Extra Cilantro

Have more fresh cilantro than you can use right away? Freeze the extras to use later. Wash and drain whole sprigs, then pat dry with paper towels. Place a few sprigs at a time into small plastic freezer bags and freeze. Or chop cilantro and freeze in ice cube trays. Place a tablespoon in each section, cover with water and freeze. Frozen cilantro is best used in cooked dishes, not salads or salsas.

Barbecued Pork Sandwiches | *Melissa Norris, Churubusco, Indiana*

I found this recipe in one of my great-aunt's cookbooks. The original recipe called for beef, but I like to use leftover pork roast. My family loves these tangy sandwiches.

1/4 cup sugar
4 teaspoons cornstarch
1-1/2 teaspoons dried minced onion
1 teaspoon salt
1/4 teaspoon pepper
1-1/2 cups ketchup
3/4 cup water
1/4 cup cider vinegar
1/4 cup butter, cubed
3 tablespoons Worcestershire sauce
2 tablespoons lemon juice
1 tablespoon prepared mustard
3 cups sliced cooked pork (about 1-1/2 pounds, see Pork with Apricot Sauce, p. 200)
8 sandwich buns, split

1 In a large saucepan, combine the first 12 ingredients. Bring to a boil; cook and stir for 2 minutes or until thickened. Add pork; heat through. Serve on buns. **Yield:** 8 servings.

Mom's Meatballs | *Dorothy Smith, El Dorado, Arkansas*

This recipe makes a large batch of moist, flavorful meatballs. Serve some for dinner and freeze the extras and turn them into other delicious recipes like the two shared here.

1-1/2 **cups chopped onion**

1/3 **cup ketchup**

3 **tablespoons lemon juice**

1 **tablespoon Worcestershire sauce**

3/4 **cup crushed saltines (about 24 crackers)**

3 **pounds ground beef**

1 In a large bowl, combine the onion, ketchup, lemon juice, Worcestershire sauce and crackers. Crumble beef over mixture and mix well. Shape into 1-in. balls.

2 Place meatballs on a greased rack in a shallow baking pan. Bake, uncovered, at 400° for 10 minutes or until meat is no longer pink; drain. Serve immediately. Refrigerate or freeze remaining meatballs for up to 3 months. **Yield:** 7 dozen.

Meatball Minestrone | *Linda de Beaudrap, Calgary, Alberta*

As the busy parents of two boys, my husband and I are always on the lookout for quick meals. You don't have to thaw the frozen meatballs for this satisfying soup, so it's table-ready in moments.

6 **cups water**

1 **can (16 ounces) kidney beans, rinsed and drained**

1 **package (16 ounces) frozen mixed vegetables**

2 **tablespoons beef bouillon granules**

1 **tablespoon dried minced onion**

1 **bay leaf**

1 **teaspoon dried basil**

1 **teaspoon salt**

1/2 **teaspoon pepper**

4 **ounces spaghetti, broken into 2-inch pieces**

24 **frozen fully cooked meatballs (1/2 ounce each, see Mom's Meatballs above)**

1 **can (14-1/2 ounces) stewed tomatoes**

1 In a Dutch oven or stockpot, combine the water, beans, vegetables, bouillon granules, onion, bay leaf, basil, salt and pepper. Bring to a boil; add spaghetti. Reduce heat; cover and simmer for 10 minutes or until spaghetti is tender.

2 Add the meatballs and tomatoes; heat through. Discard bay leaf. **Yield:** 10-12 servings.

tasteofhome.com

Meatball Lasagna | *Addella Thomas, Mt. Sterling, Illinois*

I like to crumble leftover meatballs into a homemade spaghetti sauce I use in this cheesy lasagna. My family wants me to make this dish all the time. It goes over well at reunions, too.

2 cans (14-1/2 ounces each) diced tomatoes, undrained
1 can (8 ounces) tomato sauce
1 cup water
1 can (6 ounces) tomato paste
1 medium onion, chopped
1 garlic clove, minced
1 tablespoon dried basil
4 teaspoons dried parsley flakes
2 teaspoons sugar
Garlic salt to taste
8 uncooked lasagna noodles
24 frozen fully cooked meatballs (1 inch, see Mom's Meatballs, p. 204), thawed
1 egg
1 cup ricotta cheese
2 cups (8 ounces) shredded part-skim mozzarella cheese
3/4 cup grated Parmesan cheese

1 In a large saucepan, combine the tomatoes, tomato sauce, water, tomato paste, onion, garlic, basil, parsley, sugar and garlic salt. Bring to a boil. Reduce heat; cover and simmer for 20 minutes. Meanwhile, cook lasagna noodles according to package directions; drain.

2 Crumble meatballs into the sauce. In a small bowl, combine egg and ricotta cheese. Spoon 1 cup of the meat sauce into a greased 13-in. x 9-in. baking dish. Layer with half of the noodles, ricotta mixture, meat sauce, mozzarella and Parmesan cheeses. Repeat layers.

3 Cover and bake at 350° for 45 minutes. Uncover; bake 5-10 minutes longer or until golden brown. Let stand for 15 minutes before cutting. **Yield:** 8-10 servings.

Triple-Batch Beef | *Heidee Manrose, Burns, Wyoming*

Because I work full-time, I like to cook ahead and freeze meals so things aren't so hectic when I get home. I keep portions of this economical meat mixture in heavy-duty resealable plastic bags in the freezer. After a busy day, it's easy to fix one of the three variations I've included here.

1	boneless chuck roast (4 to 5 pounds), cut into 3/4-inch cubes
2	medium onions, chopped
4	garlic cloves, minced
2	tablespoons canola oil
1-1/2	cups water
1	teaspoon salt
1/2	teaspoon pepper

1 In a Dutch oven, cook the beef, onions and garlic in oil; drain. Stir in the water, salt and pepper. Bring to a boil. Reduce heat; cover and simmer for 1-3/4 to 2 hours or until meat is tender. Cool.

2 Divide beef and cooking liquid among three freezer containers; cover and freeze. May be frozen for up to 3 months. **Yield:** 3 batches.

Thick Beef Stew | *Heidee Manrose, Burns, Wyoming*

A portion of Triple-Batch Beef and a few extra ingredients create a real meat-and-potatoes meal. This comforting stew is sure to satisfy the heartiest of appetites.

1	portion Triple-Batch Beef (see recipe above), thawed
3	medium red potatoes, quartered and cut into 1/4-inch slices
1-1/4	cups water
1	to 1-1/2 teaspoons dried oregano
1	teaspoon salt
1	cup frozen peas
1	tablespoon cornstarch
2	tablespoons lemon juice

1 In a large saucepan, combine the beef, potatoes, water, oregano and salt. Bring to a boil. Reduce heat; cover and simmer for 10-15 minutes or until potatoes are tender. Add peas; heat through.

2 Combine cornstarch and lemon juice until smooth; gradually add to beef mixture. Bring to a boil; cook and stir for 2 minutes or until thickened and bubbly. **Yield:** 3 servings.

Chunky Chili | *Heidee Manrose, Burns, Wyoming*

This salsa-seasoned chili starts with chuck roast mixture. Since the meat is already cooked to tender perfection, this filling dinner stirs up in a jiffy. Choose a different salsa if you like your chili milder or hotter.

- 1 portion Triple-Batch Beef (see recipe, p. 204), thawed
- 1 jar (11 ounces) salsa
- 1/4 cup water
- 1 to 2 teaspoons chili powder
- 1 can (16 ounces) kidney beans, rinsed and drained

1 In a large saucepan, combine the beef, salsa, water and chili powder. Bring to a boil. Reduce heat; cover and simmer for 10 minutes. Stir in the kidney beans; heat through. **Yield:** 3-4 servings.

Herbed Beef Barley Soup | *Heidee Manrose, Burns, Wyoming*

Thyme comes through in this colorful soup that's chock-full of my tender beef mixture from the freezer. You can use any combination of vegetables you have on hand. Leftovers work especially well.

- 1 portion Triple-Batch Beef (see recipe, p. 204), thawed
- 3 cups water
- 1 cup frozen cut green beans
- 1 cup frozen sliced carrots
- 1/4 cup quick-cooking barley
- 1 tablespoon beef bouillon granules
- 1 teaspoon dried thyme
- 1/2 teaspoon salt

1 In a large saucepan, combine all ingredients. Bring to a boil. Reduce heat; cover and simmer for 10-14 minutes or until vegetables and barley are tender. Let stand for 5 minutes before serving. **Yield:** 4 servings.

Editor's Note: 2 cups of cubed cooked beef and 1/2 cup beef broth may be substituted.

Broiled Sirloin | *Sue Ross, Casa Grande, Arizona*

Serve this succulent beef with fluffy mashed potatoes, fresh greens and crusty bread—it's a meal fit for company! Or, serve for dinner and freeze the leftovers for the sandwiches and stir-fry that follow.

1	medium onion, chopped
1/2	cup lemon juice
1/4	cup canola oil
1	teaspoon garlic salt
1	teaspoon dried thyme
1	teaspoon dried oregano
1/2	teaspoon celery salt
1/2	teaspoon pepper
3	pounds boneless beef sirloin or round steak (about 1 inch thick)
2	tablespoons butter, melted

1 In a large resealable bag, combine the onion, lemon juice, oil, garlic salt, thyme, oregano, celery salt and pepper; add beef. Seal bag and turn to coat; refrigerate for 6 hours or overnight.

2 Drain and discard marinade. Broil steak 6 in. from the heat for 8 minutes. Brush with butter and turn. Broil 6 minutes longer or until meat reaches desired doneness (for medium-rare, a meat thermometer should read 145°; medium, 160°; well-done, 170°). Serve immediately. Freeze leftovers in 3/4-pound portions. May be frozen up to 3 months. **Yield:** 10 servings.

Pepper Steak Sandwiches | *Ruby Williams, Bogalusa, Louisiana*

The steak in these sandwiches is so tender and delicious, and the peppers add pretty color.

2 medium green peppers, julienned
1 small onion, sliced
4 garlic cloves, minced, divided
1 tablespoon olive oil
3/4 pound cooked beef sirloin or round steak (see Broiled Sirloin, p. 206), thinly sliced
1/2 teaspoon salt, optional
1/8 teaspoon pepper
1/4 cup butter, softened
4 French or Italian sandwich rolls, split and toasted

1 In a large skillet, saute the green peppers, onion and half of the garlic in oil until the vegetables are tender. Add the steak, salt if desired and pepper; heat through.

2 Blend butter and remaining garlic; spread over cut side of rolls. Place steak mixture on bottom halves; replace roll tops. **Yield:** 4 servings.

Sirloin Stir-Fry | *Kim Shea, Wethersfield, Connecticut*

This delectable stir-fry is quick to stir up and is perfect for a casual meal when time is at a premium.

1 medium onion, chopped
1 medium green pepper, chopped
1 medium sweet red pepper, chopped
3 garlic cloves, minced
2 tablespoons butter
1 can (14-1/2 ounces) Italian stewed tomatoes
2 to 3 teaspoons dried basil
2 teaspoons sugar
1 teaspoon garlic salt or 1/8 teaspoon garlic powder
1/4 teaspoon pepper
3/4 pound cooked beef sirloin or round steak (see Broiled Sirloin, p. 206), cut into thin strips
Hot cooked rice

1 In a skillet or wok, stir-fry the onion, peppers and garlic in butter until vegetables are tender. Add the tomatoes, basil, sugar, garlic salt and pepper. Bring to a boil. Reduce heat; cover and simmer for 5 minutes. Add steak; cover and simmer until heated through. Serve with rice. **Yield:** 4 servings.

Seasoned Hamburger Mix | *Dorothy Smith, El Dorado, Arkansas*

I prepare a large batch of this ground beef mixture and freeze it in small portions. It's the beginning of many made-in-minutes meals, including two of my favorites—Taco Bean Salad and Enchilada Dip that follow.

4 **pounds ground beef**
2 **large onions, chopped**
1 **teaspoon salt**
1/2 **teaspoon dried oregano**
1/2 **teaspoon pepper**
1/4 **teaspoon garlic salt**

1 In a large skillet, cook beef and onions in two batches over medium heat until meat is no longer pink; drain. In a large bowl, combine the beef mixture, salt, oregano, pepper and garlic salt. Freeze in 2-cup portions. May be frozen for up to 3 months. **Yield:** 5 portions (10 cups total).

Taco Bean Salad | *Dorothy Smith, El Dorado, Arkansas*

Storing Seasoned Hamburger Mix in the freezer helps me beat the clock when I'm creating this change-of-pace tossed salad. Guests love how it's chock-full of good stuff, including fresh tomatoes, chopped avocado and canned kidney beans.

Editor's Note: This recipe was tested in a 1,100-watt microwave.

3 **large tomatoes**
1 **head iceberg lettuce, torn**
6 **cups coarsely crushed tortilla chips**
2 **cups (8 ounces) shredded cheddar cheese**
1 **can (16 ounces) kidney beans, rinsed and drained**
1 **large ripe avocado, peeled and chopped**
2 **cups Seasoned Hamburger Mix (see recipe above), thawed**
1 **bottle (7 ounces) green taco sauce**
4 **green onions, chopped**
Ranch salad dressing or dressing of your choice

1 Chop two tomatoes; cut remaining tomatoes into wedges. In a large salad bowl, toss the lettuce, tortilla chips, cheese, beans, avocado and chopped tomatoes; set aside.

2 In a large microwave-safe bowl, combine hamburger mix and taco sauce. Cover and microwave on high for 2-3 minutes or until heated through. Spoon over salad; toss gently. Top with tomato wedges and onions. Serve with dressing. **Yield:** 10 servings.

Enchilada Dip | *Dorothy Smith, El Dorado, Arkansas*

This tasty dip combines convenient canned chili, tomato sauce, enchilada sauce and my Seasoned Hamburger Mix. Served with tortilla chips, it's an easy Mexican appetizer that will please a crowd.

2 cups Seasoned Hamburger Mix (see recipe, p. 208), thawed
1 can (15 ounces) chili with beans
1 can (10 ounces) enchilada sauce
1 can (8 ounces) tomato sauce
3/4 cup corn chips
1 cup (8 ounces) sour cream
1/2 cup shredded cheddar cheese
Tortilla chips

1 In a large bowl, combine the hamburger mix, chili, enchilada sauce, tomato sauce and corn chips. Transfer to a greased shallow 2-qt. baking dish.

2 Bake, uncovered, at 375° for 20-25 minutes or until heated through. Dollop with sour cream; spread carefully. Sprinkle with cheese. Bake 3-5 minutes longer or until cheese is melted. Serve with the tortilla chips. **Yield:** 10-12 servings.

Tomato Ground Beef Mix | *Lorraine Caland, Thunder Bay, Ontario*

After 50 plus years of cooking, I'm happy to find recipes like this one that help put a variety of meals on the table. This mixture is handy to keep in the freezer to jump-start the three main dishes shared here.

4   **pounds ground beef**
4   **medium onions, chopped**
4   **garlic cloves, minced**
3   **cans (28 ounces each) diced tomatoes, drained**
2   **cans (6 ounces each) tomato paste**
1   **pound fresh mushrooms, sliced**
4   **celery ribs, chopped**
2   **tablespoons minced fresh parsley**
1   **tablespoon salt**
1   **tablespoon Italian seasoning**
2   **to 3 teaspoons dried rosemary, crushed**
1   **teaspoon pepper**

1 In a Dutch oven, cook the beef, onions and garlic over medium heat until meat is no longer pink; drain. Stir in the remaining ingredients. Bring to a boil. Reduce heat; cover and simmer for 15 minutes. Uncover; simmer 15 minutes longer. Cool.

2 Freeze the mixture in 2-cup portions in freezer containers. May be frozen for up to 3 months. **Yield:** about 16 cups.

Beefy Vegetable Soup | *Lorraine Caland, Thunder Bay, Ontario*

For a satisfying lunch or dinner, serve bowls of this thick soup with fresh-baked bread. Brimming with chunks of veggies, it's easy to stir together with the meat mixture from your freezer.

2   **cups Tomato Ground Beef Mix (see recipe above), thawed**
3   **cups tomato juice**
2   **cans (10-1/2 ounces each) condensed beef consomme, undiluted**
2   **medium potatoes, peeled and cubed**
2   **celery ribs, thinly sliced**
2   **large carrots, grated**
1   **cup fresh or frozen peas**
1   **teaspoon sugar**
1/4   **cup uncooked long grain rice**

1 In a large saucepan, combine the beef mix, tomato juice, consomme, potatoes, celery, carrots, peas and sugar. Bring to a boil. Stir in rice. Reduce heat; cover and simmer for 20-25 minutes or until vegetables and rice are tender. **Yield:** 8-10 servings (about 2-1/2 quarts).

Italian Shepherd's Pie | *Lorraine Caland, Thunder Bay, Ontario*

The chunky beef mix adds heartiness to this quick, comforting supper. To give this flavorful shepherd's pie a pretty look, pipe on the mashed potatoes using a large star tip.

3 cups warm mashed potatoes (prepared with milk and butter), divided
2 medium carrots, grated
1/4 pound fresh mushrooms, chopped
1 tablespoon onion soup mix
2 cups Tomato Ground Beef Mix (see recipe, p. 210)
2 tablespoons grated Parmesan cheese

1 In a large bowl, combine 1 cup potatoes, carrots, mushrooms and soup mix. Spread in a greased 2-qt. baking dish. Top with beef mix and remaining potatoes. Sprinkle with Parmesan cheese.

2 Bake casserole, uncovered, at 350° for 40-50 minutes or until the potatoes are lightly browned. **Yield:** 4-6 servings.

Tangy Beef Salad | *Lorraine Caland, Thunder Bay, Ontario*

Store-bought Catalina dressing adds tangy-sweet flavor to this fast, fresh-tasting salad. It's loaded with good stuff, including crisp lettuce, tomatoes and beans. Add the corn chips last so they stay crunchy.

2 cups Tomato Ground Beef Mix (see recipe, p. 210)
6 cups torn iceberg lettuce
1 medium green pepper, diced
1 small onion, chopped
1 large tomato, cut into wedges
1 can (16 ounces) kidney beans, rinsed and drained
1 cup (4 ounces) shredded cheddar cheese
1 bottle (8 ounces) Catalina salad dressing
1/2 to 1 cup coarsely crushed corn chips

1 In a large saucepan, cook beef mix until heated through. In a large bowl, combine the lettuce, green pepper, onion, tomato, beans and cheese. Add beef mix. Drizzle with dressing. Sprinkle with corn chips. Serve immediately. **Yield:** 6-8 servings.

Apricot-Glazed Ham | *Galelah Dowell, Fairland, Oklahoma*

Glazing a bone-in ham with apricot jam gives it an attractive look and delicious flavor. It's the star of many of our Sunday suppers.

1/2   fully cooked bone-in ham (6 to 8 pounds)
1/2   cup packed brown sugar
  2   to 3 tablespoons ground mustard
Whole cloves
1/2   cup apricot preserves

1 Place ham on a rack in a shallow roasting pan. Score the surface of the ham, making diamond shapes 1/2 in. deep. Combine brown sugar and mustard; rub over surface of ham. Insert a clove in the center of each diamond.

2 Bake ham, uncovered, at 325° for 1 hour. Spoon the preserves over ham. Bake 15-30 minutes longer or until a meat thermometer reads 140° and ham is heated through. Slice and serve.

3 Remove ham from bone and cube. Refrigerate or freeze leftover ham for up to 2 months. **Yield:** 18-20 servings.

Scalloped Potatoes with Ham | *Emma Magielda, Amsterdam, New York*

I fix this saucy skillet dish often, especially when I'm running late, because it takes so little time to prepare. The recipe won first prize in our local paper some years back.

  4   medium potatoes, peeled and thinly sliced
  2   tablespoons butter
1/3   cup water
1/2   cup milk
  2   to 3 tablespoons dry onion soup mix
  3   tablespoons minced fresh parsley
  1   cup cubed process cheese (Velveeta)
  1   cup cubed fully cooked ham (see Apricot-Glazed Ham above)

1 In a large skillet, cook potatoes in butter until potatoes are evenly coated. Add water; bring to a boil. Reduce heat; cover and simmer for 14-15 minutes or until potatoes are tender.

2 Meanwhile in a small bowl, combine the milk, soup mix and parsley; stir in cheese. Pour over potatoes. Add ham; cook and stir gently over medium heat until cheese is melted and sauce is smooth. **Yield:** 4 servings.

Ham and Bean Chili | *Carol Forcum, Marion, Illinois*

Leftover ham gets an unusual treatment in this creative chili blend that features three kinds of convenient canned beans. I sometimes serve it in bowls over rice or corn bread and garnish it with cheese.

2 cups cubed fully cooked ham (see Apricot-Glazed Ham, p. 212)
1 medium onion, chopped
1 medium green pepper, chopped
1 garlic clove, minced
1 tablespoon olive oil
1 can (28 ounces) diced tomatoes, undrained
1 can (16 ounces) kidney beans, rinsed and drained
1 can (15 ounces) black beans, rinsed and drained
1 can (15 ounces) pinto beans, rinsed and drained
1 jar (8 ounces) picante sauce
1 can (8 ounces) tomato sauce

1/2 cup water, optional
1 can (2-1/4 ounces) sliced ripe olives, drained
1 teaspoon beef bouillon granules
1 teaspoon dried thyme
1 teaspoon salt
1/4 teaspoon pepper
Shredded cheddar cheese

1 In a large saucepan, cook the ham, onion, green pepper and garlic in oil until tender. Stir in tomatoes, beans, picante sauce, tomato sauce and water if desired. Bring to a boil. Stir in the olives, bouillon, thyme, salt and pepper. Reduce heat; simmer, uncovered, for 15-20 minutes. Garnish with cheese. **Yield:** 10 servings (about 2-1/2 quarts).

Herbed Pork Roast | *Carolyn Pope, Mason City, Iowa*

A combination of dry herbs gives pork an out-of-this-world flavor! This wonderful, moist roast is a family favorite—and it makes great company fare, too. Leftovers are delicious in the two recipes that follow.

2 tablespoons sugar
2 teaspoons dried marjoram
2 teaspoons rubbed sage
1 teaspoon salt
1/2 teaspoon celery seed
1/2 teaspoon ground mustard
1/8 teaspoon pepper
1 boneless whole pork loin roast (5 pounds)

1 Combine the sugar, marjoram, sage, salt, celery seed, mustard and pepper; rub over roast. Cover and refrigerate for 4 hours or overnight.

2 Place roast on a rack in a shallow roasting pan. Bake, uncovered, at 325° for 2-1/2 hours or until a meat thermometer reads 160°. Let stand for 15 minutes before slicing. Refrigerate or freeze leftover pork for up to 3 months. **Yield:** 12-14 servings.

Spicy Pork Sandwiches | *Myra Innes, Auburn, Kansas*

Here's a flavorful sandwich spread that's a fun alternative to standard mustard or mayo. It adds interest to leftover pork or most any sandwich meat, including turkey and roast beef.

1/2 cup mayonnaise
1-1/2 teaspoons finely chopped onion
1-1/2 teaspoons minced fresh parsley
1-1/2 teaspoons finely chopped celery
1-1/2 teaspoons picante sauce
1-1/2 teaspoons Dijon mustard
1/4 teaspoon salt
1/4 teaspoon pepper
10 slices whole wheat bread
5 slices cooked pork (see Herbed Pork Roast above)
Lettuce leaves

1 In a small bowl, combine the mayonnaise, onion, parsley, celery, picante sauce, mustard, salt and pepper. Spread about 1 tablespoon on each slice of bread. Top five slices with pork and lettuce; top with remaining bread. Refrigerate any leftover spread for another use. **Yield:** 5 sandwiches.

TIP

Sandwich Add-Ins

Be creative when making a sandwich and use what's in your pantry. Try ranch, creamy Italian, blue cheese, honey-mustard or creamy Caesar salad dressing in place of mayonnaise. Create your own signature spread by adding a secret ingredient, such as sun-dried tomatoes, chopped pickles, chopped olives or chopped chipotle peppers in adobo sauce.

Pork Noodle Casserole | *Barbara Beyer, Two Rivers, Wisconsin*

My grandmother taught me to make this hearty dish using leftover pork. We never have a family get-together without it. It's a great addition to a buffet and makes a filling meal with warm rolls.

3 cups cubed cooked pork (see Herbed Pork Roast, p. 214)

1 can (14-3/4 ounces) cream-style corn

1 cup chicken broth

4 ounces process cheese (Velveeta), diced

2/3 cup chopped green pepper

2/3 cup chopped onion

1 jar (4-1/2 ounces) whole mushrooms, drained

2 tablespoons diced pimientos

1/2 teaspoon salt

1/4 teaspoon pepper

8 ounces uncooked egg noodles

1 In a large bowl, combine the pork, corn, broth, cheese, pepper, onion, mushrooms, pimientos, salt and pepper. Add noodles; gently toss to coat.

2 Transfer to a greased 2-1/2-qt. baking dish. Cover and bake at 325° for 1 hour or until noodles are tender, stirring every 20 minutes. **Yield:** 6 servings.

Roasted Chicken | *Marian Platt, Sequim, Washington*

These two moist and tender chickens are a real time-saver on a busy weekend. A simple blend of seasonings makes them a snap to prepare, and they smell heavenly as they roast. Extra chicken from the second one is fabulous in the two recipes that follow.

2 **roasting chickens (about 5 pounds each)**
1 **teaspoon each salt, seasoned salt, celery salt and onion salt**
1/2 **teaspoon pepper**

1 Pat chickens dry. Place with breast side up in an ungreased 13-in. x 9-in. baking pan. Combine seasonings; rub over and inside chickens.

2 Cover tightly and bake at 400° for 1 hour. Uncover; bake 30 minutes longer or until a meat thermometer reads 180°. Cover and let stand for 10 minutes before carving one chicken. Serve one chicken immediately.

3 Cool the second chicken; debone and cube the meat and refrigerate or freeze up to 3 months. **Yield:** 4-6 servings per chicken.

Fast Chicken Divan | *Bertille Cooper, California, Maryland*

Frozen broccoli and leftover chicken get an easy—but elegant—treatment in this dish. The chicken is dressed up with a saucy blend of cream soup and mayonnaise, then covered with a golden, cheesy crumb topping.

2 **packages (10 ounces each) frozen broccoli florets or chopped broccoli**
3 **cups cubed cooked chicken**
2 **cans (10-3/4 ounces each) condensed cream of chicken soup, undiluted**
1 **cup mayonnaise**
1 **teaspoon lemon juice**
1 **cup (4 ounces) shredded sharp cheddar cheese**
3/4 **cup dry bread crumbs**
3 **tablespoons butter, melted**
1 **tablespoon sliced pimientos, optional**

1 In a large saucepan, cook broccoli in boiling water for 1 minute; drain. Transfer to a greased 11-in. x 7-in. baking dish; top with the chicken. Combine the soup, mayonnaise and lemon juice; spread over chicken. Sprinkle with cheese. Combine bread crumbs and butter; sprinkle over top.

2 Bake, uncovered, at 325° for 30 minutes or until bubbly and golden brown. Let stand for 10 minutes before serving. Garnish with pimientos if desired. **Yield:** 4-6 servings.

Editor's Note: Reduced-fat or fat-free mayonnaise is not recommended for this recipe.

Chicken Enchiladas | *Julie Moutray, Wichita, Kansas*

Leftover chicken is used to create a rich and creamy meal-in-one. This colorful dish has zippy flavor. It's a nice change of pace from beef enchiladas.

1	**can (16 ounces) refried beans**
10	**flour tortillas (8 inches), warmed**
1	**can (10-3/4 ounces) condensed cream of chicken soup, undiluted**
1	**cup (8 ounces) sour cream**
3	**to 4 cups cubed cooked chicken (see Roasted Chicken, p. 216)**
3	**cups (12 ounces) shredded cheddar cheese, divided**
1	**can (15 ounces) enchilada sauce**
1/4	**cup sliced green onions**
1/4	**cup sliced ripe olives**

Shredded lettuce, optional

1 Spread about 2 tablespoons refried beans on each tortilla. Combine soup and sour cream; stir in chicken. Spoon 1/3 to 1/2 cup down the center of each tortilla; top with 1 tablespoon cheese.

2 Roll up and place seam side down in a greased 13-in. x 9-in. baking dish. Pour enchilada sauce over top; sprinkle with the onions, olives and remaining cheese.

3 Bake enchiladas, uncovered, at 350° for 35 minutes or until heated through. Just before serving, sprinkle lettuce around enchiladas if desired. **Yield:** 10 servings.

Tex-Mex Chicken Starter | *Nancy Pease, Lafayette Hill, Pennsylvania*

I developed this seasoned chicken mixture to reduce meal preparation time. It's handy to keep in the freezer for a head start on three different meals. No one realizes they come from the same beginnings.

1/2	cup lemon juice
1/2	cup canola oil
3	tablespoons chili powder
1-1/2	teaspoons each garlic powder, ground cumin, dried coriander and dried oregano
3/4	teaspoon salt
3/4	teaspoon pepper
1/4	to 1/2 teaspoon cayenne pepper, optional
3	pounds boneless skinless chicken breasts, cut into 1-inch strips
3	medium onions, halved and sliced into rings
4	garlic cloves, minced

1 In a large resealable plastic bag, combine lemon juice, oil and seasonings. Add chicken. Seal bag and turn to coat; refrigerate for 1 hour.

2 In a large skillet over medium-high heat, bring chicken and marinade to a boil in batches. Reduce heat; cook and stir for 6 minutes or until juices run clear. Remove chicken with tongs to a large bowl.

3 In the drippings, saute onions and garlic until onions are crisp-tender. Pour over chicken and mix well. Cool for 30 minutes.

4 Divide mixture among three freezer containers. May cover be frozen for up to 3 months. Thaw before using. **Yield:** 6 cups.

Tex-Mex Chicken Pasta | *Nancy Pease, Lafayette Hill, Pennsylvania*

For a different treatment, the spicy chicken mixture from the freezer is coated with a cream sauce and served over hot cooked linguine. Sometimes I garnish this dish with fresh cilantro and fried tortilla strips.

1	package (16 ounces) linguine
1	medium sweet red pepper, chopped
2	teaspoons canola oil
2	cups Tex-Mex Chicken Starter (see recipe above)
1	cup fresh or frozen corn
1	cup heavy whipping cream
1/2	cup shredded Monterey Jack cheese

Minced fresh cilantro, optional

1 Cook linguine according to package directions. Meanwhile, in a large skillet, saute red pepper in oil until crisp-tender. Add the chicken starter and corn; heat through. Stir in cream and cheese.

2 Cook and stir over medium-low heat until the cheese is melted and sauce is thickened. Drain linguine; top with chicken mixture. Sprinkle with cilantro if desired. **Yield:** 4-6 servings.

Tex-Mex Chicken Fajitas | *Nancy Pease, Lafayette Hill, Pennsylvania*

To make this satisfying main dish, simply spoon the zesty chicken starter into warm flour tortillas, then sprinkle with cool toppings like fresh tomatoes, lettuce and sour cream.

1 **medium sweet red pepper, thinly sliced**
2 **teaspoons canola oil**
2 **cups Tex-Mex Chicken Starter (see recipe, p. 218)**
2 **tablespoons water**
8 **flour tortillas (7 inches), warmed**
Shredded Monterey Jack cheese, shredded lettuce, chopped tomato, sour cream and salsa, optional

1 In a skillet, saute red pepper in oil until crisp-tender. Add chicken starter and water; heat through.

2 Spoon filling down the center of tortillas; fold in half. Serve with the cheese, lettuce, tomato, sour cream and salsa if desired. **Yield:** 4 servings.

Tex-Mex Chicken Salad | *Nancy Pease, Lafayette Hill, Pennsylvania*

To create this colorful salad, top packaged greens with the warm chicken and onion combo, then toss in tomato, red pepper and shredded cheese. An easy dressing of zippy salsa and bottled vinaigrette adds the final, flavorful touch.

1 **medium sweet red pepper, julienned**
2 **teaspoons canola oil**
2 **cups Tex-Mex Chicken Starter (see recipe, p. 218)**
1 **package (10 ounces) ready-to-serve salad greens**
1 **medium tomato, chopped**
1 **medium onion, chopped**
1 **cup (4 ounces) shredded Monterey Jack cheese**
1-1/2 **cups salsa**
1/3 **cup prepared vinaigrette salad dressing**

1 In a large skillet, saute red pepper in oil until crisp-tender. Add chicken starter; heat through.

2 In a salad bowl, combine the greens, tomato, onion and cheese. Top with chicken mixture. In a small bowl, combine salsa and vinaigrette until blended. Serve with salad. **Yield:** 6 servings.

Ham with Cherry Sauce | *Joan Laurenzo, Johnstown, Ohio*

This tangy fruit sauce with almonds is so wonderful over baked ham. I usually round out this dinner with sweet potatoes, coleslaw and rolls. The extra ham can be frozen to use in the two recipes that follow.

- 1/2 **fully cooked bone-in ham (6 to 7 pounds)**
- 1 **jar (12 ounces) cherry preserves**
- 1/4 **cup red wine vinegar**
- 2 **tablespoons light corn syrup**
- 1/4 **teaspoon each ground cloves, cinnamon and nutmeg**
- 3 **tablespoons slivered almonds**

1 Place ham on a rack in a shallow roasting pan. Score the surface of the ham, making diamond shapes 1/2 in. deep. Bake, uncovered, at 325° for 1-1/2 to 2 hours or until a meat thermometer reads 140°.

2 In a large saucepan, combine the preserves, vinegar, corn syrup, cloves, cinnamon and nutmeg. Bring to a boil, stirring often. Reduce heat; simmer, uncovered, for 2 minutes. Remove from the heat; stir in almonds. Serve with ham.

3 Remove remaining ham from bone and cube. Refrigerate or freeze leftover ham for up to 2 months. **Yield:** 10-12 servings (1-1/2 cups sauce).

Pretty Ham Primavera | *Joan Laurenzo, Johnstown, Ohio*

Leftover ham gets a face-lift in this tasty pasta dish that can be mixed up in a wink. The mild cream sauce gets fresh flavor from sauteed mushrooms and a boost of color from frozen peas.

- 1/2 **pound sliced fresh mushrooms**
- 1/3 **cup chopped onion**
- 2 **tablespoons olive oil**
- 2 **tablespoons all-purpose flour**
- 2 **teaspoons Italian seasoning**
- 2 **teaspoons chicken bouillon granules**
- 1/2 **teaspoon salt**
- 1/8 **teaspoon pepper**
- 2 **cups milk**
- 1 **package (7 ounces) thin spaghetti, cooked and drained**
- 2 **cups cubed fully cooked ham (see Ham with Cherry Sauce above)**
- 1 **package (10 ounces) frozen peas, thawed**

Grated Parmesan cheese, optional

1 In a large skillet, saute the mushrooms and onion in oil until tender. Stir in the flour, Italian seasoning, bouillon, salt and pepper until smooth. Gradually add the milk, stirring constantly. Bring to a boil; cook and stir for 2 minutes or until thickened.

2 Stir in the spaghetti, ham and peas; heat through. Sprinkle with the Parmesan cheese if desired. **Yield:** 4 servings.

Plantation Ham Pie | *Sharon White, Morden, Manitoba*

Pretty parsley pinwheels top this hearty casserole filled with a saucy mixture of broccoli, ham and onion. It also can be made with asparagus instead of broccoli. With a green salad, it's a satisfying supper.

4 cups cubed fully cooked ham
(2 pounds, see Ham with Cherry
Sauce, p. 220)

1 medium onion, chopped

2 tablespoons butter

2 cans (10-3/4 ounces each) condensed
cream of chicken soup, undiluted

1 cup milk

2 cups fresh or frozen broccoli florets

2 cups biscuit/baking mix

1/2 cup water

1/2 cup minced fresh parsley

1 In a large skillet, saute ham and onion in butter until onion is tender. Combine soup and milk; stir into ham mixture. Add broccoli; heat through. Pour into an ungreased shallow 2-1/2-qt. baking dish.

2 Combine biscuit mix and water until a soft dough forms. On a lightly floured surface, knead dough 10 times. Roll out into a 12-in. square; sprinkle with parsley.

3 Roll up jelly-roll style. Cut into 12 pieces; place over the ham mixture. Bake, uncovered, at 425° for 20-25 minutes or until biscuits are golden and ham mixture is bubbly. **Yield:** 6 servings.

Ground Beef Mix | *Candace Robinson, Newark, Ohio*

This beef mixture is one of my secrets to succulent suppers. I season a batch of ground beef, divide it into meal-size portions and keep it in the freezer. With a few additional ingredients, I can quickly whip up one of three entrees that use this mixture.

3	eggs
1-1/4	cups milk
2	cups crushed saltines (about 30 crackers)
2	large onions, chopped
2	teaspoons salt
1/2	teaspoon pepper
3-1/2	pounds ground beef

1 In a large bowl, combine the eggs, milk, cracker crumbs, onions, salt and pepper. Crumble beef over mixture and mix well.

2 Divide into three freezer containers. May be frozen for up to 1 month. **Yield:** 3 portions (14 cups total).

Bacon Meat Loaf | *Candace Robinson, Newark, Ohio*

For this fast family fare, I remove my seasoned Ground Beef Mix from the freezer. Since there's little preparation before popping it in the oven, this main dish is ideal for busy weeknights.

1	portion Ground Beef Mix (see recipe above), thawed
1	can (8 ounces) tomato sauce
4	bacon strips, halved

1 Shape beef mix into a loaf; place in a greased 11-in. x 7-in. baking dish. Top with tomato sauce.

2 Bake at 350° for 45 minutes. Cook bacon until almost done; place over loaf. Bake 10 minutes longer or until meat is no longer pink and a meat thermometer reads 160°. Let stand for 10 minutes before slicing. **Yield:** 4 servings.

Beef-Stuffed Shells | *Candace Robinson, Newark, Ohio*

To assemble this easy casserole, fill jumbo pasta shells with the seasoned beef mixture, then top them off with spaghetti sauce and mozzarella cheese. Add a green salad and breadsticks for a made-in-moments meal.

20 jumbo pasta shells
1 jar (26 ounces) spaghetti sauce, divided
1 portion Ground Beef Mix (see recipe, p. 222), thawed
1-1/2 to 2 cups (6 to 8 ounces) shredded part-skim mozzarella cheese

1 Cook pasta shells according to package directions; drain. Spread about 1 cup of spaghetti sauce in a greased 13-in. x 9-in. baking dish. Fill shells with beef mix; place in pan. Top with the remaining spaghetti sauce.

2 Cover and bake at 350° for 30 minutes. Uncover; sprinkle with cheese. Bake 10 minutes longer or until meat is no longer pink. **Yield:** 6-8 servings.

Meatballs with Gravy | *Candace Robinson, Newark, Ohio*

Preparing comfort food is a cinch when you have a batch of Ground Beef Mix in the freezer. Here, mouthwatering meatballs smothered in a savory sauce top hot cooked noodles for a satisfying dinner.

1 portion Ground Beef Mix (see recipe, p. 222), thawed
1 cup boiling water
1 teaspoon beef bouillon granules
1 can (10-3/4 ounces) condensed cream of mushroom soup, undiluted
Browning sauce, optional
Hot cooked noodles

1 Shape beef mix into 30 meatballs, about 1 in. each. In a large saucepan, combine the water, bouillon and soup. Bring to a boil; cook and stir until bouillon is dissolved.

2 Add the meatballs and browning sauce if desired. Reduce heat; cook until heated through and meat is no longer pink. Serve with noodles. **Yield:** 6-8 servings.

South Shore Pork Roast | *Pat Botine, Storm Lake, Iowa*

This moist pork roast is surrounded with a pretty combination of carrots and onion. It feeds a family of four with plenty left over for the two dishes that follow. And since the creamy gravy is served at the table, the leftover pork is easy to freeze and use.

1	boneless pork loin roast (3 to 3-1/2 pounds)
1/4	cup butter, cubed
1	cup chopped onion
1	cup diced carrots
1	teaspoon paprika
3/4	cup chicken broth
2	tablespoons all-purpose flour
1/2	cup sour cream
1	tablespoon minced fresh parsley
1/2	teaspoon salt

1 In a large skillet over medium heat, brown roast in butter for 5 minutes on each side. Transfer to a roasting pan. In the same skillet, saute onion and carrots until crisp-tender. Place around roast. Sprinkle with paprika. Add broth to pan.

2 Cover and bake at 350° for 1-1/2 hours. Uncover; bake 50 minutes longer or until a meat thermometer reads 160°.

3 Remove roast and vegetables to a serving platter; keep warm. Pour pan drippings to a measuring cup; skim fat. Add water to measure 2-2/3 cups.

4 In a small saucepan, combine flour and sour cream until smooth. Add drippings, parsley and salt. Bring to a boil; cook and stir for 2 minutes or until thickened. Serve with the roast.

5 Refrigerate or freeze remaining pork for up to 3 months. **Yield:** 10-12 servings (3-1/3 cups gravy).

Have It Your Way

TIP

The Pork Chow Mein recipe at right is a great dish to personalize. For instance, try instant brown rice instead of the white rice. The brown rice will add a nutty flavor. It does take a few minutes longer to cook though. Also add some shredded carrots or small broccoli florets to the vegetable mix. To jazz up the sauce, add a little sherry, sesame oil, chili oil or oyster or stir-fry sauce to the cornstarch mixture.

Roast Pork Soup | *Sue Gulledge, Springville, Alabama*

This satisfying, well-seasoned soup has a rich, full-bodied broth brimming with tender chunks of pork, potatoes and navy beans. Served with corn bread, it's one of our comfort foods in winter.

- **3** cups cubed cooked pork roast (see South Shore Pork Roast, p. 224)
- **2** medium potatoes, peeled and chopped
- **1** large onion, chopped
- **1** can (15 ounces) navy beans, rinsed and drained
- **1** can (14-1/2 ounces) Italian diced tomatoes, undrained
- **4** cups water
- **1/2** cup unsweetened apple juice
- **1/2** teaspoon salt, optional
- **1/2** teaspoon pepper

Minced fresh basil

1 In a Dutch oven, combine the pork, potatoes, onion, beans, tomatoes, water, apple juice, salt if desired and pepper. Bring to a boil. Reduce heat; cover and simmer for 45 minutes or until vegetables are crisp-tender. Sprinkle with basil. **Yield:** 9 servings.

Pork Chow Mein | *Deborah Stark, Cavalier, North Dakota*

This crunchy combination is quick to fix and a great way to use up leftover pork roast. I've substituted leftover turkey for the pork with equally pleasing results.

- **2/3** cup uncooked instant rice
- **2** tablespoons butter
- **1/2** teaspoon salt
- **1** large onion, chopped
- **2** celery ribs, sliced
- **1** medium green or sweet red pepper, chopped
- **1** teaspoon chicken bouillon granules
- **1-1/2** cups boiling water
- **1** cup cubed cooked pork roast (see South Shore Pork Roast, p. 224)
- **1** tablespoon cornstarch
- **1** tablespoon cold water
- **1** tablespoon soy sauce

Chow mein noodles

1 In a large skillet, saute rice in butter until golden brown. Sprinke with salt. Add the onion, celery and green pepper; cook until the vegetables are crisp-tender.

2 Dissolve bouillon in boiling water; stir into the rice mixture. Add pork; bring to a boil. Reduce heat; cover and cook for 5 minutes or until the rice is tender.

3 Combine the cornstarch, cold water and soy sauce until smooth; add to the skillet. Bring to a boil; cook and stir for 2 minutes or until thickened. Serve with chow mein noodles. **Yield:** 3 servings.

Make-Ahead Meatballs | *Ruth Andrewson, Leavenworth, Washington*

My husband and I often have company. Keeping a supply of these homemade meatballs in the freezer means I can easily prepare a quick, satisfying meal. I start with a versatile meatball mix that makes about 12 dozen meatballs, then freeze them in batches for future use.

4 **eggs**
2 **cups dry bread crumbs**
1/2 **cup finely chopped onion**
1 **tablespoon salt**
2 **teaspoons Worcestershire sauce**
1/2 **teaspoon white pepper**
4 **pounds lean ground beef**

1 In a large bowl, beat eggs. Add the next five ingredients. Crumble beef over mixture and mix well. Shape into 1-in. balls, about 12 dozen.

2 Place meatballs on greased racks in shallow baking pans. Bake at 400° for 10-15 minutes or until no longer pink, turning often; drain. Cool.

3 Place about 30 meatballs into each freezer container. May be frozen for up to 3 months. **Yield:** 5 batches (about 30 meatballs per batch).

Meatball Sandwiches | *Ruth Andrewson, Leavenworth, Washington*

These sandwiches are so yummy no one will guess frozen meatballs are your secret ingredient! The saucy meatballs also make easy appetizers if unexpected guests stop by.

1 **batch of 30 meatballs (see Make-Ahead Meatballs above), frozen or thawed**
1 **cup ketchup**
3/4 **cup packed brown sugar**
1/4 **to 1/2 cup chopped onion**
1/4 **teaspoon garlic powder**
1/8 **teaspoon Liquid Smoke, optional**
6 **sandwich rolls, split**

1 Place meatballs in an ungreased 1-qt. baking dish. Combine the ketchup, brown sugar, onion, garlic power and Liquid Smoke if desired; pour over the meatballs.

2 Cover and bake at 350° for 1 hour. Serve on rolls. **Yield:** 6 servings.

Editor's Note: These meatballs may be served as an appetizer with toothpicks instead of on rolls.

Sweet-and-Sour Meatballs | *Ruth Andrewson, Leavenworth, Washington*

A tangy sauce, combined with green pepper and pineapple, tranforms my Make-Ahead Meatballs into a delightful main dish served over rice.

1 can (20 ounces) pineapple chunks
3 tablespoons cornstarch
1/3 cup water
3 tablespoons cider vinegar
1 tablespoon soy sauce
1/2 cup packed brown sugar
1 batch of 30 meatballs (see Make-Ahead Meatballs, p. 226), frozen or thawed
1 large green pepper, cut into 1-inch pieces
Hot cooked rice

1 Drain pineapple, reserving juice. Set pineapple aside. Add water to juice if needed to measure 1 cup. In a skillet, combine cornstarch and 1/3 cup water until smooth. Stir in the pineapple juice mixture, vinegar, soy sauce and brown sugar. Cook over medium heat until thick, stirring constantly.

2 Add the pineapple, meatballs and green pepper. Simmer, uncovered, for 20 minutes or until heated through. Serve with rice. **Yield:** 6 servings.

Spaghetti 'n' Meatballs | *Ruth Andrewson, Leavenworth, Washington*

Use the frozen meatballs to dress up any purchased spaghetti sauce for a fast supper with real homemade appeal—and very little effort.

1 package (12 ounces) spaghetti
1 jar (28 ounces) spaghetti sauce
1 batch of 30 meatballs (see Make-Ahead Meatballs, p. 226), frozen or thawed
Grated Parmesan cheese, optional

1 Cook spaghetti according to package directions. Meanwhile, in a saucepan, combine spaghetti sauce and meatballs; cover and simmer for 15-20 minutes or until the meatballs are heated through.

2 Serve with spaghetti; top with Parmesan cheese if desired. **Yield:** 6 servings.

Cream Puff Shells | *Taste of Home Test Kitchen*

This easy recipe yields 16 buttery cream puff shells that freeze beautifully! They thaw in minutes and taste as yummy as the day you baked them. They're great filled with shrimp, turkey or ham salad.

1-1/4 **cups water**
  3/4 **cup butter**
  1/4 **teaspoon salt**
1-1/4 **cups all-purpose flour**
    5 **eggs**
    2 **tablespoons milk**
    1 **egg yolk**

1 In a large saucepan, bring the water, butter and salt to a boil. Add flour all at once and stir until a smooth ball forms. Remove from the heat; let stand for 5 minutes. Add eggs, one at a time, beating well after each addition. Continue beating until mixture is smooth and shiny.

2 Drop by 2 rounded tablespoonfuls 3 in. apart onto greased baking sheets. In a small bowl, whisk the milk and egg yolk; brush over puffs. Bake at 400° for 30-35 minutes or until golden brown. Remove to wire racks. Immediately split puffs open; remove tops and set aside. Discard soft dough from inside. Cool puffs. May be frozen for up to 3 months.

3 To use frozen cream puff shells: Remove from the freezer 15 minutes before filling. **Yield:** 16 cream puff shells.

Shrimp 'n' Slaw Puffs | *Taste of Home Test Kitchen*

Coleslaw mix and bottled dressing cut the prep time for this delicious shrimp salad to almost nothing!

    8 **ounces frozen cooked small shrimp, thawed and chopped**
    2 **cups coleslaw mix**
    2 **tablespoons chopped green onion**
    2 **tablespoons chopped sweet yellow pepper**
  1/4 **cup coleslaw salad dressing**
    1 **tablespoon capers, drained and patted dry**
    1 **teaspoon snipped fresh dill or 1/4 teaspoon dill weed**
  1/4 **teaspoon salt**
  1/4 **teaspoon pepper**
    4 **Cream Puff Shells**

1 In a large bowl, combine the shrimp, coleslaw mix, onion and yellow pepper. In a small bowl, combine the coleslaw dressing, capers, dill, salt and pepper. Pour over shrimp mixture and gently toss to coat. Refrigerate until serving. Just before serving, spoon 1/2 cup shrimp salad into each cream puff; replace tops. **Yield:** 4 servings.

Turkey Salad Puffs | *Taste of Home Test Kitchen*

Fresh mango, grapes and lemon juice add a splash of summer to this sweet and savory salad. The mixture is great tucked into cream puffs from the freezer—or served simply on lettuce leaves.

1-1/2 **cups cubed cooked turkey breast**
1/2 **cup chopped peeled mango**
1/4 **cup quartered seedless red grapes**
1/4 **cup pine nuts, toasted**
2 **tablespoons chopped celery**
5 **tablespoons mayonnaise**
1 **teaspoon lemon juice**
1/2 **teaspoon lemon-pepper seasoning**
1/4 **teaspoon garlic powder**
4 **Cream Puff Shells (see recipe, p. 228)**

1 In a large bowl, combine the turkey, mango, grapes, pine nuts and celery. In a small bowl, combine the mayonnaise, lemon juice, lemon-pepper and garlic powder. Pour over turkey mixture and gently toss to coat. Chill until serving.

2 Just before serving, spoon 1/2 cup turkey salad into each cream puff shell; replace tops. **Yield:** 4 servings.

Ham Salad Puffs | *Taste of Home Test Kitchen*

Flecked with pimientos and chives, this fast, flavorful ham salad boasts crunchy pecans, tart pineapple and chewy raisins. It's a delicious change-of-pace twist on traditional ham salad recipes.

1-1/2 **cups diced fully cooked ham**
1/2 **cup unsweetened crushed pineapple, drained and patted dry**
1/4 **cup golden raisins**
1/4 **cup chopped pecans, toasted**
1 **tablespoon diced pimientos, drained**
3 **tablespoons mayonnaise**
1 **tablespoon ranch salad dressing**
1 **tablespoon sour cream**
1 **tablespoon minced chives**
1/8 **teaspoon pepper**
4 **Cream Puff Shells (see recipe, p. 228)**

1 In a large bowl, combine the first five ingredients. In a small bowl, combine the mayonnaise, ranch dressing, sour cream, chives and pepper. Pour over ham mixture and toss gently to coat. Refrigerate until serving.

2 Just before serving, spoon 1/2 cup ham salad into each cream puff shell; replace tops. **Yield:** 4 servings.

Cook-Ahead Pork Chops | *Marge Anderson, Fergus Falls, Minnesota*

I found the recipe for these moist make-ahead pork chops in a magazine years ago and adapted a couple of our favorite recipes to work with them. It's handy to have them in the freezer for quick dinners.

- **4** bone-in loin pork chops (1 to 1-1/4 inches thick and 8 ounces each)
- **3/4** cup chicken broth

1 Place pork chops in an ungreased 9-in. square baking pan. Pour chicken broth over chops. Cover and bake at 350° for 45-55 minutes or until a meat thermometer reaches 160°. Cool.

2 Wrap each chop individually and place in a freezer bag; May be frozen for up to 4 months. **Yield: 4** servings.

Doubly Convenient

For larger families—or those who enjoy pork chops often, consider doubling this recipe so you have enough on hand to make more than a meal or two. Place eight pork chops in a 13-in. x 9-in baking pan and pour 1-1/2 cups chicken broth over chops. Cover and bake as directed, making sure a meat thermometer reaches 160°. Then wrap and freeze as directed.

Chops with Potato Gravy | *Marge Anderson, Fergus Falls, Minnesota*

For a change-of-pace supper, I simmer cooked pork chops in a white sauce made easy with a can of cream of potato soup. Served with noodles, it's a filling meal for two.

- **2** cooked bone-in pork loin chops (1 to 1-1/4 inches thick and 8 ounces each, see Cook-Ahead Pork Chops above)
- **1/2** teaspoon garlic salt
- **1/2** teaspoon poultry seasoning
- **1/8** to 1/4 teaspoon pepper
- **1** can (10-3/4 ounces) condensed cream of potato soup, undiluted

1 Thaw pork chops if frozen. Place in a skillet; sprinkle with garlic salt, poultry seasoning and pepper. Spread soup over chops.

2 Cover and cook over low heat for 20-25 minutes or until heated through. **Yield: 2 servings.**

Apricot Pork Chops | *Marge Anderson, Fergus Falls, Minnesota*

I like to give this sweet apricot treatment to cooked pork chops. I place the frozen chops in the refrigerator the night before. The next night, I can have supper on the table in less than a half hour.

2   **cooked bone-in pork loin chops (1 to 1-1/4 inches thick and 8 ounces each, see Cook-Ahead Pork Chops, p. 230)**

Salt and pepper to taste

1   **can (8-1/4 ounces) apricot halves, undrained**

1 Thaw pork chops if frozen. Place chops in an ungreased 8-in. square baking dish. Sprinkle with the salt and pepper.

2 Pour apricots over the chops. Cover and bake at 350° for 25-30 minutes or until heated through. **Yield:** 2 servings.

Fruitful Variation

A can of apricot halves adds a sweet touch to this simple pork chop entree. If you don't have canned apricots on hand, you can easily substitute canned peach halves instead. No apricots or peaches? Canned pear halves will work in a pinch.

Big-Batch Beef Sauce | *Debbie Hodge, Kitscoty, Alberta*

I prepare this beef mixture on weekends when I have a little more time. Having it in the freezer is a real time-saver during the week and a great way to serve unexpected guests. You can use the versatile sauce to get a head start on lasagna, chili and other swift suppers.

4	pounds ground beef
4	medium onions, chopped
5	celery ribs, thinly sliced
4	garlic cloves, minced
3	cans (28 ounces each) diced tomatoes, undrained
2	cans (6 ounces each) tomato paste
2	jars (4-1/2 ounces each) sliced mushrooms, drained, optional
1/4	cup minced fresh parsley
1	tablespoon salt
2	teaspoons dried oregano
2	teaspoons dried basil
1	teaspoon pepper
1/2	teaspoon crushed red pepper flakes

1 In a Dutch oven over medium heat, cook beef, onions, celery and garlic until meat is no longer pink and vegetables are tender; drain. Stir in the remaining ingredients. Bring to a boil; reduce heat. Simmer, uncovered, for 1 to 1-1/2 hours, stirring occasionally. Cool.

2 Transfer to freezer bags or containers, about 2 cups in each. May be frozen for up to 3 months. **Yield:** about 15 cups total.

Oven-Ready Lasagna | *Debbie Hodge, Kitscoty, Alberta*

When company drops in, I use this sauce to assemble this fabulous lasagna. Oven-ready noodles, which don't need to be cooked before they're layered in the baking dish, further speed preparation.

2	cups Big-Batch Beef Sauce (see recipe above), thawed
1	can (6 ounces) tomato paste
2	teaspoons dried basil
2	cups (16 ounces) 4% small-curd cottage cheese
1	egg
6	no-cook lasagna noodles
4	cups (16 ounces) shredded part-skim mozzarella cheese
1/3	cup shredded Parmesan cheese

1 In a saucepan, combine beef sauce, tomato paste and basil. Bring to a boil; reduce heat. Cover and simmer for 5 minutes. Combine cottage cheese and egg; mix well.

2 Spoon a third of the meat sauce into a 13-in. x 9-in. baking dish coated with cooking spray. Layer with three noodles, half of the cottage cheese mixture and a third of the mozzarella cheese. Repeat layers. Top with remaining meat sauce and mozzarella.

3 Cover and bake at 350° for 30 minutes. Uncover; sprinkle with Parmesan cheese. Bake 5-10 minutes longer or until bubbly and the cheese is melted. Let stand for 10 minutes before serving. **Yield:** 9-12 servings.

Time-Saving Tacos | *Debbie Hodge, Kitscoty, Alberta*

An envelope of taco seasoning gives Mexican flair to the frozen beef mixture in this tasty dinner. It has such a different flavor from the other variations that your family will never realize it's made from the same sauce.

- 2 cups Big-Batch Beef Sauce (see recipe, p. 232)
- 1 envelope taco seasoning
- 1/4 cup water
- 6 to 8 taco shells or flour tortillas

Shredded lettuce, chopped tomatoes, sliced ripe olives, shredded cheddar cheese, chopped onions, sour cream and salsa

1 In a large saucepan, combine the beef sauce, taco seasoning and water. Bring to a boil; reduce heat. Simmer, uncovered, until heated through.

2 Spoon about 1/4 cup meat mixture into each taco shell or tortilla. Serve with toppings of your choice. **Yield:** 3-4 servings.

Speedy Spaghetti | *Debbie Hodge, Kitscoty, Alberta*

On a busy weekday, I rely on this prepared meat sauce to put a spaghetti dinner on the table in minutes.

- 2 cups Big-Batch Beef Sauce (see recipe, p. 232)
- 1 can (8 ounces) tomato sauce
- 1 jar (4-1/2 ounces) sliced mushrooms, drained
- 2 teaspoons Italian seasoning

Hot cooked spaghetti

1 In a saucepan, combine the beef sauce, tomato sauce, mushrooms and Italian seasoning. Bring to a boil; reduce heat. Simmer, uncovered, for 5 minutes. Serve with spaghetti. **Yield:** 2-3 servings.

Weekday Chili | *Debbie Hodge, Kitscoty, Alberta*

It's so convenient to pull a batch of the meat out of the freezer to make this zippy chili.

- 2 cups Big-Batch Beef Sauce (see recipe, p. 232)
- 1 can (16 ounces) kidney beans, rinsed and drained
- 1 can (8 ounces) tomato sauce
- 1 to 2 tablespoons chili powder
- 1/4 teaspoon crushed red pepper flakes

Shredded cheddar cheese

1 In a large saucepan, combine the beef sauce, beans, tomato sauce, chili powder and red pepper flakes. Bring to a boil; reduce heat. Cover and simmer until heated through. Sprinkle each serving with cheese. **Yield:** 2-3 servings.

Taco-Seasoned Meat | *Taste of Home Test Kitchen*

Are Mexican-style entrees popular at your house? You'll appreciate the convenience of this seasoned meat that's tasty in traditional tacos and the two recipes that follow. Since you brown all the ground beef at once, you save time and cleanup when using the extras.

4 pounds ground beef
4 medium onions, chopped
4 envelopes taco seasoning

ADDITIONAL INGREDIENTS:
2/3 cup water
8 taco shells

OPTIONAL INGREDIENTS:
Shredded lettuce, shredded cheddar cheese, sliced ripe olives, sour cream and/or chopped tomatoes

1 In a Dutch oven, cook beef and onions until meat is no longer pink; drain. Stir in taco seasoning. Cool.

2 Spoon 2-1/2 cups into four resealable freezer bags. May be frozen for up to 3 months. **Yield:** 4 batches (10 cups total).

3 **To prepare tacos:** In a saucepan or skillet, combine water and 2-1/2 cups of seasoned meat. Bring to a boil; reduce heat. Simmer, uncovered, for 8-10 minutes, stirring occasionally. Spoon 1/3 cupful into each taco shell. Top with the lettuce, cheese, olives, sour cream and/or tomatoes if desired.

Taco Twist Bake | *Karen Buhr, Gasport, New York*

People of all ages enjoy this Mexican-flavored noodle bake that's convenient to make with seasoned ground beef from the freezer.

2-1/2 cups cooked Taco-Seasoned Meat (see recipe above)
2 cans (8 ounces each) tomato sauce
1/4 cup chopped green pepper
1 package (8 ounces) spiral pasta, cooked and drained
1 cup (8 ounces) sour cream
1 cup (4 ounces) shredded cheddar cheese, divided

1 In a large saucepan, combine the taco meat, tomato sauce and green pepper; bring to a boil. Meanwhile, combine pasta and sour cream; place in a greased 8-in. square baking dish. Sprinkle with 1/2 cup cheese. Top with meat mixture.

2 Bake, uncovered, at 325° for 25 minutes. Sprinkle with remaining cheese. Bake 5-10 minutes longer or until the cheese is melted. **Yield:** 4-6 servings.

Taco Corn Bread Squares | *Denise Hughes, Waynesville, Missouri*

Corn bread makes a delicious crust for this hearty meal that calls for Taco-Seasoned Meat from your freezer. I cut it into bite-size squares so it's less messy to eat. My family loves it!

1	package (8-1/2 ounces) corn bread/muffin mix
1	egg
1/3	cup milk
2-1/2	cups cooked Taco-Seasoned Meat (see recipe, p. 234)
1	can (16 ounces) refried beans
1	cup (8 ounces) sour cream
1-1/2	cups shredded Mexican cheese blend, divided
1/4	cup chopped onion
1	medium tomato, chopped
1	cup shredded lettuce
1	can (2-1/4 ounces) sliced ripe olives, drained

1 In a large bowl, combine the corn bread mix, egg and milk until blended. Spread into a greased 9-in. square baking dish.

2 Bake at 350° for 15 minutes. Combine taco meat and beans; spread over corn bread. Combine sour cream, 1 cup cheese and onion; spread over meat mixture.

3 Bake for 20-25 minutes longer or until heated through and cheese is melted. Sprinkle with the tomato, lettuce, olives and remaining cheese. **Yield:** 4-6 servings.

Sweet

Praline-Peach Brownie Sundaes

Praline-Peach Brownie Sundaes | *Jodi Trigg, Toledo, Illinois*

Adding fresh sliced peaches to a homemade praline sauce creates an irresistible topping for leftover brownies and some ice cream. The sundaes make a perfect ending to a summer supper.

1/4   cup packed brown sugar
1/4   cup heavy whipping cream
  2   tablespoons butter
1/4   teaspoon ground cinnamon
  2   medium peaches, peeled and sliced or 1 cup frozen unsweetened peach slices, thawed and patted dry
1/2   cup chopped pecans
  1   teaspoon vanilla extract
  6   prepared brownies (see Fudgy Brownies below)
  3   cups vanilla ice cream
Additional peach slices, optional

1 In a large saucepan, whisk the brown sugar, cream, butter and cinnamon until smooth. Bring to a boil; cook and stir for 6-7 minutes or until thickened. Remove from the heat; stir in the peaches, pecans and vanilla. Cool for 10 minutes.

2 Place brownies in dessert dishes; top with ice cream and peach sauce. Garnish with additional peach slices if desired. **Yield:** 6 servings.

Fudgy Brownies | *June Formanek, Belle Plaine, Iowa*

I've made these moist brownies many times, and they're always a hit. If your family doesn't gobble up the whole pan, you can freeze the leftovers to use to make other sweet treats.

  4   squares (1 ounce each) unsweetened chocolate, coarsely chopped
  1   cup butter, cubed
  4   eggs
  2   cups sugar
  1   teaspoon vanilla extract
  1   cup all-purpose flour
  1   cup (6 ounces) semisweet chocolate chips
  1   cup chopped pecans, optional
Confectioners' sugar

1 In a microwave, melt unsweetened chocolate and butter; stir until smooth and cool. In a large bowl, beat the eggs, sugar and vanilla for 1-2 minutes or until light and lemon-colored. Beat in chocolate mixture. Add flour; beat just until combined. Fold in chocolate chips and pecans if desired.

2 Transfer to a greased 13-in. x 9-in. baking pan. Bake at 350° for 25-30 minutes or until a toothpick inserted near the center comes out with moist crumbs. Cool on a wire rack.

3 Cut into bars. To serve, dust with confectioners' sugar or freeze. Brownies may be frozen for up to 6 months. **Yield:** 16-20 servings.

Brownie Cheesecake | *Dorothy Olivares, El Paso, Texas*

Crumbled brownies are stirred into the batter before baking, which gives this chocolate cheesecake a delectable sweet surprise.

1-1/2 cups crushed vanilla wafers (about 45 wafers)
6 tablespoons confectioners' sugar
6 tablespoons baking cocoa
6 tablespoons butter, melted

FILLING:
3 packages (8 ounces each) cream cheese, softened
1/4 cup butter, melted
1 can (14 ounces) sweetened condensed milk
3 teaspoons vanilla extract
1/2 cup baking cocoa
4 eggs, lightly beaten
1-1/2 cups crumbled brownies (see Fudgy Brownies, p. 237)
Whipped topping and pecan halves, optional

1 In a small bowl, combine the wafer crumbs, confectioners' sugar and cocoa; stir in the butter. Press onto the bottom of a greased 9-in. springform pan; set aside.

2 In a large bowl, beat cream cheese and butter until smooth. Beat in milk and vanilla. Beat in cocoa until well blended. Add eggs; beat on low just until combined. Fold in brownies. Spoon into crust. Place pan on a baking sheet.

3 Bake at 350° for 50-55 minutes or until center is almost set. Cool on a wire rack for 10 minutes. Carefully run a knife around the edge of pan to loosen. Cool 1 hour longer. Refrigerate overnight.

4 Remove sides of pan. Garnish with whipped topping and pecans if desired. Refrigerate leftovers. **Yield:** 10-12 servings.

Heavenly Angel Food Cake | *Fayrene De Koker, Vancouver, Washington*

This light, moist cake is my favorite. It tastes divine and is special enough for most any occasion. Leftover slices can be frozen to create the two desserts that follow.

1-1/2 cups egg whites (about 12)
1-1/4 cups confectioners' sugar
1 cup all-purpose flour
1-1/2 teaspoons cream of tartar
1-1/2 teaspoons vanilla extract
1/2 teaspoon almond extract
1/4 teaspoon salt
1 cup sugar

1 Place egg whites in a large bowl; let stand at room temperature for 30 minutes. Sift confectioners' sugar and flour together twice; set aside.

2 Add cream of tartar, extracts and salt to egg whites; beat on medium speed until soft peaks form. Gradually add sugar, about 2 tablespoons at a time, beating on high until stiff glossy peaks form and sugar is dissolved. Gradually fold in flour mixture, about 1/2 cup at a time.

3 Gently spoon into an ungreased 10-in. tube pan. Cut through the batter with a knife to remove air pockets. Bake on the lowest oven rack at 350° for 40-45 minutes or until lightly browned and entire top appears dry. Immediately invert pan; cool completely, about 1 hour.

4 Run a knife around side and center tube of pan. Remove cake to a serving plate. Leftover cake may be frozen for up to 6 months. **Yield:** 20 servings.

Caramelized Angel Dessert | *Sharon Bickett, Chester, South Carolina*

This quick-and-easy treat features a broiled, caramel-like sauce that's simply wonderful.

1/2   cup butter, softened
1/2   cup packed brown sugar
   1   tablespoon lemon juice
1/4   teaspoon ground cinnamon
Dash ground nutmeg
   6   slices angel food cake (see Heavenly
        Angel Food Cake, p. 238)
   1   cup mandarin oranges
Sour cream, optional

1 In a bowl, cream butter and sugar. Beat in the lemon juice, cinnamon and nutmeg until blended.

2 Spread about 1 tablespoon on the top and sides of each cake slice. Place on a baking sheet. Broil 4-6 in. from the heat for 1-2 minutes or until bubbly. Top with the oranges and sour cream if desired. **Yield:** 6 servings.

Cranberry Ribbon Loaf | *Patricia Kile, Greentown, Pennsylvania*

Leftover angel food cake is used to create this refreshing cranberry dessert...perfect for the holidays.

   1   package (3 ounces) cream cheese,
        softened
1/4   cup sugar
Dash salt
   1   can (16 ounces) whole-berry cranberry
        sauce
   1   cup heavy whipping cream, whipped
   6   slices angel food cake (1/2 inch thick,
        see Heavenly Angel Food Cake, p. 238)

1 Line bottom and sides of a 9-in. x 5-in. loaf pan with heavy-duty foil; set aside. In a large bowl, beat cream cheese, sugar and salt until smooth. Stir in cranberry sauce. Fold in whipped cream.

2 Spread a third of the mixture in prepared pan; top with three cake slices (cut cake if needed to fit). Repeat layers. Top with remaining cranberry mixture. Cover and freeze.

3 Remove from the freezer 15 minutes before serving. Use foil to remove loaf from pan; discard foil. Cut into slices. **Yield:** 8 servings.

Gingerbread Cake | *Shannon Sides, Selma, Alabama*

I drizzle a basic orange sauce over homemade gingerbread for this old-fashioned dessert. Cut just the number of squares needed and freeze the rest for the two delicious desserts that follow.

2-1/3 cups all-purpose flour
1 teaspoon baking soda
1 teaspoon ground ginger
1 teaspoon ground cinnamon
3/4 teaspoon salt

ORANGE SAUCE:
1 cup confectioners' sugar
2 tablespoons orange juice
1/2 teaspoon grated orange peel

1/2 cup butter-flavored shortening
1/3 cup sugar
1 cup molasses
3/4 cup water
1 egg

1 In a large bowl, cream shortening and sugar until light and fluffy. Add molasses, water and egg. Combine flour, baking soda, ginger, cinnamon and salt. Gradually add to creamed mixture; mix well.

2 Pour into a greased 15-in. x 10-in. x 1-in. baking pan. Bake at 350° for 18-22 minutes or until a toothpick inserted near the center comes out clean. Cool on a wire rack.

3 In a small bowl, combine the sauce ingredients until blended. Serve with cake. Leftover cake may be frozen for up to 6 months. **Yield:** 4 servings with sauce plus leftovers.

Gingerbread Men | *Taste of Home Test Kitchen*

Cookie cutters work well to form these fun and festive fellows. Kids of all ages will enjoy spreading the cutouts with soft, sweet white chocolate frosting, then giving them character by decorating with colorful store-bought candies.

1 piece (10 inches x 7 inches) Gingerbread Cake (see recipe above)
1/4 cup butter, softened
1-1/2 squares (1-1/2 ounces) white baking chocolate, melted
1/2 cup confectioners' sugar
Assorted candies

1 Using a 3-1/2-in. gingerbread man cookie cutter, cut out six men from the gingerbread cake. In a small bowl, combine the butter, chocolate and confectioners' sugar; beat for 2 minutes or until light and fluffy. Frost gingerbread men and decorate with candies as desired. **Yield:** 6 gingerbread men.

Gingerbread Trifle | *Betty Kleberger, Florissant, Missouri*

This tasty dessert was a hit when I served it to our Bible study group. It's a wonderful blend of flavors and a great ending to holiday meals. If you don't have leftover gingerbread, bake some from a boxed mix to assemble this delectable trifle.

2 cups cold milk

1 package (3.4 ounces) instant French vanilla pudding mix

7 cups cubed Gingerbread Cake (see recipe, p. 240)

3/4 cup English toffee bits or almond brickle chips

1 carton (8 ounces) frozen whipped topping, thawed

1 maraschino cherry

1 In a large bowl, whisk milk and pudding mix for 2 minutes. Let stand for 2 minutes or until soft-set.

2 In a 2-qt. serving bowl, layer half of the cake cubes and pudding. Sprinkle with 1/2 cup toffee bits. Top with remaining cake and pudding. Spread whipped topping over the top; sprinkle with remaining toffee bits. Garnish with cherry. **Yield:** 8-10 servings.

Delicate Chocolate Cake | *Annette Foster, Taylors, South Carolina*

A special friend gave me this recipe years ago. The cake has a light cocoa flavor, and the frosting is rich and delicious. The recipe makes a two-layer cake plus extra portions to freeze for the two treats that follow.

1/4 **cup baking cocoa**
1 **cup water**
1 **cup canola oil**
1/2 **cup butter, cubed**
2 **cups self-rising flour**
2 **cups sugar**
1/2 **cup buttermilk**
2 **eggs**

FROSTING (for the layer cake):

1/2 **cup butter, cubed**
1/4 **cup baking cocoa**
1/4 **cup milk**
4 **to 4-1/2 cups confectioners' sugar**
1 **teaspoon vanilla extract**

1 In a small saucepan over medium heat, combine cocoa and water until smooth; add the oil and butter. Bring to a boil; cook and stir for 1 minute. Remove from the heat.

2 In a large bowl, combine flour and sugar; gradually add cocoa mixture, beating well. Add buttermilk and eggs until well combined.

3 Pour into a greased 15-in. x 10-in. x 1-in. baking pan. Bake at 350° for 28-30 minutes or until a toothpick inserted near the center comes out clean. Cool on a wire rack.

4 Cut cake into four 7-1/2-in. x 5-in. rectangles. Wrap two of the rectangles separately in plastic wrap, then place in a resealable plastic bag; refrigerate or freeze for up to 6 months. Set the other two rectangles aside.

5 For frosting, in a small saucepan, combine the butter, cocoa and milk. Bring to a boil; cook and stir for 1 minute (the mixture will appear curdled).

6 Pour into a large bowl. Gradually add confectioners' sugar and vanilla; beat until frosting achieves spreading consistency. Spread frosting between layers and over the top and sides of cake. **Yield:** 1 two-layer cake (6-8 servings) plus 2 plain cake portions.

Editor's Note: As a substitute for 2 cups of self-rising flour, place 3 teaspoons baking powder and 1 teaspoon salt in a measuring cup. Add all-purpose flour to measure 1 cup. Add another cup of all-purpose flour to the mixture.

Butterscotch Banana Dessert | *Carol Haugen, Fargo, North Dakota*

This yummy sauce is terrific served warm over leftover chocolate cake or ice cream.

- 2/3 cup packed brown sugar
- 1/3 cup corn syrup
- 1/4 cup butter, cubed
- 1/4 cup water
- 1 egg yolk, beaten
- 1 piece chocolate cake (7-1/2-inch x 5-inch rectangle, see Delicate Chocolate Cake, p. 242), thawed and cut into four pieces
- 2 medium firm bananas, sliced

1 In a saucepan, combine sugar, corn syrup, butter, water and egg yolk. Cook over low heat, stirring frequently, until mixture thickens slightly and a thermometer reads 180°, about 20 minutes.

2 Place cake on serving plates; cover with bananas. Top with the warm butterscotch sauce. Sauce may be stored in the refrigerator for up to 3 days. To reheat sauce, heat in the microwave until simmering; whisk before serving. **Yield:** 4 servings (about 1 cup sauce).

Raspberry Chocolate Trifle | *Karena Bauman, Minneapolis, Minnesota*

Guests will think you slaved over this impressive-looking dessert...and it's a snap to assemble.

- 1 package (3 ounces) cream cheese, softened
- 2 tablespoons sugar
- 2 tablespoons milk
- 1-1/2 cups whipped topping
- 1 piece chocolate cake (7-1/2-inch x 5-inch rectangle, see Delicate Chocolate Cake, p. 242), thawed and cut into 1/2-inch cubes
- 2 cups fresh raspberries
- 1/4 cup slivered almonds, toasted

1 In a large bowl, beat the cream cheese, sugar and milk until smooth. Fold in whipped topping.

2 In a small trifle bowl or individual dessert dishes, layer half of the cake cubes, raspberries, cream cheese mixture and almonds. Repeat layers. Chill for at least 15 minutes. **Yield:** 4-6 servings.

Quick Baking Mix | *Alice Wrisley, Mohawk, New York*

A fast-to-fix bread is one of the best ways to dress up a meal any time of day. With this versatile mix in the freezer, you can make corn bread, biscuits and coffee cake. It's a great helper in the kitchen.

9 **cups all-purpose flour**
1/3 **cup baking powder**
1/4 **cup sugar**
3 **teaspoons salt**
1 **teaspoon cream of tartar**
2 **cups butter-flavored shortening**

1 In a large bowl, combine the flour, baking powder, sugar, salt and cream of tartar. Cut in shortening until the mixture resembles coarse crumbs.

2 Store in an airtight container in a cool dry place or in the freezer for up to 6 months. **Yield:** 12 cups.

Country Corn Bread | *Alice Wrisley, Mohawk, New York*

Using my from-scratch baking mix, it takes only minutes to whip up this corn bread. The squares have a lovely golden color and light texture.

1-1/2 **cups Quick Baking Mix (see recipe above)**
3/4 **cup cornmeal**
2 **tablespoons sugar**
1/2 **teaspoon salt**
1 **egg**
1 **cup milk**

1 In a large bowl, combine the mix, cornmeal, sugar and salt. Whisk the egg and milk; stir into dry ingredients just until moistened. Pour batter into a greased 8-in. square baking pan.

2 Bake at 400° for 20-22 minutes or until a toothpick inserted near the center comes out clean (corn bread will not brown). Cool for 10 minutes on a wire rack before cutting. **Yield:** 6-8 servings.

Golden Biscuits | *Alice Wrisley, Mohawk, New York*

These flaky biscuits are a snap to make with Quick Bread Mix. They're wonderful served warm with butter and honey...or use as a base for creamed dishes.

3 **cups Quick Baking Mix (see recipe above)**
2/3 **cup milk**

1 Place mix in a small bowl. Add the milk; stir just until combined. Turn onto a lightly floured surface; knead 10-15 times. Pat or roll out to 1/2-in. thickness; cut with a 2-1/2-in. biscuit cutter.

2 Place 2 in. apart on ungreased baking sheets. Bake at 425° for 12-14 minutes or until golden brown. Serve warm. **Yield:** 9 biscuits.

Cinnamon Coffee Cake | *Alice Wrisley, Mohawk, New York*

Tempt taste buds in the morning by stirring up this sweet and cinnamony breakfast treat. It calls for my homemade baking mix and just a few additional ingredients.

2-1/4 cups Quick Baking Mix (see recipe, p. 244)
1/3 cup sugar
1 egg
1/3 cup milk

TOPPING:
1/2 cup packed brown sugar
1 tablespoon all-purpose flour
1/2 teaspoon ground cinnamon
3 tablespoons cold butter

1 In a bowl, combine mix and sugar. Whisk the egg and milk; stir into dry ingredients just until moistened. Spread into a greased 9-in. square baking pan. For topping, combine the brown sugar, flour and cinnamon. Cut in butter until mixture is crumbly. Sprinkle over batter.

2 Bake at 400° for 18-20 minutes or until a toothpick inserted near the center comes out clean. Cool on a wire rack. **Yield:** 9 servings.

Peanut Butter Maple Cookies | *Lois Bowman, Swanton, Maryland*

I bake these crispy, yet chewy peanut butter cookies often. My grandchildren, both near and far, can't wait to dig into the cookie jar. If there are any leftovers, try them in the two special recipes that follow.

1	cup butter, softened
1/2	cup peanut butter
1	cup sugar
1	cup packed brown sugar
2	eggs
1	tablespoon maple syrup
2	teaspoons vanilla extract
2	cups all-purpose flour
3/4	cup quick-cooking oats
1-1/2	teaspoons baking powder
1	teaspoon baking soda
1	teaspoon salt
1	package (10 ounces) peanut butter chips

1 In a large bowl, cream the butter, peanut butter and sugars until light and fluffy. Add the eggs, one at a time, beating well after each addition. Beat in syrup and vanilla. Combine the flour, oats, baking powder, baking soda and salt. Gradually add to creamed mixture and mix well. Stir in the peanut butter chips.

2 Drop by heaping tablespoonfuls 2 in. apart onto ungreased baking sheets. Bake at 325° for 15-18 minutes or until golden brown. Cool for 1 minute before removing to wire racks to cool completely. May be frozen for up to 6 months. **Yield:** about 5 dozen.

Editor's Note: Reduced-fat or generic brands of peanut butter are not recommended for this recipe.

Peanut Butter Cookie Parfait | *Jamie Wright, Kalamazoo, Michigan*

You'll need just three ingredients to assemble this cool, creamy and crunchy dessert. It makes just a single sundae and is a perfect way to treat yourself...or someone special.

3	peanut butter cookies (see Peanut Butter Maple Cookies above), coarsely chopped
2/3	cup vanilla ice cream
3	tablespoons hot fudge ice cream topping, warmed

1 Set aside one large cookie piece. Sprinkle half of the chopped cookies in a parfait glass; top with half of the ice cream and hot fudge topping. Repeat. Garnish with reserved cookie piece. **Yield:** 1 serving.

Peanut Butter Icebox Dessert | *Nancy Mueller, Bloomington, Minnesota*

Leftover crushed cookies create the yummy crust for this crowd-pleasing dessert. It's covered with a smooth cream cheese mixture, chocolate pudding and whipped topping for a lovely layered look.

2-1/4 **cups crushed peanut butter cookies (about 11 cookies, see Peanut Butter Maple Cookies, p. 246)**

1/4 **cup sugar**

1/4 **cup butter, melted**

2 **packages (3 ounces each) cream cheese, softened**

1 **cup confectioners' sugar**

1 **carton (8 ounces) frozen whipped topping, thawed, divided**

2-1/2 **cups cold milk**

2 **packages (3.9 ounces each) instant chocolate pudding mix**

Additional peanut butter cookies, broken into pieces

1 In a large bowl, combine crushed cookies, sugar and butter; press into an ungreased 13-in. x 9-in. baking dish. Bake at 350° for 6-8 minutes or until golden brown; cool on a wire rack.

2 In a large bowl, beat cream cheese and confectioners' sugar until smooth; fold in 1 cup whipped topping. Spread over cooled crust.

3 In another large bowl, beat milk and pudding mix on low speed for 2 minutes or until thickened. Spread over cream cheese layer. Top with remaining whipped topping; sprinkle with cookie pieces. Cover and refrigerate for at least 1 hour before serving. **Yield:** 12-15 servings.

INDEXES

Alphabetical Index

Refer to this index for a complete alphabetical listing of all recipes in this book.

General Index

This handy index lists every recipe by food category, major ingredient and/or cooking method, so you can easily locate recipes to suit your needs.